THE ORIGIN AND DESTINY OF HUMANNESS

THE ORIGIN AND DESTINY OF HUMANNESS

AN INTERPRETATION OF
THE GOSPEL ACCORDING TO MATTHEW

HERMAN C. WAETJEN

Published by CRYSTAL PRESS, San Rafael, CA
for OMEGA BOOKS

ISBN 0-89353-016-6

2nd Edition Printed 1978

Printed in the U.S.A.

To Tommy

who in life and in death taught us the meaning of Jesus' saying: "Except you become as little children, you will not enter the kingdom of God."

CONTENTS

FOREWORD

This interpretation of the First Gospel attempts to reconstitute the coherence of Matthew's literary composition and to retrieve a sense of its meaning as a whole. It is concerned with the individual parts and pieces only in so far as they contribute to the unity of its thought. It is hoped that this literary-critical approach utilizing the historical-critical tools that biblical scholarship has devised will throw a little more light on this complex writing of the first century and at the same time present some new insight into the problematic self-understanding of Christian identity in this final quarter of our 20th century. Although this book has been rewritten and revised many times during the past ten years — it was begun on a sabbatical leave in Tübingen, Germany late in 1965 — it is not easy to let it go to print. There is still more work to be done in research and reflection, more maturity to be gained in insight and judgment. Nevertheless, it is time for a critical response, and therefore the risk of publishing it must be taken.

The introduction which concentrates on interpretive and methodological problems may be by-passed temporarily and read after the rest of the book has been digested. Chapter Two focuses on hermeneutical matters only initially and then quickly moves into an attempt to reconstruct the setting in and for which the gospel was composed. The remaining chapters reflect the literary framework of the gospel as it is construed by this interpreter. An effort has been made to avoid sexist language and to speak as inclusively as possible. When a possessive pronoun for God is necessary a combination of "his/her" is used. The phrases "the Son of the Human Being" and "the Human Being" are substituted for "the Son of Man."

What it has been possible to achieve here is to be attributed to the help, challenge and inspiration of many human beings: my teachers, my students, my friends, my colleagues and most of all my wife and our children. I am thankful to my father-in-law, Harry C. Struyk, for his proof-reading work. A special debt of gratitude is owed to Mrs. Thelma Furste for her indispensable role in typing and retyping the manuscript and by her great assistance, patience and personal interest in facilitating its preparation for the publisher.

Herman C. Waetjen

San Anselmo, California

ABBREVIATIONS

Ant.	Antiquities of Josephus
HTR	Harvard Theological Review
JAAR	Journal of the American Academy of Religion
JBL	Journal of Biblical Literature
LXX	Septuagint
NT	Novum Testamentum
NTD	Das Neue Testament Deutsch
NTS	New Testament Studies
TWzNT	Theologisches Wörterbuch zum Neuen Testament
ZNW	Zeitschrift für die neutestamentliche Wissenschaft
ZTK	Zeitschrift für Theologie und Kirche

"And then, into this tasteless heap of gold and
marble, He came, light and clothed in an aura,
emphatically human, deliberately provincial,
Galilean, and at that moment gods and nations
ceased to be and man came into being . . ."

Dr. Zhivago
by Boris Pasternak

Chapter I

INTRODUCTION

The unusual similarity between the gospels of the New Testament, especially the first three, the Synoptics, makes it seem logical to interpret them in relation to each other. Likeness or resemblance provides a point of departure for understanding, while the singular or the individual, since it cannot be assigned to any class and therefore be grasped in terms of something else, appears to be ineffable. גאבאת

The gospel according to Matthew, therefore, is generally interpreted in relation to the writings most like it, namely Mark and Luke. The circular movement of proceeding from the particular to the general and from the general back to the particular contributes to the knowledge of both: the individual gospel and the class of texts with which it is identified, the Synoptics.

For generations this has been — and indeed continues to be! — the logic by which biblical scholarship has endeavored to comprehend these ancient writings and to explain their verbal meaning as accurately and lucidly as possible. The almost endless flow of monographs and articles, especially since the turn of the century, discloses a rather broad spectrum of methodological approaches and correspondingly a wide diversity of conclusions. Much progress has been made, and each new study has contributed to increased insight, further direction, additional clues, supplementary slants and emphases. At the same time new tools have been developed and standardized, but they have not always fulfilled original expectations, and the search for other and perhaps superior instruments of interpretation continues to be pressed.

After source criticism had exhausted its possibilities, form criticism tended to be the prevailing method for several decades. More recent research, however, has been dominated by its derived coordinate, redaction criticism. The two are often considered to be the beginning and the end of gospel study. While the former investigates the origin and history of the individual traditions, the latter concentrates a scientific analysis on their final compilation. Because of this interconnection redaction criticism, at first at least, labored under the same presuppositions of its precursor. The gospels are to be considered as collections of tradition bound into coherent presentations by means of redaction. They constitute the culminating stage of a continuous process of transmission which originated in the formation of oral units of tradition. Assembling and editing the collected material encompass the work of the evangelists but were already carried on before the fixation of oral tradition in writing. The evangelists and their writings, therefore, belong to the history of editorial work.

During the Fifties, however, when redaction criticism began to flourish, the role of the evangelists as "interpreters" rather than mere editors was more generally acknowledged and emphasized. Redaction involves revision, and revision is based on interpretation. The gospel writers are not only transmitters of traditional material but also its oldest exegetes.[1] In giving a particular story or saying a new meaning they establish themselves as theologians who in author-like fashion chose, arranged and altered tradition.[2]

Working hand in hand with historical criticism, redaction criticism attempts to recover the concrete life situation of a gospel by analyzing the distinctive features of the evangelist's editorial alterations and then proceeding to interpret the gospel as a whole according to the conclusions that have been drawn. This circular hermeneutical process which moves from the gospel, or at least parts of it, to an historical setting and subsequently back to the gospel has been only partially successful in illuminating verbal meaning. By locking a gospel into its original context the search for the appropriate intrinsic genres or types of meaning is conveniently narrowed in order to make the language game that is being played more easily recovered. But the givens of a situation do not determine verbal meaning. "The conventions and traditions which the speaker relies on are not directly given by a milieu. We may know from the milieu what conventions are available to him, but the ones he chooses to rely on are construed by us from his utterance."[3]

Yet it is usually never the complete utterance of the evangelist that is analyzed by redaction criticism in order to interpret the verbal meaning of a gospel. Analysis is focused on a circumscribed part and the derived results are generalized to hold true for the entire composition without further correlation with other parts or with the whole.[4] Moreover there is no indication that a prior comprehension of the gospel as a whole has governed the selection of those texts that have been used to elicit what is considered to be the main thrust of the book. The redaction critical studies of Matthew that have been published so far labor to be scientifically correct and objective but nevertheless lapse into subjectivity by their discriminating choices of texts. Different parts of the gospel are regarded to be pivotal for grasping the composition as a whole, but there is little agreement as to what they are.

The problem is compounded by another deficit of redaction criticism: the differentiation between tradition and redaction and the subsequent concentration on the latter because it is regarded to be determinative of the evangelist's generic conceptions. Certainly this material, the sum total of the editorial changes in the body of tradition that has been adopted, should reveal the distinctive language game that is being played, especially if it can be locked into a concrete historical situation.[5] In the process, however, a large part of the gospel is ignored. Tradition, that material which has been taken over without revision, is either dismissed as having no bearing on the final redaction or explained away as belonging to a previous stage of tradition. But does not *all* the tradition which the evangelist utilized stand under his editorial work, that which he did not alter as well as that which he revised? Does the absence of alteration in a particular text automatically imply faithfulness to tradition? Must it not also be attributed to the evangelist's redaction by the very fact of its inclusion? Matthew has chosen to adopt certain materials unchanged. That does not presuppose that he is construing the verbal meaning of his source traditionally or according to its original intention. On the one hand it is questionable whether an arbitrary transmission of tradition without accompanying interpretation took place in early Christianity. On the other hand, any shift from one ethnic or socio-economic context to another necessitates a new construction of meaning even if a particular text is appropriated without revision. Its intrinsic type of meaning may be apprehended by the borrowing evangelist, but its utilization in a new literary context aimed at a new life situation generates some kind of change in verbal meaning.

Redaction criticism seems to be especially guilty of methodological confusion in this sphere of its literary-critical enterprise. The evangelists are acknowledged to be interpreters of tradition and therefore also theologians. Their compositions are researched for the recovery of their theological ideas in relation to specific life situations. Yet their literary technique and the literary integrity of their work are often denigrated because of apparent unresolved contradictions between the tradition they simply adopted and the tradition they adapted by redaction. These incongruities and inconsistencies are attributed to "the carelessness of popular journalism"[6] or to the weight of previous stages of tradition which the evangelists were unable to overcome in order to produce a successfully integrated composition.[7]

To what extent, therefore, authorship may be attributed to them is not clear. Not all redaction critics employ the term. Some appear to want to restrict the concept of redactor to the role of interpreter.[8] Others express a willingness to regard the evangelists as authors but in a limited sense as exegetes who may originate new generic conceptions but continue to remain in the history of tradition in their employment of literary forms.[9] A few appraise the redactional work of the evangelists as "authorship in its own right" in as far as it brings about a discontinuity in the handing down of tradition. That is, by the personal creation of a literary framework and by the personal selection, formulation and unification of an anonymous tradition a new, unprecedented and individualistically constructed type of composition called "gospel" came into existence. Since authorship, however, is to be understood relatively according to the degree of originality, Matthew and Luke who adopted Mark's innovative outline to one extent or another do not have equal stature as authors.[10]

But is this valid criticism? Originality and success in literary construction, coherence and verbal meaning are matters related to authorial intention as it is linked to the concrete circumstances of time and place. Redaction criticism which concerns itself with both interpretation and literary criticism often confuses the two. While the former is aimed at understanding and explanation, the latter endeavors to make judgments on all the features that are involved in gospel writing: authorial will as it is expressed in literary design and purpose, the use and integration of tradition and the lucidity of verbal meaning. A critical assessment of these things is not based simply on a comparison of similar texts, such as the Synoptic gospels, but also on a contrast between an evangelist's accomplishment and his aim or intention.

Literary-critical judgments do affect interpretation. A premature denigration of an evangelist's work frustrates the recognition of the generic conceptions that have been used to convey verbal meaning. A lack of integration, unresolved inconsistencies or a left-over "surplus" which have surfaced through redaction critical analysis may be indicative of a basic failure to recover the distinctive types of meaning which the evangelist employed, not necessarily the authorial incompetence or inadequacy of the evangelist himself.[11] Redaction criticism by its accustomed choice of specific parts over against other parts or by the separation of redaction from tradition loses or at least is in danger of losing the comprehensive unity of a gospel composition which embraces all of its parts and particulars. For:

> "A part is never a means to another part which is the
> end — unless in the organistic sense that all
> parts and the whole are reciprocally ends and
> means, the heart, the head, and the hand."[12]

This is another hermeneutical circle. An idea of the whole that is derived from a part may control the interpretation of a text in all of its individual parts. If, however, the one cannot be unified by the other, if a literary coherence cannot be established, the generic conception of the whole with which the interpreter has worked may be wrong and must therefore be discarded. The search for the appropriate intrinsic types of meaning must be pressed until the whole can be understood in its parts and the parts through the whole. Only when integrity cannot be reconstituted will it be valid to make a critical judgment about the evangelist's authorial capabilities and the literary-critical character of his composition.

The establishment of coherence or integrity, on the other hand, is also a reasonable basis for measuring "validity in interpretation." This is not simply elicited by a correct identification of types of meaning. "The correct determination of implications is a crucial element in the task of discriminating a valid from an invalid interpretation."[13] Here is still another hermeneutical circle, for ". . . the correct drawing of implications depends upon a correct guess about the type."[14] In this respect a gospel is like an iceberg.[15] The vocabulary, grammar, syntactical patterns, formulas, etc. are but the empirically discernible tip beneath which the intrinsic types of meaning and their attendant implications exist and by which they are conveyed to the reader. The identification of the types that have consciously been selected by the evangelist also involves ferreting out as far as possible the proprieties which belong to them. Yet because an author cannot be aware of all the implications which attend a particular type, aspects of meaning may be surfaced which were not consciously intended. For ". . . there is the problem of the role of the unconscious in the process of the composition; there is the possibility of the (author) having written better than he knew; there is even the matter of the happy accident."[16] If these fall within the verbal meaning as a whole, if they are logical implications of the type that has been willed, they should not be considered illegitimate.

Are there any special rules or principles which apply to the interpretation of the gospel according to Matthew? It occupies a unique position at the head of the New Testament canon; and like the three writings which follow it, it is traditionally classified as a "gospel." While the former resulted from the arbitrary choice of the second century church leaders and therefore contributes little to an understanding of the book, the other poses certain methodological ambiguities which both facilitate and hinder the task of interpretation.

What does the literary classification "gospel" presuppose? To what extent is it applicable to Matthew's work? Form criticism and redaction criticism generally acknowledge the form "gospel" to be essentially without analogy,[17] "the one unique literary product of New Testament Christianity."[18] This acknowledgement, however, is often accompanied by a prejudicial evaluation of their literary quality which is traceable to form criticism's original judgment that the gospel's are "unliterary writings" which ". . . should not and cannot be compared with 'literary works.' The composers are only to the smallest extent authors . . . St. Luke more than the other Synoptics. Thereby it can be estimated in how lowly a degree after all St. Mark and St. Matthew may pass as authors."[19] They do not command the cultivated techniques of composition necessary for grand literature nor let the personalities of their author appear.[20] Even where personal and individualistic authorship has been acknowledged by redaction critics, it has been, as observed above, a relative distinction accorded primarily to Mark or it has been restricted to a theological rather than a literary expression of creativity.

What a gospel is and how it should be interpreted depend in part at least on whether such a literary type existed and was cultivated within the ancient church. Do four instances of formal literary similarity, as evident in the first four books of the New Testament, establish the historical existence of a literary genus? Certain resemblances to the later apocryphal gospels are evident, but the differences seem so predominant, at least in relation to those that are more or less preserved in their entirety, that the continuity between them may be a limited transference of tradition without an accompanying transmission of form.[21]

The four gospels of the New Testament appear to stand alone in unparalleled distinctiveness as a group of Christian writings without antecedents or successors. In contrast to the apocryphal gospels they share a corresponding account of Jesus' activity and teaching culminating in his death and resurrection. In all four, John the Baptist serves as an essential preliminary figure to the person and work of Jesus.

Nevertheless, while this significant resemblance may confirm the historical existence of a unique literary form which, although short-lived, was innovated by its oldest representative Mark, the gospel as a literary type is at best a heuristic device by which new intrinsic types of meaning may be investigated and recognized. Matthew, who reproduced more than 600 of Mark's 661 verses along with its general outline of Jesus' career,[22] has given his literary composition a character and structure that are peculiarly its own. This "Book of Origin" possesses an originality of conception and purpose which was generated by the author's consummate interaction with a singular set of social-religious circumstances.

"The aims and norms of a text are determined not by the category we happen to place it in, but by the aims and norms which the author entertained and under the broadest conception of communicability managed to convey."[23] So while it may be true that the individual or the singular is ineffable and must be apprehended in terms of a class or genus to which it can be assigned at least provisionally, Matthew's gospel must finally be interpreted in and for itself. Historical criticism reinforced by sociology and social theory will narrow the possible intrinsic types of meaning utilized by the evangelist by locating very concretely the cultural context of the composition. Redaction criticism will be useful if not indispensable in recovering the evangelist's intention through an analysis of the text's discernible authorial revision. Finally, a literary-critical approach, which makes use of all this data and investigates the text holistically as an integrated composition in which all the parts are interconnected by the intrinsic types of meaning employed by the evangelist, should be able to reconstitute the comprehensive unity of the book and the verbal meaning it was intended to convey.

If such a unity between the parts and between the parts and the whole can be established; if the implications of the intrinsic genres which have been used can be construed in such a way as to resolve the apparent contradictions and to demonstrate a literary as well as a theological coherence, perhaps a convincing degree of validity in interpretation will have been achieved. The richness of the text will, of course, not be exhausted by any such attempt, but the probability of a right direction for further study may be established.

FOOTNOTES

1 Adapted from Gunther Bornkamm's, "The Stilling of the Storm in Matthew" in *Tradition and Interpretation in Matthew*, trans. from the German, *Überlieferung und Auslegung im Matthäusevangelium* (Philadelphia: The Westminster Press, 1963), p. 55, who asserts this of Matthew.

2 See the survey of the major redaction critical studies in Joachim Rohde's, *Rediscovering the Teaching of the Evangelists*, trans. from the German, *Die redaktionsgeschichtliche Methode*, by Dorothea M. Barton, (Philadelphia: The Westminster Press, 1968), pp. 47-239.

3 E.D. Hirsch, Jr., *Validity in Interpretation*, (New Haven and London: Yale University Press, 1967), p. 87. Compare R. Hummel, *Die Auseinandersetzung Zwischen Kirche und Judentum in Matthäusevangelium*, (München: Chr. Kaiser Verlag, 1963), and D.R.A. Hare, *The Theme of Jewish Persecution of Christians in the Gospel according to St. Matthew*, Volume 6 in the monograph series of the Society for New Testament Studies, (Cambridge: at the University Press, 1967), who use the givens of the situation which they have deduced from Matthew through redaction criticism to elicit verbal meaning.

4 See G. Bornkamm, "End-expectation and Church in Matthew," *Tradition and Interpretation in Matthew*. Also Gerhard Barth, *Matthew's Understanding of the Law*, also in *Tradition and Interpretation in Matthew;* Heinz Joachim Held, *Matthew as Interpreter of the Miracle Stories*, also in *Tradition and Interpretation in Matthew;* Wolfgang Trilling, *Das Wahre Israel, Studien zur Theologie des Matthäusevangeliums* (Leipzig: St. Benno Verlag, 1959). Trilling follows Otto Michel, "Der Abschluss des Matthäusevangeliums," *Evangelische Theologie* 10 (1950/51), pp. 16-26, in the attempt to interpret the gospel "backwards" in the light of the theological presupposition of 28:16-20 under which the entire gospel is assumed to have been written. See *op. cit.*, pp. 6ff. J.D. Kingsbury, *The Parables of Jesus in Matthew 13*, (London: S.P.C.K., 1969); M.J. Suggs, *Wisdom Christology, and Law in Matthew's Gospel*, (Cambridge: Harvard University Press, 1970). J.D. Kingsbury, *Matthew: Structure, Christology, Kingdom*, (Philadelphia: Fortress Press, 1975).

5 See G. Barth, *op. cit.*, p. 58.

6 H.J. Held, *op. cit.*, p. 165.

7 George Strecker, *Der Weg der Gerechtigkeit, Untersuchung zur Theologie des Matthäus*, (Göttingen: Vandenhoeck and Ruprecht, 1962), pp. 16ff.

8 G. Bornkamm, *op. cit.*, p. 35. Also G. Barth, *op. cit.*, p. 58. H.J. Held, *op. cit.*, p. 165.

9 W. Trilling, *op. cit.*, pp. 2, 19lff. and G. Strecker, *op. cit.*, p. 10.

10 Especially Willi Marxsen, *Mark the Evangelist*, trans. from the German, *Der Evangelist Markus, Studien zur Redaktionsgeschichte des Evangeliums* ed. by Roy Harrisville, (Nashville: Abingdon Press, 1969), pp. 18ff. See the discussion in J. Rohde, *op. cit.*, pp. 16-21. Especially Rohde's quotation of G. Iber on pp. 20f.

FOOTNOTES

11 Compare G. Strecker, *op. cit.*, pp. 72, 83, and E.D. Hirsch, Jr., *op. cit.*, pp. 144ff. and 151.

12 W.K. Wimsatt, Jr., "Explication as Criticism" in *Explication as Criticism. Selected papers from the English Institute*, ed. by W.K. Wimsatt, Jr., (New York: Columbia University Press, 1963), pp. 1-26 and W.K. Wimsatt, Jr., *The Verbal Icon: Studies in the Meaning of Poetry*, (Lexington: University of Kentucky Press, 1967), pp. 235-51.

13 E.D. Hirsch, Jr., *op. cit.*, p. 89.

14 *Ibid.*, p. 91.

15 See Hirsch, Jr., for the use of this analogy of an iceberg, *ibid.*, pp. 53f.

16 Cleanth Brooks, "Literary Criticism: Marvell's 'Horatian Ode,' " *Explication as Criticism*, ed. by W.K. Wimsatt, Jr., p. 125.

17 See Rudolf Bultmann, *The History of the Synoptic Tradition*, trans. from the German, *Die Geschichte der synoptischen Tradition*, by John Marsh, (New York: Harper and Row, 1963), pp. 371ff.

18 Norman Perrin, *What is Redaction Criticism?*, (Philadelphia: Fortress Press, 1969), p. 74. Also Marxsen, *op. cit.*, pp. 9f. and Helmut Koester, "One Jesus and Four Gospels," *Harvard Theological Review* 61 (1968), pp. 206ff., which is also found in *Trajectories Through Early Christianity*, (Philadelphia: Fortress Press, 1971), pp. 161f.

19 Martin Dibelius, *From Tradition to Gospel*, trans. from the German, *Die Formgeschichte des Evangeliums*, 2nd rev. ed., (New York: Charles Scribner's and Sons, 1933), pp. 2f.

20 Bultmann, *op. cit.*, p. 372. Again see Held, *op. cit.*, p. 167.

21 H. Koester, *op. cit.*, pp. 211ff. or in *Trajectories*, pp. 163ff.

22 See B.H. Streeter, *The Four Gospels*, (London: Macmillan, 1953), p. 159.

23 Hirsch, Jr., *op. cit.*, p. 151.

Chapter II

THE LIFE SITUATION OF THE GOSPEL

What a text means should be differentiated from the questions of when, where and under what circumstances it was caused. Yet because meaning and context are interdependent, interpretation must be concerned with both. The gospel according to Matthew, like the other writings of the New Testament, is linked by language, structure and content to a distinctive historical and geographical setting. The life situation, therefore, in which it originated must be identified as far as it is possible. By locking the literary composition into a social, economic, religious milieu, an essential hermeneutical circle is established through which its type concepts and their intended verbal meaning can be determined with greater precision.

This, however, does not imply that an investigation of the gospel's life situation precedes the literary-critical analysis of the evangelist's utterance. Because of their interdependence a separate treatment of them in part or in whole is illegitimate, if not impossible. A correlated interpretation is required from the outset, a continuous spinning through the hermeneutical circle that moves from the text to the life situation and back to the text.

As these complex hermeneutical procedures are undertaken and continued, the "meaning expectations" of the interpreter have a decisive bearing on the identification of the author's distinctive language game and its intrinsic genres in relation to a specific "socio-cultural" setting.[1] Such meaning expectations may interfere with understanding because the interpreter's conception of what is being said is determined by previous experience of the subject matter or the lack of it altogether. The willed type of the author must be shared in order for communication to take place.[2] Education, as excellent and comprehensive as it may be, is always limited and limiting by the sociology of knowledge and its construction of reality in which the interpreter participates as a member of a particular social class with its own discrete ideological horizons. Therefore, the generic conceptions which the interpreter brings to bear on the text may not correspond at all or only inexactly to the determinate meaning of the author.

If, for example, Matthew's gospel or a certain part of it is approached with the expectation that its distinctive language game is rabbinic in character, the resulting understanding will be determined by it. "An interpreter's preliminary generic conception of a text is constitutive of everything that he (or she) subsequently understands, and this remains the case unless or until that generic conception is altered."[3] Such an initial meaning expectation must be tested in at least two ways. Firstly, it should be worked through the various hermeneutical circles in order to ascertain whether it can explain the gospel in all of its individual parts as an integrated unity. Secondly, other language games, such as apocalypticism and gnosticism, depending, of course, on the possibilities of time and place, must be tried out on the text and put through the same hermeneutical circles in order to discover whether there is a more appropriate language game that provides a more exact overarching type concept that embraces and controls the composition as a whole.

However, even the correct identification of a particular language game may not necessarily lead to an immediate sharability of the generic conceptions that are conveyed by the text. Room must also be left for the originality of the author. Matthew's intrinsic genres, as will become evident, are not merely derived from a specific language game but are creative innovations designed to unsettle, not to endorse, to foster disruption and iconoclasm, not continuity.

Because of the evangelist's dependence on the gospel according to Mark and the Q source, his type concepts should also not be considered as simple borrowings of tradition, not even that body of material which has been adopted without revision. No matter how similar the one may appear to be to the others in content and arrangement, Matthew's literary work is a new articulation of the good news. Tradition cannot simply be transferred from one cultural milieu to another. Translation is required. Some kind of adjustment must be made to the language game of the new socio-cultural environment. Corresponding generic conceptions must be substituted and wherever necessary modified according to the purpose of the author.

The Marcan gospel, on the one hand, appears to have originated in the rural countryside. Its frequent references to "villages" (6:6, 36, 56; 8:23, 26, 27; 11:2) and "towns" (1:38) and to Jesus' itinerant ministry among them point to this; and the preponderance of agricultural parables and metaphors supports it. Moreover, its crude grammar and syntax indicate a lower class audience consisting of peasants, artisans and craftspeople. Jesus himself is presented as "the carpenter" (6:3), and the metaphor of 9:3, "his garments became very shining white such as a bleacher on earth is unable to make so white," is drawn from a particular handicraft.

Matthew's gospel, on the other hand, has an undeniable urban character. While there are only four references to "villages," the word "city" occurs 26 times. Jesus for the greater part of his life resides in cities. Nazareth where he grew into adulthood is designated a city in 2:23. Capernaum is his place of residence during his ministry; according to 8:1, "his own city." Although he also carries his messianic mission into the countryside as an itinerant, he continually returns to his home in Capernaum. The evangelist, therefore, seems to be writing for an urban community, for people who like Jesus have their home in the city.

Furthermore, the general character and emphases of the gospel intimate that the addressees are affluent Christian Jews who probably belong to upper class society. Such an identification is suggested by the genealogical table which stands at the very head of the book and which upholds Jesus' descent from Abraham, the grand patriarch of the Jews, and David the king. Genealogies were indispensable to the upper classes of agrarian society. They were the historical records of the elite in urban culture which served to establish a family's pedigree and simultaneously to maintain its social prestige and privileged position in the community.[4]

Matthew's genealogy, however, is decidedly ambiguous. While it enhances Jesus' messianic identity by tracing his royal lineage from David through Zerubbabel, it also points to various scandals connected with the five women who are specified and the men associated with them.[5] Jesus' ancestry includes the expendables of society, foreigners, adulterers as well as King David who committed murder for the sake of adultery. It is hard to imagine that such an unusual family tree with its startling contrasts would not have impressed but also offended these upper class Jewish Christians.

Similar incongruities are evident throughout the gospel. On the one hand, Jesus is worshipped as "the king of the Jews" by the Magi from the east who present him with regal gifts of gold, frankincense and myrrh. On the other hand, he subsequently concentrates his ministry on the lower class masses who are "harrassed and oppressed as sheep without a shepherd" (9:36). He even gives a banquet for tax collectors and sinners at his home in Capernaum (9:10). One tax collector in particular, Matthew by name, is called to discipleship and eventually named to the ranks of the original Twelve. If the gospel was attributed to him from its very beginning, such a deliberate ascription of authorship to one of the degraded of the lower classes would have a shattering effect upon the elitism and class consciousness of these Christian Jews.

Certain peculiarly Matthean traditions hint at a more precise identification of these affluent, upper class addressees of the gospel. It would seem that they are landlords and merchants engaged in business and commerce. In any mature pre-industrial city they would be able to acquire considerable wealth, but because they happened to belong to a minority status group, they would be prevented from gaining political power through purchase or marriage.[6] They would appreciate the analogy which Jesus drew from the world of business at the conclusion of the first antithesis of the Sermon on the Mount, "Be on the best terms with your adversary (your creditor) while you are on the way with him (to the local court where you must appear for failure to make repayment on a loan at the agreed time), so that your adversary does not hand you over to the judge and the judge to the jailer, and he throws you into prison. Truly I say to you, you will not get away until you have paid the last penny" (5:25-6). But they would be startled by the radical examples which he attached to the fifth antithesis in order to illustrate different ways of terminating the vicious cycle of evil, particularly the suggestion of giving a creditor one's outer robe after he has already appropriated one's underwear (5:40). Jesus' exhortation in 5:39 suggests that like most urban people in business, they are hesitant to extend credit to simply anyone, especially people of the lower classes, a risky venture in any city: "Give to the one who asks you, and do not turn away from the one who would borrow money from you." The command of 6:19, "Do not store up for yourselves treasures on earth where moth and rust destroy and thieves break in and steal . . ." is relevant only to those who enjoy affluence. Merchants would be captivated by the analogy of the wholesale dealer who trades in beautiful pearls (13:45-6).

On the other hand, those among Matthew's addressees who are land owners engaged in agriculture would be dismayed at the business logic of the landlord who owns a vineyard and insists on paying all his day laborers the same wage regardless of how long they have worked in the fields (20:1-16). Yet because they would justify the lord who ostracized a servant unwilling to take even a minimal business risk in order to increase the capital of his absent master, the eschatological parable of 25:14-30 would serve as an especially ⟶ effective warning to them. Finally, the concluding story of 25:31-46 seems to be intended for those who have the resources to help "the least of these my fellow human beings," the poor and wretched of the lower classes, by feeding the hungry, clothing the naked, rendering service to the imprisoned and opening their homes to strangers.

As people who enjoy wealth because of their land holdings and business interests, Matthew's addressees also appear to have the advantage of advanced schooling, another privilege of upper class status. The sophistication that is presupposed for the comprehension of the gospel's literary construction and theological dialectic involves a degree of literacy and learning that requires higher education.

Besides beginning his gospel with a genealogy that is ingeniously constructed according to numerical patterns, one that is explicit (1:17) and one that is implicit,[7] the evangelist has put together a literary framework that is essentially ambiguous. The teaching of Jesus has obviously been arranged in five great discourses which have been incorporated into the narrative at certain points with great skill. Each is terminated by a transition formula (7:28-9, 11:1, 13:53, 19:1, 26:1) that also leads back into the narrative. The transition which ends the final discourse (26:1) includes the added word "all" which signals the end of Jesus' teaching. A certain symmetry is evident in the selection and arrangement of the material. The setting of the fifth and last discourse, at least in its second half, is like the first, the Sermon on the Mount. Both occur on a specific mountain. Jesus' eschatological teaching is located appropriately on the Mount of Olives, a site that according to Zech. 14:4 has an apocalyptic character. His ethical teaching is presented on a definite but unnamed mountain in Galilee which in the gospel is an *axis mundi,* a navel of the earth, from which a new creation originates.[8] The conclusion of the final discourse, the story of 25:31-46, looks back to the Sermon on the Mount where the criteria of the Human Being's judgment were originally set forth. The second discourse which presents instructions for the mission outreach of Jesus' disciples contrasts with the guidelines of the fourth that are offered for the communal life and relationship of the mission oriented church. Seven parables compose the third discourse which stands in the middle of the gospel looking back as well as forward to the success and failure of Jesus' ministry.

The function of the number five and its relation to the framework of the gospel has been disputed. B.W. Bacon's reconstruction of a Pentateuch-like design constituting five books consisting of narrative and discourse,[9] introduced by a preamble (chapters 1-2) and concluded with a lengthy epilogue (chapters 26-8) has gained only limited acceptance.[10] On the basis of a literary-critical examination of this proposed five-fold structure W.D. Davies judges, "Taken in isolation on its 'literary' merits, the pentateuchal approach to Matthew must remain questionable."[11] Davies uncovers the "substance of the New Law, the New Sinai, the New Moses," yet nothing explicit that would provide any conclusive evidence for a pentateuchal framework.[12]

The five book design, therefore, like the motifs of the New Law, the New Moses and the New Sinai, is ambiguous. But by the purposeful intention of the author! For the literary framework of the gospel is determined by his theology. The tension between the old and the new, the past and the present, continuity and discontinuity, is expressed in and by the literary structure. The pentateuchal form in which Israel's constitution was cast has deliberately been adopted by the evangelist and with it, as will become evident, the typologies of Moses, Exodus, Sinai and Law. For Matthew Jesus' fulfillment of the Old Testament requires such continuity. Yet the literary

structure of the gospel is more than a repetition of the five
book design of the Torah. While chapters 1-2 may be
considered as part of Book One, chapters 26-8, which present
the climactic events of Jesus' death and resurrection, do not fit
into this scheme. These final three chapters destroy the five
book structure and confer on the gospel its unique literary
character of a shattered Pentateuch. Accordingly, iconoclasm
is the type concept or intrinsic genre that governs the
composition and unifies both its form and content. Its
framework may be outlined as follows:

Book I

Narrative 1:1 - 4:25   Origin and Beginnings
Discourse 5:1 - 7:27   The Sermon on the Mount
          Transition 7:28-9

Book II
Narrative 8:1 - 9:35   The Character of Jesus'
                              Ministry
Discourse 9:36 - 10:42   A Manual of Mission Conduct
          Transition 11:1

Book III
Narrative 11:2 - 12:50   Controversy
Discourse 13:1 - 52   Analogies of God's Rule
          Transition 13:53

Book IV
Narrative 13:54 - 17:27   Preparing and Training the
                              Disciples for the Future
Discourse 18:1 - 35   On Community Conduct and
                              Discipline
          Transition 19:1

Book V
Narrative 19:2 - 22:46 Return to Judaea and
Rejection in Jerusalem
Discourse (double) A Polemic against the Scribes
23:1 - 39 and Pharisees
24:1 - 25:46 On Eschatology
Transition 26:1

Consummation 26:2 - 28:20 Jesus' Death and Resurrection

 Geographically the life situation of this iconoclastic literary composition is best located in Syria rather than any other area in the Roman Empire. The peculiarly Matthean reference in 4:24 that Jesus' fame swept "into the whole of Syria" and the distinctive reference to a Syrian coin, the *stater,* in 17:28 point to that province. Although any large city in Syria might qualify as the exact place of origin, its capital Antioch, as has often been proposed, seems to be the most logical possibility. The evidence is piecemeal but persuasive.
 Antioch was one of the three largest cities of the Empire. Because of its strategic location at the crossroads of major caravan routes from the east and from the south it was a hub of business and commerce. Because of its position as the capital of an imperial province on the eastern frontier it was a center of diplomatic activity and military staging.[13] Herod the Great paid frequent visits to the city, and with his munificent gifts of public buildings affirmed its stature and reputation. When the ethnarchy of Judaea was taken from his son Archelaus and added to the imperial province of Syria in A.D. 6, the mint of Antioch, which produced the coinage for this part of the Empire, celebrated the city's new position as the capital of an enlarged province by issuing coins bearing the older title of Metropolis.[14]
 Jesus' remarkable story (18:23-35) of a king who wished to settle accounts with his servants and who found one who

owed "myriads of talents," a sum equivalent to millions of
dollars, would most likely occur in a great urban center like
Antioch. The servant with such a fantastic debt would be a
governor or a legate who was responsible for collecting
revenue in a royal or imperial province that belonged to the
king's administration.[15] The citizenry of Antioch would relish
Jesus' story delighting in its exaggeration and responding with
exasperation at the injustice of the forgiven governor who had
one of his revenue collectors thrown into prison for a mere sum
of 100 denarii.

     As a meeting place of eastern and western cultures
Antioch afforded a cosmopolitan climate in which traditional
lines of nationality and religion could easily be crossed.
Hellenistic philosophies and religious cults flourished having a
wide appeal to all classes of people and degrees of education.
Cynic-Stoic philosophers like Euphrates of Tyre and
Artemidorus preached and taught in Antioch;[16] and,
according to Philostratus, an earthquake accompanied the
visit of the great sage and wonder worker Apollonius of Tyana
(6, 38).

     A city where Stoic vocabulary could penetrate the
language of educated people would explain the unusual
appearance of the Stoic technical term *paliggenesia* in the —
teaching of Jesus in 19:28, one of only two occurrences of the
word in the New Testament.[17]

     Jews had been residents of the city and accorded civic
privileges from the time of Seleucus I Nicator and Antiochus
Epiphanes. Organized under the Romans as a separate
commonwealth with guaranteed rights and religious freedom,
they flourished and increased in numbers to the extent that,
according to C.H. Kraeling's estimate, 45,000 of them may
have lived in Antioch during Nero's reign.[18] Josephus testifies,
"The Jewish race . . . is particularly numerous in Syria where
intermingling is due to the proximity of the two countries. But
it was at Antioch that they especially congregated partly owing
to the greatness of the city, but mainly because the successors

of King Antiochus I had enabled them to live there in security."[19] They evidently made a religious impact, for Josephus subsequently adds, " . . . in Antioch multitudes of Greeks were attracted to the religious ceremonies of the Jews, and some even attached themselves to them."[20]

Two historical references indicate that both the Jews and Jewish Christians of Antioch enjoyed prosperity and wealth. According to Josephus, "The Jewish colony grew in numbers . . . and their richly designed and costly offerings formed a splendid adornment to the Temple."[21] And Acts 11:27-30 relates that the Christian community of Antioch "sent relief to the brothers who lived in Judaea" during a widespread famine in the East that occurred in the early reign of Claudius.

To what extent the Jewish revolt in Palestine affected their economic circumstances is not clear. While Jewish prestige undoubtedly declined, legal status remained virtually unchanged.[22] Christians, both Jewish and Gentile, presumably were not included in the general disaffection and hostility of the city's populace against the Jews. For since "the disciples were first called Christians" at Antioch, perhaps in order to enable the Roman authorities to identify the sect and differentiate it from Judaism,[23] discrimination must have grown through the intervening years to the point where the two communities could be and indeed were distinguished. Such a clear-cut distinction is supported by Matthew's consistent use of the phrase "their synagogues" in 4:23, 9:35, 10:17, 12:9, 13:54, 23:34. Although Christian Jews, at least some of them, had not disassociated themselves from their fellow Jews, they were nevertheless differentiating themselves as well as being differentiated by others.

The wide differences in religious and social backgrounds must have precluded any uniformity among the Christians of Antioch. While some preferred an emancipated Gentile type of Christianity which was oriented towards Hellenistic culture and its various forms of pagan thought and belief even to the degree of renouncing everything Jewish,[24] others struggled to maintain their bond with Judaism and their mission to the Jewish community which Jesus had instituted. Yet among themselves they may have been divided on the vexing issues of the interpretation of the Torah and the observance of tradition, as Peter and Paul had been in the same city many years earlier.[25] Moreover, their relationship to the synagogue was complicated by the establishment of rabbinic Judaism in Antioch. For as the Jews became more alienated and isolated from their co-residents of the city, they probably turned to kindred groups in Palestine who like them were struggling in the face of great adversity to preserve their Jewish identity.[26] Such contact would expose them to the new orthodoxy that was being consolidated by the vigorous leadership and control of the rabbis of Yavneh who were demanding a submission and acquiescence to the heritage of the scribes and Pharisees in order to resolve the religious and political crisis of Judaism that had been produced by the destruction of the Jerusalem Temple. Their insistence on uniformity seems to have been so strong that opposition or resistance was met with persecution and, as a last resort, expulsion.[27]

For Christian Jews the connection between their ethnic identity and their Christian discipleship was at stake. On the one hand, subordination and conformity would mean the renunciation of Jesus as the Messiah but simultaneously the preservation of their ethnic identity and therefore a continued participation in the history of Israel. Allegiance to Jesus the Messiah, on the other hand, would result in immediate reprisals but eventually in excommunication from the synagogue and consequently the loss of religious roots and racial ties.

Matthew's gospel mirrors such a dilemma among its addressees. Indeed, the severity of their situation is conveyed by the stark formulation of the Q tradition in 10:34-6, "Do not think I came to cast peace on the earth. I came not to cast peace but a sword. For I came to divide a man against his father and a daughter against her mother and a bride against her mother-in-law, and a human being's enemies (will be) his or her household." Even though the fundamental purpose of Jesus' messiahship was unification, separation was a calculated concomitant. Those who follow him in ministry and mission will become involved in painful family and community cleavage. Reprisal and rejection are to be expected. Those who cannot bear it and prefer to cling to blood and racial ties are unworthy of the Messiah. The only valid kind of discipleship consists of radical commitment and singleness of devotion.

The redaction of 5:12 indicates that Matthew's Christian Jews are being persecuted by their own people, "So they persecuted the prophets before you."[28] According to 23:34, the instigators are the scribes and the Pharisees who have assumed the religious leadership of the Jewish community. They have been pursuing Jewish Christian prophets and scribes from city to city as well as flogging those who persevere in ministry and mission to the synagogue.[29]

Throughout his ministry, as Matthew emphasizes, Jesus had stressed his Jewish identity and defined his messiahship in terms of an ardent nationalism that verged on racism (15:26). He had limited his mission (15:24) and that of his disciples (10:5-6) to the Jewish masses, "the lost sheep of the house of Israel." If he had dealings with outsiders and foreigners, such as Gentiles (8:5-13) and Canaanites (15:21-8), it was begrudgingly and in response to a faith that refused to capitulate to his nationalism.

Moreover, as 23:2-3 shows, he had acknowledged that, "The scribes and the Pharisees sit on Moses' chair" and even commanded his disciples and the Jewish masses to "do and observe all things whatever they say . . ." That privileged position of authority, however, was subsequently cancelled by their involvement in Jesus' death. Although the chief priests and the elders of the people actually were responsible for delivering Jesus up to the Romans for execution (27:1), the Pharisees had been accomplices in earlier efforts "to seize him" (21:45) and "to trap him in his speech." Moreover, their joint request with the chief priests to have Jesus' tomb sealed for three days and especially their use of *Kyrie* ("Lord"), the title which the Jews reserve for God alone, in their address of Pontius Pilate in 27:63 expose their bankruptcy. Any historical claims they might have had have been forfeited, and the followers of Jesus are no longer subject to their authority.

The continuity of true Israel and the heritage of the Old Testament is now upheld by those who identify themselves with the crucified and resurrected Jesus. They constitute the community of the Human Being which the risen Jesus founded on the mountain of Galilee and in which they enjoy full participation in his sovereignty as the Son of God. With the Gentiles who come from the east (2:1) and the west (27:54) as well as with the saints of the past like Abraham, Isaac and Jacob (8:11, 27:52-3), they are united in a new relationship which transcends not only all racial and national boundaries but death itself.

It is to establish this self-understanding among these Christian Jews that the evangelist duplicates the five book form of the Pentateuch and then promptly smashes it. History is full of discontinuities which reveal the purpose and activity of God. The women in the opening genealogy are distinctive examples of irregularity, and Mary the mother of Jesus is the foremost of them, for in contrast to the beginnings of creation recorded in Genesis where the woman was taken from the man, she gives birth to the new Human Being who inaugurates a new humankind. Initially Jesus as her offspring has no link to the past; he does not belong to the history of Israel. But he is incorporated into it by Joseph's obedient act of adoption. He is therefore simultaneously the sovereign Human Being anticipated in the future and the Messiah of Israel awaited from the past. He is enthroned as Lord and yet only coming to enthronement (26:64). His life embodies the tension between the old and the new, between the past and the future, between continuity and discontinuity; and although this tension is momentarily dissolved by his death, it is reconstituted almost immediately after his resurrection when he as the deified Human Being of the future joins his eleven disciples to form a new Israel and to confer on them his own singular identity. As they leave the cosmic mountain in Galilee and proceed into the world the story of the gospel will repeat itself, although in new and unprecedented ways. In this respect the end of the gospel ✝ marks a return to the beginning. Matthew has produced a book that is essentially a charter document; and in and through it the church of affluent, upper class Christian Jews to which it is addressed is to discover its own origin, its own identity and ministry, its own suffering, death and resurrection. What Jesus was in his own time and place in the past now becomes applicable to them as they live their lives in and out of this same dialectical tension. But because iconoclasm, a smashing of images, is at the very center of the gospel, there can never be a simple continuity of repetition or imitation.

Matthew's "Book of Origin" clarifies the relationship between Jesus and the history of Israel and simultaneously between Jesus and contemporaneous Judaism. As the Son of the Human Being and the Son of David, Jesus is a figure of the past whose messiahship was conducted in a specific time and place but finally vitiated by his death. Through the new Israel which he has reconstituted by his resurrection from the dead he continues his work. But those who belong to this new community are to take their own history seriously and to exercise a messiahship in relation to their own distinctive socio-cultural environment. They are to take responsibility for their lives, their decisions, their relations to the institutions in and under which they live. No authority or government of any kind can be allowed to claim absolute control over their lives (17:24-7). Like Simon Peter, one of the Twelve who lived and worked in Antioch earlier — perhaps between A.D. 47 to 54[30] — they have the authority of the keys of the kingdom of God. Whatever principles and categories, institutions and structures they choose to establish or abolish will be validated by God.[31]

By linking their identity and self-understanding to Jesus and
Peter horizontally, the evangelist seeks to draw these upper
class Christian Jews into the kind of ministry which they
conducted among the dehumanized and dispossessed masses
of their society. They may be landlords and merchants of
means, but as new people participating in Jesus' sovereignty
they are called to be servants. There is no place for elitism or
privilege in this community of the new Human Being.

     The author of this charter document seems to have been
a converted Jewish scribe, but not, as is often supposed, a
former rabbi.[32] The twofold quotation of Hosea 6:6 in 9:12 and
12:8, which is directed by Jesus in both instances against the
Pharisees, was a crucial principle in the rabbinic
reconstruction of Judaism under the leadership of Jochanan
ben Zakkai after the critical loss of the Temple in A.D. 70. Its
employment, instead of intimating that the evangelist once
belonged to this movement, may indicate nothing more than
an effective use of rhetoric against the rabbis.

     A more likely background and schooling out of which
Matthew came is one of the inter-testamental conventicles of
Jewish apocalypticism. Originating in the time of Seleucid
oppression, especially during the reign of Antiochus
Epiphanes, millennially oriented sectarian groups of Jews
rallied around the hope of the imminent rule of God that
would bring about a total transformation of human life on
earth. Old Testament history was not only reinterpreted but
also restructured in terms of numerical patterns, such as four,
seven, ten, twelve, fourteen and seventy, in order to convey
meaningful measurements of time.[33]

     From this language game the evangelist has drawn his
generic conceptions and interpretive devices. Two numerical
measurements have been combined in his construction of the
genealogy of Jesus. The number four serves as the basic
division of the history of Israel from Abraham to Jesus Christ,
while the individual epochs of this history are divided into
fourteen or, as will be seen, twelve plus two generations.[34] The

visionary dreams of Joseph in chapters 1-2 are a medium of revelation typical of apocalypticism. The four mountains in Galilee (5:1, 14:23, 15:29, 28:16) perhaps also the Mount of Temptation and the Mount of Transfiguration, are instances of the cosmic mountain or navel of the earth which are also featured in apocalyptic writings.[35] Earthquakes, which in apocalyptic millennialism reduce the world to primeval chaos and signal a reordering of reality, are especially prominent in the First Gospel occurring four times in the course of Jesus' career: 8:24, 21:10, 27:51, 28:2. Also, instead of adopting Mark's handicraft metaphor, Matthew distinguishes Jesus' transformation with an analogy that parallels descriptions of epiphanies found in apocalyptic literature. These and other features that will emerge in the subsequent interpretation of the gospel identify the author as a writer and thinker who came out of a conventicle of Jewish apocalypticism. That he was a scribe is upheld by the generally sympathetic attitude towards scribes that is conveyed by the gospel; that he was a learned student and a skillful interpreter of the Old Testament is evident in the exegetical ability that he displays in his unique fulfillment quotations. Perhaps the scribe that expresses the intention in 8:19, "I will follow you wherever you go," echoes the commitment of the author as much as the peculiar tradition of 13:52, which is often cited in this regard, discloses his self-understanding: "Every scribe who has been taught with respect to the kingdom of God is like a houselord who throws out of his treasure new and old things." The treasure which the evangelist oversees, which he has the authority to distribute freely, consists of the traditions of Jesus as found in Mark, Q, oral materials and the Old Testament. In his scribal office he has the freedom to be iconoclastic as he responds to a new life situation and creates a new literary composition that will communicate the good news to the upper class Christian Jews of Antioch. Above all he has the freedom to mythologize Jesus according to his apocalyptic perspective, that is, to match the life of Jesus, as presented by his primary source Mark, with a mythology derived from apocalypticism in order to bring it as fully as possible into accord with its essence. Thus the life of Jesus, which is essentially image-smashing in character, corresponding to the implicit literary structure of Matthew's gospel, is paradigmatic of the kind of life style God wills. Jesus' resurrection from the dead is its validation.

The gospel, therefore, is a charter document that is basically mythical; it constructs a realm of reality or a universe in which certain values, attitudes and beliefs are institutionalized. But because this new order is grounded in the iconoclastic person of Jesus, these values, attitudes and beliefs are anarchical. That is, they are always subject to the sovereignty of men and women who participate in this new order and like Jesus embrace the ambiguity of their identity and the openness of human existence which even death cannot negate. Only in a world where people live by faith and are therefore casting their cosmic mountains into the sea of chaos is the kind of humanness that God willed at creation and Jesus attained realizable.

FOOTNOTES

1 E.D. Hirsch, Jr., *Validity in Interpretation*, p. 72.

2 *Ibid.*, p. 66.

3 *Ibid.*, p. 74.

4 Gideon Sjoberg, *The Pre-Industrial City Past and Present* (New York: The Free Press, 1960) pp. 161-2. Also Joachim Jeremias, *Jerusalem in the Time of Jesus* (Philadelphia: Fortress Press, 1969) pp. 214, 275-302.

5 Compare Matthew's genealogy with Luke 3:23-38.

6 Gerhard Lenski, *Power and Privilege. A Theory of Social Stratification* (New York: McGraw-Hill Book Co., 1966) pp. 248-56. Also Sjoberg, *op. cit.*, pp.118-21.

7 See below, pp. 52-3.

8 See below, pp. 76, 84, 162, 168, 177-8, 254.

FOOTNOTES

9 Bacon, *Studies in Matthew* (New York: Harper Bros., 1930) pp. 81f. See also M.S. Enslin, " 'The Five Books of Matthew,' Bacon on the Gospel of Matthew," *JBL* 24 (1934), pp. 67-97.

10 See W.G. Kümmel, *Introduction to the New Testament*, trans. from the 17th edition of the German by H. Clarke Kee (Nashville: Abingdon Press, 1975) p. 106. Also G. Bornkamm, "End-Expectation and Church in Matthew," *Tradition and Interpretation in Matthew*, trans. from the German by Percy Scott (Philadelphia: Westminster Press, 1963) p. 35, n. 1.

11 W.D. Davies, *The Setting of the Sermon on the Mount* (Cambridge: At the University Press, 1964) p. 25.

12 *Ibid.,* p. 108.

13 Glanville Downey, *A History of Antioch in Syria from Seleucus to the Arab Conquest* (Princeton: University Press, 1961) pp. 163, 175.

14 *Ibid.,* p. 168.

15 J. Jeremias, *The Parables of Jesus,* trans. from the German by S.H. Hooke (London: SCM Press, 1963) pp. 210-12. Eta Linnemann, *Jesus of the Parables,* trans. from the German, third edition, by John Sturdy (New York: Harper & Row, 1966) pp. 108-9.

16 Downey, *op. cit.,* p. 210.

17 Friedrich Büchsel, "Paliggenesia," *TWzNT,* ed. by Gerhard Kittel (Stuttgart: W. Kohlhammer, 1933) I, 686-7.

18 Carl H. Kraeling, "The Jewish Community at Antioch," *JBL* 22 (1932), p. 136.

19 Josephus, *The Jewish War,* 7, 43, trans. by H. St. J. Thackeray, Loeb Classical Library (Harvard: At the University Press, 1928).

20 *The Jewish War,* 7, 45.

21 *The Jewish War,* 7, 45.

22 *The Jewish War,* 7, 96, 100-11. Also Kraeling, *op. cit.,* p. 153 and Downey, *op. cit.,* pp. 192-5 and 204-6.

23 Downey, *op. cit.,* pp. 198, 275.

24 Kraeling, *op. cit.,* p. 154 and Downey, *op. cit.,* pp. 277-8.

25 Galatians 2:11-18.

26 Kraeling, *op. cit.,* pp. 152-4.

27 Douglas R.A. Hare, *The Theme of Jewish Persecution,* pp. 48-62 on social and economic reprisals as well as exclusion from the synagogue.

28 See also the distinctive tradition of 10:23.

29 Hare, *op. cit.,* pp. 105-6, is not correct in regarding these floggings to be only past experience.

30 Downey, *op. cit.,* pp. 281-5. Also pp. 583-6.

31 See below, pp. 172-3.

FOOTNOTES

32 Against Ernst von Dobschütz, "Matthäus als Rabbi und Katechet," *ZNW* (27) 1928, p. 339.

33 See Dan. 2 and 7; 1 Enoch 93:3-91:17; 2 Bar. 53-74; Rev. 2-3, 6-10, 16. Also D.S. Russell, *The Method and Message of Jewish Apocalyptic* (Philadelphia: Westminster Press, 1964) pp. 195-202 and 224-9.

34 See below, pp. 49-51.

35 Is. 25:6; Dan. 2:35; 1 Enoch 24:1-6, 52:1-6, 77:4; Jub. 4:26.

Chapter III

THE PROLOGUE OF THE GOSPEL: "THE ORIGIN OF JESUS CHRIST"
Matthew 1:1-25

Unlike the other evangelists Matthew introduces his gospel with a table of/ancestry.[1] Certain features distinguish it as a novel presentation of a family tree. In contrast to Luke 3:23-38, the only other genealogy of Jesus in the New Testament, it begins with Abraham, the grand patriarch of Israel, and moves forward through the individual generations to its culmination in "Jesus who is called Messiah." Forty names succeed each other in unbroken father-son relationships; the forty-first is Jesus, but his link to this chain of successive generations is ambiguous. The verb *egennēsen* ("he generated") is used 39 times to connect these father and son pairs, but at the crucial point in verse 16 it does not relate Jesus to Joseph. Instead Joseph is identified as "the husband of Mary," and Mary is designated as the one "from whom Jesus who is called Messiah was born." Four other women of different reputations have been included previously among the male descendants through whom the family line moves, even though they are not to be counted separately as individual generations. Finally, in contrast to Luke's register of names — and most others — Matthew's genealogy is numerically structured according to a pattern which *seems* to demarcate three divisions each consisting of fourteen names (1:17).

All of these distinctive features have something to do with the origin of Jesus. He is the climactic goal and termination of Israel's history, and yet he does not appear to be

directly or immediately linked to it. The ambiguity of verse 16,
which in spite of the textual variants in the manuscript tradition that seek to resolve it, raises the question of Jesus'
relationship to Joseph.[2] Is he his son or not? If he is, what is the
purpose of 1:18-25? If he is not, how can he belong to the
genealogy and be regarded as its culmination?

　　To comprehend this unusual table of ancestry it is
necessary to recognize its arbitrary character. This becomes
more apparent through a comparison of its content with its
Old Testament sources. The first fourteen generations from
Abraham to David correspond to those named in various lists
recorded in the Old Testament, especially 1 Chron. 1:28-2:15.[3]
There are, however, gaps in the second division of fourteen.
Three successive kings of Judah: Ahaziah, Joash and
Amaziah, listed in 1 Chron. 3:11-2, have been excluded.
Jehoiachim who succeeded Josiah and who was the father of
Jehoiachin or Jechoniah, is also missing. Various reasons for
their omission have been offered, but none has been especially
convincing.[4] Why certain ones and not others may no longer
be ascertainable. What matters is that verse 17 indicates an
imposed limit of fourteen generations to each division, and
that requires the exclusion of some names.

　　This arbitrary employment of the number fourteen,
however, is called into question by an apparent deficiency in
the third and final section of the genealogy which lists only
thirteen generations. That might be accounted for by the
inadequacy of the extra-biblical source from which most of
these names have been derived, for only two of them, Salathiel
and Zerubbabel, appear in the ancestry tables of 1 Chron. 3:17-
24. But such reasoning from silence is groundless. On the other
hand, at this point it might seem more cogent to dismiss the
entire genealogy with all of its idiosyncracies as the work of
earlier tradition. Matthew simply adopted it and without
critical revision placed it at the head of his gospel.[5]

　　Nevertheless, in spite of these difficulties verse 17 must
not be set aside too quickly; it provides the key to the

genealogy. A correct counting of its individual generations is crucial to an understanding of its numerical schemes and their theological purpose. According to verse 17, ". . . all the generations from Abraham to David (are) fourteen generations and from David to the Babylonian deportation fourteen generations and from the Babylonian deportation to the Messiah fourteen generations." David is mentioned twice; he ends the first division of names and begins the second. An enumeration indicates that he is the fourteenth generation and so the end of the first section of the genealogy. If he is counted a second time, the number of names in the second group totals fifteen. Obviously, if verse 17 is to be observed, this cannot be correct unless Jechoniah were omitted at the end of the second division and counted at the beginning of the third. That would furnish an additional name for the final section and happily bring the total to fourteen. But at the same time it would distort the reckoning for David would be counted twice, but Jechoniah, representing the transition of the Babylonian exile, only once.[6] If, however, each name represents one generation and is reckoned accordingly, the correspondence with the numerical scheme of verse 17 is almost perfect. David and Jechoniah stand at the end of the first and second sections of the genealogy respectively. Although they are named twice, they are only to be counted once. As a matter of fact, since verse 17 substitutes an historical event, the Babylonian deportation, in place of Jechoniah as the conclusion of the second division of generations and the beginning of the third, it is evident that Matthew's genealogy is more than a table of ancestry. Its structure, as indicated by verse 17, presents an historical outline.

Both David and the Babylonian deportation mark an end as well as a beginning in this procession of people and events. David closes that era of history which had been opened by Abraham, a time of "beginnings." But he also inaugurates a new epoch, "an age of kings," as the second division of the genealogy might aptly be called. He is referred to in 1:6 as "the

king," and as such he is the founder of the dynasty that follows.
The Babylonian deportation serves the same purpose in this
historical scheme: it is an event of transition that terminates —
the age of kings and ushers in a new period of Israel's history as
Jehoiachin Jechoniah is carried into captivity with the Jewish people. This
third epoch, which is closed by Jesus the Messiah, might
appropriately be designated "a time of exile."

However, as already noted, this third division of the
genealogy appears to be incomplete: only thirteen names are —
listed. This deficiency may be attributed to the carelessness of
Matthew's redaction[7] or the inaccuracy of his sources.[8] It may
also be resolved by counting Jesus as the thirteenth generation
and the risen Christ as the fourteenth.[9] But neither explanation corresponds to the character and purpose of the
evangelist's work. On the one hand, as will become evident,
Matthew is a masterful literary artist and is in complete control
of his writing as well as his use of the materials of tradition that
are available to him. On the other hand, he presents Jesus as
the Christ already from the time of his birth.

The incomplete number of generations in the third
section of the genealogy is deliberate and is clarified by the
origin and significance of the number fourteen which,
according to verse 17, is the basis of the author's schematization of Israel's history. The best clues are provided by the
Messiah Apocalypse of 2 Baruch 53-74. Whether Matthew —
actually utilized this millennial writing or was only familiar
with its pattern of fourteen or twelve plus two is probably
indeterminable. What matters is that his scheme matches the
apolocalyptist's organization and interpretation of Israel's
history.

The pattern which this visionary sees in the history of
Israel is analogous to an alternating series of rainfalls originating from an enormous cloud that has emerged from "a very
great sea . . . full of waters white and black" (53:1). "Now this
was done twelve times, but the black were always more
numerous than the white" (53:6). The first waters that fall upon

the earth are dark because they symbolize the sin of Adam, and they become darker because of the sin that results in the waters of the flood (56:5-16). The bright waters that follow are "the fount of Abraham" and the births of his son and grandson (57:1). They are succeeded by the dark waters of slavery in Egypt (58:1). Bright waters usher in the fourth period, the time of Moses and the Exodus (59:1-12). But the fifth waters soon fall to make an end of this through the evil works of the Amorites (60:1). The sixth waters are interpreted to be the illustrious reigns of David and Solomon (61:1-8). Jeroboam's sin of the two golden calves, however, brings back the dark rains (62:1-8). The eighth waters are bright again because righteousness flourishes in the time of Hezekiah's rule (63:1-11). Manasseh's wickedness represents the murky ninth waters (64:1-10). The bright tenth waters signify the restoration that takes place under Josiah (66:1-8). "And the eleventh black waters which thou hast seen: this is the calamity now befalling Zion," namely Jerusalem laid waste by the king of Babylon (67:1-6). The bright twelfth waters are interpreted as a time of restoration when Zion will be rebuilt, the Temple offerings re-instituted and the priests reinstated (68:4-8).

Twelve episodes of epochs have occurred, but the goal of history has not yet been reached. "For the last waters which thou hast seen which were darker than all that were before them, those which were *after* the twelfth number which were collected together belong to the *whole world*" (69:1). Although this final rainfall is not numbered, it is to all intents and purposes the thirteenth. As such it is the unluckiest, the most tragic period in history: "And it shall come to pass that whoever gets safe out of the fire shall be destroyed by famine . . for all the earth shall devour its inhabitants."

At the consummation of this darkest rainfall a lightning bolt flashes across the sky which is identified as the messiah: ". . he shall summon all nations, and some of them he shall spare and some of them he shall slay" (72:2). After he has carried out the great judgment, the fourteenth and final age is inaugurated, "the beginning of that which is not corruptible" (74:2). "Then healing shall descend in dew, and disease shall withdraw, and anxiety and anguish and lamentation pass away and gladness proceed through the whole earth" (73:2).

Matthew's numerically structured genealogy parallels this arbitrary schematization of Israel's history. Moreover, the supposed discrepancy between the statement of verse 17 that there are fourteen generations from the Babylonian deportation to the Messiah and the actual number of thirteen names listed in the table is resolved by it. Indeed, it is in the third division of the genealogy that the scheme of twelve plus two or fourteen has its real application. That is, there are twelve ancestors and Jesus the Messiah who, in contrast to all the other individuals in the family tree is to be counted twice. He represents two generations, not consecutively, but simultaneously from the beginning of his life.

His birth marks the end of the age of exile. He is "the king of the Jews" who draws the Magi from the east, and "they rejoice with exceeding great joy" when they arrive at his home in Bethlehem in order to pay him homage. But his birth also elicits the dreadful response of Herod the Great who dispatches his soldiers to slaughter all the infant boys in Bethlehem and the surrounding regions. Jesus as the sole survivor of this massacre becomes the bearer of its holocaust character and will embody its judgment at the end of his life when this sequence of new age and death will be reversed. His abandonment by God at death will constitute the darkest moment in history for it will be accompanied by the return of the creation to its primeval chaos: ". . . and the earth was shaken and the rocks were torn apart" (27:51). The awakening of the saints which immediately follows signals the beginning of this new creation: "And the tombs were opened and many bodies of the saints having been asleep were raised; and coming out of the tombs after his resurrection they entered the holy city and were manifested to many" (27:52-3). Because Jesus' life is the ground on which the consummating events of history occur, he is the bearer of two generations. His death not only relates him to the thirteenth episode in the scheme of the Messiah Apocalypse; the resurrection of the saints effected by the emission of his final divine breath of life (27:50), links him to the fourteenth, the beginning of a new time.[10]

But an ambiguity arises at this point. If Jesus represents two generations, in as far as he is the fourteenth (as well as the thirteenth) he is also a figure of transition like David the king. He ends the third period, the age of exile, and inaugurates a new era. That implies that the genealogy is not terminated by Jesus. Jesus is not the end of history and the beginning of a new creation. He upholds the continuity of history by initiating a fourth division in the genealogy and therefore also a fourth age in the history of Israel. This is the final period of history which, according to Jesus' discourse on eschatology is consummated by the *Parousia* of the Human Being and the ingathering of his community (24:29-31).

Two numerical patterns govern the construction of Matthew's genealogy. Both appear to have been derived from apocalyptic millennialism. Twelve plus two or fourteen, as it is specified in verse 17, parallels the schematization of history in the Messiah Apocalypse of 2 Baruch. The four ages implied in the division of the generations correspond to the plan of history conveyed by Nebuchadnezzar's dream of a giant image composed of four precious metals (Dan. 2) and Daniel's vision of four chaos monsters emerging from the sea (Dan. 7).

But these numerical arrangements, which the evangelist combines in 1:17, are eschatological interpretations of history which cannot be reconciled with each other. According to the number fourteen or twelve plus two, Jesus is the end of history and the agent of a new creation. According to the number four, he belongs to the history of salvation. He is an arching figure who bridges two epochs, the one he has terminated with the one he inaugurates. In contrast to Daniel's millennial vision, Jesus is "the one like a human being" who brings the kingdom of God in history, not at the end of it. Matthew makes no effort to resolve this discrepancy. The two numerical schemes and their incipient eschatologies are united with two different christologies and held in tension throughout the gospel.

In this light the meaning of the gospel's opening words: "Book of the origin of Jesus Christ" can more adequately be understood. It is not immediately apparent whether they are intended as a superscription of the whole composition or only the introduction to the genealogical table which follows.[11] The latter seems more logical since the genealogy presents the origin of Jesus as the culmination of the historical process of Israel's begetting. Although such a continuity is implied, verse 18, which clarifies the ambiguity of verse 16, discloses that there is no immediate link between Joseph and Jesus. The progression of father begetting son moves forward uninterrupted for forty generations. At the forty-first the continuity is broken. Jesus who was generated by the holy Spirit introduces a disjunction. In this respect he is like Abraham who stands at the beginning of the genealogy as the grand patriarch of Israel, the originator of a new people and their unique history. As a result, the superscription: "Book of the origin of Jesus Christ" cannot apply only to the genealogical table. It reaches beyond it to 1:18-25 which explains the origin of Jesus and his relationship to the preceding generations. Yet as soon as these closing verses of the prologue are connected to the opening words of the evangelist, the body of the gospel that follows must necessarily be included because the subsequent content of Jesus' life elucidates the disclosure of 1:18b as well as the discrepant eschatologies that are conveyed by the two numerical schemes of verse 17.

While the origin of Jesus was linked initially to the progression of father and son generations in the genealogy, it is subsequently connected to Mary in verses 16 and 18. Like the four women: Tamar, Rahab, Ruth and "the wife of Uriah" who precede her, she is another irregularity in the history of Israel. The differences in the evangelist's syntactical constructions, however, hint that her pregnancy is the greatest anomaly of the entire genealogy. The four who serve as her forerunners were presented as the objects of the preposition *ek* ("from"): ". . . Solomon generated Boaz *from* Rahab;" "Boaz generated Obed *from* Ruth;" "David generated Solomon *from* the wife of Uriah."[12] In contrast Joseph did not generate Jesus from Mary, although she is identified as his wife and Jesus' mother.

The ambiguity of 1:16 demands clarification, and scribal revision has attempted to furnish it by unequivocally specifying Mary in advance as "a virgin" and thereby removing the vagueness of Jesus' relation to Joseph.[13] But the clarification is provided by the evangelist himself in verse 18, "But of Jesus Christ the *genesis* was *thus*." "Genesis" or origin is a repetition of the word that appears in the superscription of 1:1. Some ancient scribes substituted *gennēsis,* a word that is similar in sound but is spelled differently and means "birth." Although *genesis* is the textual reading preferred by most authorities, the word "birth" is nevertheless used in many English translations of 1:18. But Matthew is interested in Jesus' origin, not his birth; and the immediate purpose is the clarification of the important ambiguity of verse 16. The adverb "thus" indicates that this will now be done.

Without reluctance or uncertainty Matthew ascribes Jesus' origin to the generating activity of the holy Spirit: "While his mother Mary was betrothed to Joseph before they had sexual intercourse she was found pregnant from the holy Spirit." By its position at the end of the sentence the phrase "from the holy Spirit" receives special emphasis; it is curiously similar to several previous prepositional phrases in the genealogy which call attention to various irregularities in the history of Israel: "from Tamar," "from Rahab," "from Ruth," "from the wife of Uriah."

The conceptualization of the relationship between Mary and the holy Spirit which Matthew intends to convey is crucial to a proper understanding of Jesus' origin: "Mary was found pregnant from the holy Spirit;" "for that which has been generated in her is from the holy Spirit" (1:20). The verb

gennan ("to generate") which was used 39 times to link father
and son pairs and which therefore carries the meaning of
"fathering by an act of sexual intercourse" is also used of Jesus'
origin. This and the phraseology of procreation which the
evangelist employs, "before they had sexual intercourse"
(1:18b), ". . . he did not know her . . ." (1:25a), might suggest
that the holy Spirit is the male partner of Mary and that Jesus'
generation is to be conceived as the result of their sexual union.
Such an understanding of Jesus' origin is often attached to a
certain uniqueness that is ascribed to Mary. In contrast to the
four women who precede her in the genealogy she is construed
to be a virgin. The tradition of 1:18-25 often serves as a proof
text of the so-called virgin birth of Jesus. But there is no such
identification of Mary by the evangelist except in the
fulfillment quotation of 1:23 which interrupts the narrative;
and then it is the designation "the virgin." In spite of its absence
in many English translations the definite article is purposeful
and should not be overlooked. Mary is "the virgin," and as such
she plays a distinguished role in the origin of Jesus.

Moreover, the generation of Jesus is not to be
interpreted as the result of a sexual union. The preposition *ek*
("from"), as in "from the holy Spirit" may simply denote origin
without the accompanying connotation of male impregnator.
Matthew's use of the clause *en gastri echousa* in verses 18b and
23 seems to be chosen carefully and, as in the Septuagint text of
Gen. 38:18, 24, 25 and 2 Sam. 11:3, simply expresses the condition of being pregnant. It has been substituted by the evangelist
in his fulfillment quotation (1:23) in place of the clause *en
gastri lēmpsetai* ("she will conceive") that appears in the
Septuagint version of Is. 7:14 and implies a conception
originated by the agency of the male principle when it is followed
by the preposition "from."[14]

In the New Testament the combination of the verb "to
generate" (*gennan*) and the accompanying prepositional
phrase, "from the (holy) Spirit" is limited to the Johannine
tradition where it seems to have the character of a formula. In

John 3:5 Jesus tells Nicodemus that one must be "generated from water and Spirit." The Spirit is an inexplicable reality which "blows where it wills and you hear its sound, but you do not know where it comes from or where it goes to. So is everyone who has been *generated from the Spirit.*"[15]

Such a divine origin by the creative activity of the Spirit is attributed to Jesus by the evangelist Matthew. Mary has no husband. She is only "betrothed to Joseph" who "did not know her until she bore a son." There is no possibility of her conceiving and bearing a child. It is entirely the work of the Spirit who generates Jesus by a direct act of creation.

By reason of this unusual genesis Jesus is a second Adam who like his prototype is thoroughly human but who, in view of his divine generation, may also be called "the Son of God." That in fact is one of the christological titles conferred on Jesus in the course of the gospel: by Simon Peter in 16:16 and by the centurion of the crucifixion in 27:54; and it is implied in the identification of the virgin's son as Emmanuel in 1:23.[16] But the epithet that conveys the identity of Jesus in terms of his "having been generated in her (Mary) from the holy Spirit" as a new human being is the one that appears consistently on his lips as a form of self-designation: the Son of the Human Being.

Although the maternity of Mary is accentuated in the ambiguity of verse 16 and its elucidation in verse 18b, the narrative of 1:18-25 is told from the point of view of Joseph. This has often been noted but unfortunately interpreted as an apologetic motive. The shift back to Joseph in Matthew's explanation of Jesus' origin is based on his decisive position in the genealogy. For if Jesus is the climax of the history of Israel, at least in terms of his identity as the Son of David, he is that by reason of his relationship to Joseph and not to Mary.[17] Although Joseph is not physically involved in the generation of Jesus, he is betrothed to Mary, and the irregularity of her pregnancy must be explained to him. For as a "righteous" Jew, as he is characterized in verse 19, and therefore as one who is obedient to the law, he is obliged to dissolve this betrothal in view of Mary's apparent unfaithfulness. While contemplating a quiet divorce he is approached by the angel of the Lord, addressed as "Son of David" and commanded to make Mary's child his own by adoption. Only as a result of this obedience is Jesus linked to the history of Israel.

Joseph belongs to the substance of tradition available to the evangelist. Although not mentioned in Mark or Q and appearing only in the first two chapters of Matthew's gospel, he can hardly be the invention of the evangelist. In Luke he is named both as the man to whom Mary was engaged (1:27) and as the father - "as was supposed" - "of" Jesus (3:23, 4:22). The fourth gospel refers to him twice as the father of Jesus (1:45, 6:42). Matthew's Joseph is unique in gospel literature. Nowhere is he sketched more concretely, nowhere does he play a more active role in relation to the birth of Jesus. Only the first evangelist characterizes him as "righteous" and then proceeds to show how this basic trait is manifested in his conduct both toward Mary and Jesus. While he wants no part in Mary's seeming unchastity, he has no desire to shame her publicly. Moreover, making Mary his wife also involves adopting her child and relating to it as a father. Joseph not only acknowledges his fatherhood by naming the boy; he assumes the responsibility of his safety by taking mother and infant to Egypt in order to escape from the murderous designs of Herod the Great and subsequently by moving his family to Nazareth in order to avoid the jeopardy of living under the rule of Archelaus.

This representation of Joseph seems to be invested with certain Old Testament features and allusions which contribute to the evangelist's theological interpretation of Jesus' beginnings. The prototype that most readily suggests itself is the Old Testament patriarch Joseph. Not only is the name the same; both Josephs have a father named Jacob. It is not certain whether Matthew's designation of Jacob as the father of Joseph in 1:16 is intended to evoke the reader's memory of the

Old Testament figure. But it is noteworthy that the last four members of the genealogical table of the first gospel are identical to those of the third gospel's catalog except for the name of Joseph's father. Matthew lists "Jacob;" Luke "Heli." Joseph is like his Old Testament counterpart in at least three other respects; (1) he is chaste and refuses to be involved in immorality; (2) he has dreams in which the future is revealed to him and (3) he rescues Jesus by adopting him and by carrying him to safety in Egypt. These are of course superficial similarities, secondary to the cardinal events of Joseph's career in the Old Testament: slavery, imprisonment, enthronement. Nevertheless, it is specifically these three qualities which are — eulogized in the Testaments of the Twelve Patriarchs. The more momentous incidents of Joseph's life have receded, perhaps forced into the background by the messianic expectations surrounding Levi and Judah. At any rate, the messianic character of Joseph's life is absent; here he is acknowledged by the other patriarchs as a model of virtue: "Now Joseph was a good man and had the Spirit of God in him" (Test. of Sim. 4:1). Again, ". . . Joseph, my brother, the true and good man" (Test. of Dan. 5:1). In almost every instance chastity is the basis that is given for this evaluation. Joseph's life exemplifies the keeping of God's commandments, above all in his triumph over fornication, the sin most confessed and condemned by the other patriarchs.[18] In his own testimony the patriarch vividly narrates the agonizing temptations he endured at the hand of Potiphar's wife. Little is said of his imprisonment, and almost nothing of his elevation to vice-regent of Egypt; but the experience with the Egyptian woman has been expanded and embellished to the point of completely dominating his last will and testament.[19]

At least two other traits are acknowledged by Joseph: love and long-suffering, and they are combined with humility. Noteworthy is his claim, "You see, therefore, my children, what great things I endure that I should not put my brothers to shame" (17:1). And this is coupled with the exhortation, "You also love one another and with a long-suffering hide one another's faults" (17:2). In the light of these qualities Joseph presents himself as Jacob's successor in caring and providing for his brothers and their children. Only Joseph can assume this position because he is the only son among the patriarchs who "was like Jacob in all things" (18:4). The words attributed to him are important in this respect for they represent him as the grand patriarch:

> And after the death of Jacob my father I loved them more abundantly, and whatever he commanded I did for them. And I did not permit them to be afflicted in the least matter; and all that was in my hands I gave them. And their sons were my sons and my sons as their servants. And their life was my life, and all their sufferings were my suffering and all their sicknesses were my infirmity. My land was their land, and their counsel my counsel. And I did not exalt myself among them in arrogance because of my worldy glory, but I was among them as one of the least (17:5-8).

Dreams are not explicitly mentioned, but a vision is included which offers an apocalyptically colored glimpse of the final events of the age. More significant is Joseph's reference to a revelation received through an angel of God which warned him of the devices of Potiphar's wife: "Now therefore know that the God of my father has disclosed your wickedness to me by his angel" (6:6). Throughout the Testament of the Twelve Patriarchs the angel of God reveals what has been done or what will happen.

Matthew's portrayal of Joseph bears a resemblance to the Old Testament patriarch, but the corresponding features have not been derived from the original narrative in Gen. 37-50. He seems rather to have been invested with a character that parallels the more contemporary image of Joseph presented in the Testaments of the Twelve Patriarchs, particularly the Testament of Joseph.

Chaste, righteous and kind, Joseph is called to adopt Mary's child in order to engraft him into his family tree. He does so by giving the boy a name and thereby publicly declaring himself to be his father (1:25b). He is called Jesus, "for he will save his people from their sins" (1:21). This saving work is primarily nationalistic is character and scope: he is to be the saviour of his people, the Jews. Joseph, therefore, by adopting Jesus upholds the continuity of the Davidic line and the divine promises which have accompanied it for many generations.

At the same time, however, Jesus is more than the Son of David. His commission reaches beyond Davidic messianism. He is to save his people *from their sins.* Nowhere is such a function ascribed to the Old Testament king or his promised heir. It is said in 2 Sam. 3:18 that by David's hand God would save Israel from their enemies. To save from sins is a work which is restricted to the Lord, as is evident from Ps. 130:8, the Old Testament parallel closest to 1:21b, "And he will redeem Israel from all his lawlessnesses." Such an irregularity, however, is in keeping with the ambiguity of Jesus' origin. According to 2 Sam. 7:11-4 and Ps. 2:7, David's heir is to become God's son by adoption. The very opposite takes place in the first gospel. Jesus, a new creation of the holy Spirit and as a result the divine Human Being is adopted by David's descendant Joseph in order to fulfill the promises made to Israel,". . . and he called his name Jesus."

As Joseph upholds the continuity of Israel's history and the fulfillment of the Davidic promise, Mary is the bearer of this eschatological event of a new creation and the radical discontinuity it interposes. In the fulfillment quotation, as already indicated, she is identified as "the virgin." According to the introductory formula of 1:22, this whole thing happened in order to fulfill God's word spoken by the prophet. But that cannot include the virgin birth for Matthew does not seem to have known such a theologoumenon. It is not the doctrine of the virgin birth that led the evangelist to Is. 7:14.

There is another meaning and purpose to Matthew's abrupt interruption of the narrative and his identification of Mary as "the virgin."

In its reference to "the virgin" the fulfillment quotation of verse 23 corresponds to the Septuagint version of Is. 7:14. The original Hebrew text, however, does not convey such a designation for it does not utilize the technical term for virgin, *bethulah,* but simply the word *almah* ("young woman"). It is very likely that the Septuagint translation interpreted this young woman to be the corporate motherhood of Israel that had already found expression in such forms of address as "Daughter of Zion," "Rachel" and "Virgin Israel."[20] Israel is the virgin because she has not defiled herself through unfaithfulness and idolatry; and she will give birth to the messianic king.

Matthew appropriates this Septuagint version of Is. 7:14 in order to identify Mary in the light of her extraordinary maternity as the incarnation of Mother Israel. She represents the corporate motherhood of God's people giving birth to this incongruous Messiah.

Jesus therefore is the integration of both discontinuity and continuity. As the child of Mary he is a new creation generated by the holy Spirit. As the adopted son of Joseph he is a descendant of David and Abraham. The ambiguity of his origin corresponds to the two generations of the third division of the genealogy which he simultaneously fills, as well as the eschatological tension between the two numerical schemes of verse 17 that serve as the framework of his table of ancestry.

This dual origin and its concomitant identities: the Son of the Human Being and the Son of David, explain Matthew's strange account of Jesus' triumphal entry into Jerusalem. In contrast to Mark's version, Jesus rides on two beasts, an *onos* which is a coronation animal, and a *polos huios hypozygiou,* a pack animal.[21] This is not, as is often thought, a misunderstanding of the poetic parallelism of Zech. 9:9 but rather a dramatic reminder of the christological identities which Jesus bears and the dialectical eschatology which they express.

Although he represents two generations and wears two christological hats concurrently, he is one person and has one name, Jesus. This is the name which the angel commanded Joseph to give Mary's child because "he will save his people from their sins." Since the verb *sōsei* ("he will save") is an etymological pun on the Hebrew meaning of the name of Jesus, and since it is not explained as, for example, Immanuel is in 1:23, it must be assumed that Matthew's readers were familiar with it.[22] The Septuagint translation of Ps. 130 (129):8 appears to be quoted here. The differences between it and its rendition in Matthew can be accounted for on the basis of the evangelist's purposeful alteration. The substitution of the verb "he will save" for "he will redeem" is his work and not the result of an adoption of pre-Matthean tradition.[23] There can only be one reason for it; it is the verb that conveys the meaning of the name of Jesus.

He is to be called Jesus because he will save. His life will manifest a direct correspondence between his activity and his name, between his person and his work. That is why his naming is so important.[24] It anticipates what is yet to be told in this "Book of Origin."

FOOTNOTES

1 See Marshall D. Johnson's excellent study, *The Purpose of Biblical Genealogies, with Special Reference to the Setting of the Genealogies of Jesus* (Cambridge, at the University Press, 1969) esp. pp. 153, 176ff. Unfortunately Johnson reads the peculiarities of Matthew's genealogy in the light of a polemical setting of Jewish slander rather than the evangelist's own intention. Also H.C. Waetjen, "The Genealogy as the Key to the Gospel according to Matthew," *JBL* 95 (1976), pp. 205-30. C.T. Davis, "The Fulfillment of Creation: A Study of Matthew's Genealogy," *JAAR* 41 (1973), pp. 520-35.

FOOTNOTES

Creation: A Study of Matthew's Genealogy," *JAAR* 41 (1973), pp. 520-35.

2 See Waetjen, *op. cit.,* pp. 216-18.

3 G.F. Moore, "Fourteen Generations: 490 Years" *HTR* 14 (1921), p. 98.

4 Johnson, *Genealogies,* p. 180. G. Kuhn, "Die Geschlechtsregister Jesu bei Lukas und Mattäus, nach ihrer Herkunft untersucht," *ZNW* 22 (1923), pp. 221-2, suggested the common demoninator of a violent death which the three kings shared but recognized that this included Amon (Matt. 1:10) who was not eliminated from the genealogy. E. Lohmeyer, *Das Evangelium des Matthäus, Kritisch-exegetischer Kommentar zum Neuen Testament,* arranged and edited by W. Schmauch (Göttingen: Vanderhoeck and Ruprecht, 3rd ed., 1962), p. 3, suggests the omission is due to the inexactness of the LXX.

5 Strecker, *Gerechtigkeit,* p. 38, note 3. Also R. Bultmann, *History of the Synoptic Tradition,* p. 356.

6 Rodney T. Hood, "The Genealogies of Jesus," *Early Christian Origins: Studies in honor of H.R. Willoughby;* ed. by A. Wikgren (Chicago: Quadrangle Books, 1961), p. 10.

7 J. Jeremias, *Jerusalem,* pp. 293-5.

8. E. Lohmeyer, *Matthäus,* p. 3.

9 Krister Stendahl, *Matthew, Peake's Commentary on the Bible,* rev. ed. edited by M. Black and H.H. Rowley (London: Thomas Nelson and Sons, 1962), pp. 770-1, para. 674c. This possibility as far as I have been able to determine, was first posed by von Hofmann, *Weissagung und Erfüllung im Alten und Neuen Testamente* (Nördlingen: C.H. Beck, 1841-44) vol. 2, p. 42, who considered it at least probable that Jesus was intended by Matthew to be the thirteenth generation, and the risen Christ who would come again as the fourteenth. See also T. Zahn, *Das Evangelium des Matthäus. Kommentar zum Neuen Testament* (Leipzig: A. Deichert, 2nd ed., 1905), p. 53, fn. 19.

10 See below pp. 248-9.

11 See discussion of the problem in relation to the different points of view in Waetjen, *op. cit.,* pp. 213-5.

12 See the summary in Johnson, *op. cit.,* pp. 152-179.

13 Waetjen, *op. cit.,* pp. 216-9.

14 See also 2 Kings 8:12, 15:16; Hos. 14:1; Amos 1:13; Is. 40:11.

15 Also I John 3:9 and 5:1.

16 Although "the Son of God" is an important title, it is subordinate to "the Son of the Human Being." Against J. D. Kingsbury, *Matthew,* who argues for the primacy of "the Son of God" title in Matthew's christology.

17 T.H. Robinson, *The Gospel of Matthew, Moffat New Testament Commentary* (New York: Harper and Row, 1951), p. 3.

FOOTNOTES

18 T Reuben 4:6-9, 11 and 6:1-4; T Sim 5:1-3; T Jud 14:2-15:6 and 18:2; T Joseph 3-10. Also CD 2:14-21 and 4:17. Sirach 9:2-9 and 19:2.

19 T Joseph 10:2-4.

20 W. H. Brownlee, *The Meaning of the Dead Sea Scrolls for the Bible* (New York: Oxford University Press, 1964), pp. 274-81.

21 See below, pp. 202-3.

22 Strecker, *op. cit.,* p. 54 and especially his reference to Philo, *de mut. nom.* 121, which shows that the meaning of Jesus could be presupposed in Hellenistic Judaism.

23 Against Strecker, *ibid.,* p. 29.

24 Hans Kosmala, "The Conclusion of Matthew," *Annual of the Swedish Theological Institute,* 4 (1965), p. 142, "Matthew describes the name-giving and its significance in greater detail than the other evangelists."

Chapter IV

THE NARRATIVE OF BOOK ONE: "BEGINNINGS"
Matthew 2:1-4:25

Matthew is preoccupied with meaning, not historical fact or accuracy. From the beginning of his account of Jesus' life it is apparent that biographical interest is subordinate to the motives, both christological and eschatological, that have been introduced in the prologue. Nothing is said about the circumstances of Jesus' birth. Place and time, however, are critical and are specified in the opening clause, "And Jesus having been born in Bethlehem of Judaea in the days of Herod the King. . ."

The evangelist is more interested in telling the story of the Magi's arrival in Jerusalem. This initial episode determines the subsequent events that lead to Joseph's relocation of his family in Galilee and binds together in a cohesive unit the individual incidents of 2:1-23. It also introduces one of the dominant motives of the gospel's presentation of Jesus' life: the tension between nationalism and universalism.

The Magi are astrologers "from the east" who observed "his star in its rising" and came in search of the new born king of the Jews in order to worship him. The two prepositional phrases of verses 1 and 2: *apo anatolōn* and *en tē anatolē,* which employ the same noun, should be carefully differentiated. The former which is in the plural is a geographical expression and is appropriately translated "from the east;" while the latter, which is in the singular, denotes astronomical movement and means "in the rising."[1] The reaction which their announcement of the new born king evokes: "Herod was agitated and all Jerusalem with him ..." is curiously similar to that of Belshazzar and his court in Dan. 5:9 when they saw the divine sign of a hand writing on the plaster of the wall of the king's palace and discovered that the Magi were unable to interpret its words. According to Theodotion's Greek version, ". . . he was greatly agitated and his courtiers were agitated with him." Daniel is introduced by the queen and proceeds to demonstrate his wisdom in providing the interpretation. In Matthew's gospel, however, the situation is ironically reversed. The Magi, who once appeared inferior to Daniel and his associates,[2] have interpreted the meaning of the star, and they announce it upon their arrival in Jerusalem.

Herod's turmoil is not caused by his inability to grasp the meaning of the sign. For him "the star in the rising" can only point to a fulfillment of Num. 24:17-8 and accordingly his own dispossession as an Edomite by the new born Messiah. Although there is no explicit reference to this astrological oracle, certain features of Matthew's narration suggest a connection with it.[3] Balaam, its speaker, is not identified as a magus, but he is a man of divinization who names his place of origin both as Aram and "out of the mountains from the east" (Num. 23:7). After an encounter with "the angel of the Lord" he pronounces blessing on Israel three times; and in a fourth oracle he prophesies the future rising of "a star of Jacob," of "a human being out of Israel" who will defeat Moab and disinherit Edom.

In reply to Herod's inquiry on behalf of the Magi the chief priests and the scribes of the people cite Scripture to support their designation of Bethlehem of Judaea as the birthplace of the Messiah. The text which they cite in 2:6 should not be included among Matthew's fulfillment quotations.[4] It does not interrupt the narrative, and there is no acknowledgement of fulfillment. The formula that introduces it is the one most widely used in New Testament writings and Jewish literature.[5] In the First Gospel it always occurs on the lips of those who are involved in the story that is being narrated.[6]

Nevertheless, it is similar to the fulfillment quotations of the gospel in as far as it reproduces neither the Massoretic tradition nor the Septuagint.[7] It has a composite character: a clause from 2 Sam. 5:2 has been added to Mic. 5:1. Moreover, the phrase "land of Judah" has been substituted for "house of Ephratah." It not only supports the given location of Bethlehem in the province of Judaea; its similarity to the name of Judas enables the evangelist to hint at a personification of the land of Judah which the disciple Judas will eventually bear.[8] What is more immediately important, however, is the identification of the Messiah's birthplace with the ancestral home of David and the accompanying emphasis on his nationalistic mission: "For out of you (Bethlehem) will come forth the ruling one who will shepherd my people Israel."

After a briefing from Herod, the Magi set out for Bethlehem. As soon as they leave Jerusalem they rediscover the star which they saw in its rising and are guided by it to their desired destination: "It led them until coming it stood over where the child was." That is, the star which they saw appear above the horizon indicating the birth of the king of the Jews continues to ascend until it reaches its zenith point in the sky; and that is when it stands directly over the house in which Jesus lives. Precisely at that moment, as verse 10 points out, "they rejoiced with exceeding great joy." This is eschatological joy! The star has become identified with the young Messiah.[9] But more important, according to the significance which the ancient world attached to a star reaching its zenith point in the heavens: the king whom it represents has begun his rule![10] That is what the astrologers acknowledge when they offer him their worship and their gifts. They are outsiders, foreigners, yet they are the first and the only ones who pay homage to Jesus, the Son of David, the Jewish Messiah, at the beginning of his reign.

Herod and Jerusalem pose a stark contrast. The Magi's

announcement does not precipitate the anticipated response of celebration and festivity. The history of Israel has reached its goal: the promised and long-awaited Messiah has come. But his presence goes unacknowledged by those who know the Old Testament prophecies, "the chief priests and the scribes of the people." When the Magi do not return to inform Herod about the young king, he sends out his soldiers to slaughter "*all* the boys in Bethlehem and in *all* its surrounding regions from two years and under" (2:16). The phrase "two years and under" suggests the possible age of Jesus at this time, as discerned by Herod from the testimony of the Magi. But it may also indicate the fact that the boys who were killed had not yet been enrolled among Israel by genealogy because they were not yet three years old.[11] A lost generation of which Jesus is the only survivor![12]

Although the story of the flight into Egypt (2:13-5) is told from Joseph's point of view, the thought of the evangelist is fixed on the necessity of Jesus' withdrawal. It is incongruous for the Messiah to be dispossessed of his rule and to be forced to find asylum in Egypt by his own people. Matthew, however, establishes this anomaly by noting the fulfillment of Hos. 11:1, "Out of Egypt I called my son."

The tragedy of the boys' massacre is also incompatible with the beginning of the messianic age.[13] For the evangelist it is nevertheless confirmed by the prophecy of Jer. 31:15. The fulfillment formula begins with a favorite adverbial particle, *tote* ("then"). Only one other quotation is introduced in this manner, 27:9-10. By using it and simultaneously omitting the phrase, "by the Lord," Matthew avoids attributing these events to the intention of God. Both occurrences, Herod's slaughter of the innocents and Judas' betrayal of Jesus are initiated by the will of human beings. The adverbial particle "then" serves as the immediate connecting link between these actions and the terrible fulfillment which they bring about. Israel's rejection of Jesus the Messiah already at the beginning of his life, as signified by the persecution of Herod, leads to self-inflicted judgment. Coincidental with the eschatological joy of the Magi there is the bitter lamentation of Mother Israel weeping for her murdered children.

The flight into Egypt and the massacre of the boys are concomitant eschatological realities which, like the Old Testament events of the Exodus and the Babylonian deportation that may be presupposed as generic conceptions in 2:13-8, signal an end and concurrently a new beginning. On the one hand, Jesus' expulsion from the "land of Israel" is an exile that is terminated by his repatriation after Herod's death (2:20). But on the other hand, his flight into Egypt is a reversal of the Exodus typology. Judaea is the new land of bondage, the persecution of Jesus is analogous to that which Moses experienced as an infant, and the massacre of the boys is equivalent to the fate which the male children of the Israelites suffered at the hand of Pharoah (Ex. 1:15-2:10). As the sole survivor of the children of Rachel, and therefore the only link between the past and the future, Jesus like Moses of old incorporates the identity of the remnant. Although forced out of the the land of his inheritance, he will be called from his asylum in Egypt; and upon his return he, like Moses, will launch a new Exodus and a new history of Israel. The explicit verbal reproduction of parts of the Septuagint text of Ex. 4:18-20 in Matt. 2:19-21 hints at this implicit Exodus model. The similarity between the command given to Joseph, "Arise, take the young child and his mother and return to the land of Israel for those seeking the life of the young child have died" (2:20) and that spoken to Moses, "Return to Egypt for all those seeking your life have died" (Ex. 4:19) intimates a Moses typology and suggests the substitution of the "land of Israel" in place of Egypt.

After Herod's death Jesus is returned to the land of Israel; it is his legacy as the Son of David. However, in view of the rule of Archelaus, Herod's son, and the threat which it poses on the life of the young Messiah, Joseph is compelled to transfer him from Judaea once more. This time he takes up residence in Nazareth; and that, according to Matthew, is how

Jesus the Messiah and heir to Judaea, the "land of Israel," came to be called "the Nazarene."[14]

Numerous efforts have been made to solve the problem of the elusive quotation of verse 23.[15] Unfortunately its peculiar introduction has generally been disregarded. This is the only fulfillment formula which relates the participle, *to rēthen* ("that which was spoken") to the plural "prophets." Furthermore, this is the only fulfillment formula which ends with the particle *hoti* ("that"); all the others are concluded with the genitive singular present active participle *legontos* ("saying") which introduces the quotation as direct discourse. It is possible that the *hoti* may be used as a sign of direct discourse and intended by the evangelist. But there is only one instance where the verb "to fulfill" is combined with it in order to introduce a scriptural quotation, John 15:25.[16] In every other case, above all in the First Gospel, the participle form of *legein* ("to say") follows the verb "to fulfill" when a specific text is cited.

Verse 23, in spite of its fulfillment formula, is not a fulfillment quotation because the words, "He will be called a Nazarene" is not derived from the Old Testament. They simply convey a fact, an awkward one. The Son of David, the heir to the land of Israel, is being called "the Nazarene." This is another irregularity in his life. Matthew has no specific fulfillment quotation to offer nor does he try to invent one. His purpose is simply to indicate that the incongruity contained in the epithet "the Nazarene" is the result of Jesus' rejection in his own country by his own people and is established by the word of God spoken by the prophets in general.[17]

By means of the transitional particle *de* ("and") and the general chronological reference, "in those days," the author spans the elapse of time and simultaneously keeps his new narrative material, derived from Mark, linked to what he has already recounted. There is no structural division at this point: it is not the beginning of the gospel,[18] nor is it the opening section of Book One.[19] This is a continuation of the story of Jesus' life which was begun in 2:1.

A new personality emerges in chapter 3, John the Baptizer. He intrudes as a stranger, unanticipated and unannounced. Nothing is said of his origin. He is simply there — in the wilderness of Judaea! — proclaiming the imminent kingdom of God. His significance, however, is established by the quotation of Is. 40:3. He is the voice of the last times calling for the repentance of Israel, "Prepare the way of the Lord, make his paths straight." Further identification is indicated by the immediately following description of his clothing.[20] As the wearer of a garment of camel's hair "with a leather belt around his waist," he is none other than Elijah. The clause of 3:4b is almost a literal rendition of the description of Elijah's dress in 2 —— Kings 1:8. In the person and work of John the Baptizer, Elijah has returned for a second career. His appearance, therefore, signals the fulfillment of Mal. 3:1 and 4:5-6 and adumbrates the end of the present age. The Lord is coming at last, and through repentance and baptism Israel is getting ready for this eschatological event.

John's success is impressive: all respond! "Then there went out to him Jerusalem and all Judaea and the whole countryside of the Jordan, and they were baptized in the Jordan river by him confessing their sins" (3:5f). The religious leaders are among them. They specifically — not the masses as in Lk. 3:7 — are singled out for denunciation. Like all the others, they have been baptized confessing their sins. But, John insists, mere repentance is not enough. A genuine change of mind is authenticated by corresponding deeds. Racial or national identity as sons of Abraham is no guarantee for security in the impending crisis. Judgment is imminent; "already the ax is being laid to the root of the trees" where the fruit of repentance is not in evidence.

Matt. 3:11-2 should not be separated from 3:7-10. There is no indication in the text that these words are directed at another group or the crowds in general. These verses continue John's address to the Pharisees and Sadducees and emphasize the preparatory character of his baptism; it is "for repentance." They, the Jewish religious leaders, are to know that there is yet another baptism which will be administered by the one who comes after him, "the one who is stronger than I, whose shoes I am not worthy to carry."

John does not say who this is, but the evangelist already anticipated it in his quotation of Is. 40:3 in verse 3. Moreover, on the basis of John's identity as the incarnation of Elijah, it can only be Yahweh. In accordance with apocalyptic expectation Yahweh is coming to render judgment, and in the great separation that takes place the grain will be gathered into the barn, and the chaff will be burned with inextinguishable fire (3:12).

All Israel is gathered and waiting at the Jordan river under the ministry of John. But it is not the Lord God who appears. Jesus, having crossed over the Jordan, arrives from Galilee. It is his second return to his own territory, the land of Israel. Like all the other Jews he comes to be baptized by John. Evidently he too wishes to participate in this eschatological act of repentance expressed in baptism; his own words in verse 15b make that explicit. But John objects to baptizing Jesus, "I have need to be baptized by you and you come to me?" Such an admission suggests that John recognizes who Jesus is.

Jesus' reply, "Let it be now, for so it is fitting for us to fulfill all righteousness!" is at once an acknowledgment of the validity of John's objection and at the same time a disclosure of his self-understanding. He in fact is the one whom John heralded. Although there is no instance in the gospel in which he baptizes with the holy Spirit, the meaning that nevertheless appears to be intended by the author is that Jesus is "the stronger one . . . who will baptize with the holy Spirit and with fire."

In spite of his superiority he refuses to show any elitism. Whether or in what way he is the Lord must await further disclosure. For the moment he insists on expressing solidarity with all those of the land of Israel. What is implied is his own act of repentance, his own confession of sins and consequently his acknowledgment of the eschatological character of John's baptism. Nothing less can be involved in the meaning of his determination "to fulfill all righteousness."[21] Through the peculiar use of the first person plural pronoun "us" in verse 15b the addressees of Matthew's gospel are drawn into Jesus' identification with his fellow Jews and his submission to John's baptism. Even though, like John, they may need the baptism which Jesus brings, an initial reorientation is required that will involve them in doing justice and righteousness.

Immediately after his baptism Jesus' identity is unexpectedly disclosed. As he ascends from the water the heavens are opened, and the Spirit of God who originally created him comes upon him descending as a dove. At that moment a voice sounds from heaven. According to Mk. 1:11, Jesus alone was addressed. Matthew, however, has substituted a demonstrative pronoun, "*This* is my beloved Son in whom I took pleasure." Yahweh has come and baptized with the holy Spirit, but only Jesus is the recipient! Furthermore, Yahweh introduces Jesus to all of Israel assembled at the Jordan river and endorses him as a surrogate. As the divine offspring who bears the holy Spirit he will now begin to act on behalf of the Lord.

His immediate commission is to be tempted by Satan: "*Then* Jesus was led up into the wilderness by the Spirit to be tempted by the devil." The preposition *an* ("up") prefixed to the verb suggests that this is a continuation of the ascent begun in baptism (3:16), which reaches its climax on "a very high mountain" in the third temptation. Before the temptations actually begin, Jesus, according to Matthew's interpolation of 4:2, "fasted forty days and forty nights." Not only is the time of "forty nights" added to the period of forty days specified in the Marcan source; it is also indicated that this duration was devoted to fasting. These two features hint at implicit comparisons with the Old Testament experiences of Moses and Elijah. Moses was on Mt. Sinai "forty days and forty nights" at least two different times: Ex. 24:18 and 34:28. During the second stay "he neither ate bread or drank water." But he enjoyed the divine presence on both occasions; and he and the seventy elders of Israel had been banqueted by God at the beginning of these mountain-top experiences (Ex. 24:11). According to I Kings 19:8, Elijah walked "forty days and forty nights" to Mt. Horeb; but he was sustained by what he initially had eaten and drunk. In contradistinction to these two great prophets of the Old Testament, Jesus neither eats nor is fed by God before this forty day and forty night interval. Although his continuation in the wilderness during this period resembles Elijah's experience, — Moses sojourned on the mount of God; Elijah appears to have walked in the desert — Jesus, in contrast to Elijah who had encountered the still small voice of God, is confronted by the devil at the end of this time.

Three challenges are laid down in different geographical settings: the wilderness, Jerusalem, a very high mountain. They also occur in the other version of this Q tradition, Lk. 4:1-12, but in another order. Moreover, Lk. 4:13 intimates that there were more than three temptations, "and having completed every temptation, the devil withdrew . . . " Mk. 1:13, on the other hand, merely recounts that Jesus was tempted by Satan.

In the first temptation Jesus is challenged to corroborate his Son of God identity for the purpose of, what would appear to be, self-satisfaction. Surely such a long period of abstinence should be rewarded by a display of power which would not only satisfy Jesus' hunger but also confirm his divine sonship. The unique use of the plural, however, ". . . speak that *these stones* may become *loaves of bread,*" hints at a temptation with economic-political implications. Such a miraculous production of bread would serve to validate his presentation to Israel by the heavenly voice. Moses had been commanded by Yahweh, "Tell the rock before their eyes to yield its water; so you shall bring water out of the rock" (Num. 20:8). The enormity of Jesus' miracle, transforming stones into loaves of bread, would establish his equality with, if not his superiority to, Moses.

Jesus, however, refuses to certify himself in this way and replies with a literal quotation of Deut. 8:3b drawn from a context in which Moses is exhorting the people of Israel before entry into the Promised Land: "The human being does not live by bread alone but by every word issuing from the mouth of God." Jesus not only declines to satisfy himself physically or psychologically by taking advantage of his divinely acknowledged deity. His response indicates that as the Son of God he prefers to understand himself as a human being who endures — not by a self-contained and self-serving exercise of power — but by an interdependent relationship with the Creator.[22] Jesus' response to this first temptation is not an indication of a religious orientation that is indifferent toward the economic realities of life. Eventually on two different occasions he will provide food for the masses by multiplying a few loaves of bread and fish. What he is repudiating here is an understanding of humanness that is defined by self-sufficiency and self-satisfaction as well as self-endorsement through the performance of power miracles.

The scene of the second temptation is Jerusalem, more specifically "the pinnacle of the Temple." Like the first this is more than an inducement to self-validation. Jesus is not simply being urged to throw himself down on the basis of so much accumulated holiness in order to confirm his divine credentials to himself. This is a challenge to substantiate his introduction to Israel as "the Son of God" by an exploitation of the sacred traditions of the past: holy City, holy Temple and holy Scripture. Jesus, however, refuses to resort to or rely on traditional categories and precedents of the past no matter how holy they may be. The scriptural admonition which he directs at Satan, "You shall not tempt your Lord God," is also being applied to himself as one who in his humanness is committed to the fulfillment of all righteousness. God's faithfulness is not a measurable quantity. It is not to be tested, either by simple dependence on the religious heritage of the fathers nor by the performance of spectacular feats which attempt to demonstrate continuity with the sanctified past. The third temptation, according to the redaction of 4:8, occurs on "a very high mountain." Luke's version (4:5) simply reads, "And leading him up . . . " This is the first of many mountains in Matthew's geography. While they all express the "architectonic symbolism of the Center,"[23] they do not uniformly serve the same purpose in the gospel. Most of them are definite mountains, usually introduced by the phrase *eis to oros* ("into the mountain"), yet only one is named: the Mount of Olives in Jerusalem. Two, however, are indefinite; the mount of temptation and the mount of transfiguration; in both cases the evangelist refers to them as "a very high mountain."[24] But there is little similarity between them. One is located in Judaea, the homeland and inheritance from which Jesus the Messiah has twice been expelled but where he nevertheless hopes to begin his messianic work. The other is in Galilee, the province he adopts for the fulfillment of his messiahship and where he enjoys a successful ministry. The one is the site of the third temptation with its tantalizing offer: "All these things ("the kingdoms of the world and their glory") I will give you, if falling down you will worship me." The other is the scene of the unveiling of his apotheosis as the Human Being who will inherit the kingdom of God. The ascent of the one occurs prior to the beginning of his ministry and is accompanied by Satan offering world dominion. The ascent of the other takes place in the company of three disciples who are to glimpse the glory that awaits him as he begins to journey up to Jerusalem in order to suffer, die and be raised again.

Noticeably missing in the third temptation is the initial conditional clause, "If you are God's Son." That may be an implicit acknowledgment of the peculiar self-understanding of "Son of God" which Jesus has conveyed in his countercharges to the temptor. Worshipping the devil cannot be a temptation for one who is God, but it is for one who insists on a humanness

that involves an identification with the suffering and
oppression of others. Satan's proposal of uniting the political
power structures of the world under one religious rule even
with the best intentions of eliminating injustice and poverty is
an alluring temptation. But, as Jesus recognizes, it is nothing
more than a perpetuation of the diabolical cycle of exchanging
one oppressor for another. For a lordship over the kingdoms
of the world is simply a continuation of the hierarchical structure of that order by the very act of submission to Satan.
Worshipping and serving God to which Jesus commits himself
will involve him — and those who follow him — in a divine
egalitarian partnership. The kingdom of God, in contrast to
the kingdoms of the world, is a realm of horizontally structured
relationships in which God shares life and power with those
who are willing to take the risk of being truly human, even to
the extent of suffering and dying for others. That is the destiny
manifested in Jesus' career, and it is acknowledged by him on
the cosmic mountain in Galilee after his resurrection from the
dead, "All authority in heaven and on earth was given me."

At the conclusion of the third temptation, immediately
after Jesus' rejoinder, "the devil abandons him;" and Jesus
finally experiences refreshment through the ministrations of
the angels.

But subsequently when the news of John the Baptizer's
imprisonment reaches him he withdraws from Judaea once
more (4:12). The use of the verb *anechōrēsen* ("he withdrew")
in this context intimates that the "delivering up" of the one
poses danger to the other.[25] Jesus and John are linked to each
other eschatologically, and therefore what happens to the one
has consequences for the other. John as the forerunner Elijah
prepares the way of the Lord by calling for Israel's repentance
and baptizing all the people in the Jordan river. He also prepares the way of the Lord by going before him into rejection
and death in Judaea. For Jesus this is the third retreat from the
land of his messianic inheritance.

Jesus returns to Galilee and according to the

distinctively Matthean tradition of 4:13, "he took up residence in Capernaum." This, as 9:1 indicates, becomes "his own city;" and the edited verses of 9:10, 28; 13:1, 36 and 17:25 show that he had a dwelling there.[26] As the Messiah Jesus lives among his people! In 9:10 "tax collectors and sinners" join him "in his house" in order to recline at table and share a meal with him; the clause, "they were reclining with Jesus..." points to him as the host.[27] Later in 9:28, he is followed "into his house" by two blind men whose sight he restores. Jesus leaves "his house" in 13:1 in order to speak to the masses by the sea; he re-enters "his house" in order to impart special teaching to his disciples alone. Jesus' reprimand of Simon Peter's all too quick responses to the tax collectors in 17:24f. occurs privately after having gone "into his house."

Residence in Capernaum is as irregular for Jesus the Messiah as it was in Nazareth (2:23). His country is Judaea and, according to 2:11, he lived in a house in Bethlehem. Nevertheless, compelled to withdraw again, he chooses to move into Capernaum "by the sea." For in as far as it belongs to the territory of the tribes of Zebulon and Naphtali it will enable him to function as "the one who will shepherd" the lost sheep of the house of Israel. For Matthew this incongruity is confirmed by the prophecy of Isaiah; "The land of Zebulon and the land of Naphtali, the way of the sea, across the Jordan, Galilee of the Gentiles. The people who sat in darkness began to see a great light, and to those seated in the country and shadow of death light began to dawn."[28] A star arose over Judaea, but the people of God rejected it. Then the light dawned in Galilee, the tribal regions of Zebulon and Naphtali, and the Jewish masses who lived there saw it and began to turn to it.

"From then Jesus began to preach and to say, 'Repent, for the kingdom of God has drawn near.'" This eschatological proclamation which John the Baptizer originated, and to which he himself responded (3:13), is now adopted and introduced by him in Capernaum and Galilee. Eventually the disciples will be charged to preach it in their own mission to the lost sheep of Israel (10:6f.). John is the forerunner of this good news. Jesus and his disciples merely repeat it. Although he is the last and the greatest of the Old Testament prophets, John can initiate it because he also participates in the new age that Jesus inaugurated by his birth.

Matthew underlines this moment of transition by introducing the next phase of Jesus' messianic career with the unusual combination of a preposition and an adverb: *apo tote* ("from then"). Because it is used once more in 16:21, it has been regarded as a formal indication of a literary structure which divides the gospel into three major sections: the prologue (1:1 - 4:16) which presents the origin of the Messiah and the preparation of his mission; the second part, introduced by 4:17 which expounds the content of Jesus' kingdom of God proclamation, and the final part beginning with 16:21 which elucidates the "theme of the Son of Man and his way to resurrection."[29] However, in view of its two-fold use at strategic points in Jesus' ministry, the phrase serves to differentiate historic moments or turning points rather than major divisions of the book's literary framework. From 4:16 to the climactic moment of Peter's confession in 16:16, Jesus' healing and teaching activity manifest the eschatological reality of the kingdom of God which he has followed John the Baptist in proclaiming. Peter's confession, however, initiates a new phase in which Jesus' forthcoming suffering, death and resurrection are incorporated into the content of the gospel. In this way continuity is established between Jesus' proclamation of the kingdom of God and the eventual proclamation of Jesus by the church.

In his appropriation of Mark 1:16-20 Matthew has opportunity to demonstrate the immediate success of Jesus' Galilean ministry. Two sets of brothers immediately respond to his message and follow him: "Simon, the one called Peter and Andrew his brother" and "James the son of Zebedee and John his brother." Both pairs are fishermen: the first two are poor, the other two moderately affluent. Simon and Andrew, having only hand casting nets, must wade into the water as far as they can and concentrate their fishing around the shore of the lake. James and John are in business with their father who owns a boat and can therefore fish in the deep waters of the lake and who also has hired hands to help with the larger nets and the greater quantity of fish that will be caught.

A predilection for numbers and numerical schemes has already become obvious in the gospel's introductory genealogy. Here, in 4:18, 21, the phrase "two brothers" is inserted into the Marcan tradition. The number "two" appears to be especially meaningful, for the evangelist edits it into his gospel numerous times. In 8:28 there are two demoniacs in place of the one in Mk. 5:2. Twice two blind men receive their sight (9:27, 20:30); Mk. 10:46 and 8:22 refer only to individuals. Two false witnesses are specified in 26:60; Mk. 14:57 employs the indefinite pronoun "some." A motive may be suggested in 18:16, ". . . by the mouth of two or three witnesses everything will be established;" another in 18:20, "Where two or three are gathered together in my name, there I am in their midst." The number two denotes the legal requirement for testimony as well as the beginning of community.[30] Called to follow Jesus in order to form a new community under the rule of God, Simon and Andrew, James and John will eventually be commissioned to bear witness to the good news of that reality.

The narrative of Book One ends with a summary statement of Jesus' activity "in all of Galilee" (4:23ff.). The author emphasizes his teaching and prepares for the following Sermon on the Mount by inserting the verb *didaskōn* ("teaching") before the borrowed Marcan participle, "preaching." In contrast to Mk. 1:39, Jesus' healing is not limited to exorcism. According to 4:24, every kind of sickness and malady was cured; and this very likely is an anticipation of the content of chapters 8-9. The report, distinctively Matthean, that Jesus' fame spread throughout Syria may hint at the gospel's place of origin. At the same time it is also observed that Jesus attracted "large crowds" from Galilee, the Decapolis, Jerusalem, Judaea and Transjordan. These masses, as will become more evident, are Jewish.[31] Like the two sets of brothers they follow Jesus, and he is conscious of being sent to them. On their behalf he will strive to fulfill his messianic destiny. He has compassion for them because they are oppressed and exploited (9:36). He is able to identify with them because like him they have been dispossessed.

FOOTNOTES

1 See W. Bauer, *A Greek-English Lexicon of the New Testament and Other Early Christian Literature,* trans. by W.F. Arndt and F.W. Gingrich (Chicago: University of Chicago Press, 1957), p. 61.

2 See 1:20; 2:10, 27; 4:4; 5:7, 11, 15.

3 Also Lohmeyer, *Matthäus,* p. 25.

4 So it is often done. Stendahl, *The School of St. Matthew* (Uppsala: C.W.K. Gleerup, 1954), pp. 99-100. Strecker, *Der Weg,* p. 57.

5 See B.M. Metzger, "The Formulas Introducing Quotations of Scripture in the New Testament and the Mishnah," *JBL* 70 (1951), pp. 299-301.

6 See 4:4, 6, 7, 10; 11:10; 21:13; 26:24, 31.

7 Stendahl, *op. cit.,* p. 100.

8 See below, pp. 242-3.

9 Compare Is. 49:6 and 60:3.

10 From Suetonius' life of Julius Caesar in *The Twelve Caesars* and the appearance of a comet about an hour before sunset at the time of his death the conclusion may be drawn that a king is considered to begin his rule when his star reaches its zenith point in the sky.

11 See 2 Chron. 31:16. I owe this reference to Mr. Raymond Humphries, a doctoral student in the Graduate Theological Union. For alternate possibilities, see Lohmeyer, *op. cit.,* p. 29, n. 2.

12 A second century rabbinic story of Abraham's birth provides an interesting parable to this opening event of Jesus' life. On the night of the great patriarch's birth his father Terah entertained some of his friends. Among them were astrologers and councilors of the King Nimrod's court, who when they were returning home after midnight observed a star which

FOOTNOTES

swallowed up the four stars of the four corners of heaven. They reported to the king that a boy had been born who would conquer the world and urged him to purchase the child from his parents and then kill him. When Terah learned of the king's intentions he hid his son in a cave for three years. See *The Jewish Encyclopedia* (New York and London: Funk & Wagnalls Co., 1906), p. 86.

13 Compare Jer. 31:1-14.

14 Compare E. Schweizer, "Er wird Nazoräer," *Judentum, Urchristentum Kirche. Festschrift für Joachim Jeremias* (Berlin: Alfred Töpelmann, 1960), pp. 90-3. Bertil Gärtner, *Die rätselhaften Termini Nazoräer und Iskariot. Horae Soederblomianae* (Uppsala: C.W.K. Gleerup, 1957).

15 Stendahl, *op. cit.,* pp. 103-4. Gundry, R.H., *The Use of the Old Testament in St. Matthew's Gospel. Supplements to Novum Testamentum* (Leiden: E.J. Brill, 1967), pp. 97-9. Strack-Billerbeck, *Matthäus*, I, 92-4. C.H. Cave, "St. Matthew's Infancy Narrative," *NTS* 9 (1963), p. 390. N. Walker, "The Alleged Matthean Errata," *NTS* 9 (1963), pp. 392-4.

16 But see also Jn. 18:9 where the combination is used with regard to a saying of Jesus.

17 See T. Zahn, *Matthäus,* p. 116. Also R. Hummel, *Auseinandersetzung,* p. 137.

18 See Lohmeyer, *op. cit.,* p. 33 and Strecker, *op. cit.,* p. 91.

19 As B.W. Bacon, *Studies in Matthew,* pp. 81-2; G.D. Kilpatrick, *Origins,* p. 135; Stendahl, *op. cit.,* p. 25, and others have proposed.

20 Note how Matthew has rearranged the sequence of Mk. 1:2-6.

21 See G. Barth, *Matthew's Understanding of the Law,* p. 138. As a candidate for baptism, Jesus "enters the ranks of sinners."

22 Compare Bultmann, *Synoptic Tradition,* p. 256.

23 M. Eliade, *Cosmos and History,* pp. 12-4.

24 Codex D and Eusebius include *lian* ("very") in 17:1 instead of *kat idian* ("privately") which may be a scribal effort at harmonization with Mk. 9:2. On the other hand, Codex D and Eusebius may be efforts at harmonizing 17:1 with 4:8. What matters is the contrast between them that seems to be intended by the evangelist.

25 See 2:14, 22; 12:15; 14:13; 15:21. For other uses of the verb "to deliver up," see 10:17, 19, 21; 17:22; 20:18, 19; 26:2.

26 See the discussion on the problem of Jesus' house in Strecker, *op. cit.,* pp. 95-6 and Trilling, *Das Wahre Israel,* p. 108.

27 Also A.H. McNeile, *The Gospel according to St. Matthew* (London: Macmillan, 1915), p. 118.

28 The aorist indicative verbs are best rendered as ingressive or inceptive aorists. See Blass, Debrunner, Funk, *A Greek Grammar of the New Testament and Other Early Christian Literature* (Chicago: University of Chicago Press, 1961), p. 171. Also C.F.D. Moule, *An Idiom-Book of New Testament Greek* (Cambridge: at the University Press, 2nd ed., 1959), pp. 10-1. Comp. LXX Num. 24:17 and Is. 60:1.

FOOTNOTES

29 Edgar Krentz, "The Extent of Matthew's Prologue: Toward the Structure of the First Gospel," *JBL* 83 (1964), pp. 409-14. Also J.D. Kingsbury, *Matthew.*

30 Compare with the pairs of rabbis in Pirke Aboth 1:3-12. According to Rabbi Aqiba, "All things which God created, he created in pairs."

31 Also Trilling, *op. cit.,* pp. 113, 130-8. Hummel, *op. cit.,* p. 39.

Chapter V

THE DISCOURSE OF BOOK ONE: "THE SERMON ON THE MOUNT"

Matthew 5:1 - 7:27

The setting of the first of Jesus' five discourses in the gospel is a specific yet unnamed mountain. Since the same prepositional phrase: *eis to oros* ("into the mountain") is used in 14:23, 15:29 and 28:16 and in each case the geographical location is Galilee, it would appear that all four are one and the same mountain, an *axis mundi* on which God dwells and from which a new creation is emerging.

The mountain of 5:1 is frequently regarded to be a type of Sinai because the typologies of Jesus as a New Moses and his teaching as a New Torah seem to be implicit in Matthew's presentation of Jesus' ethics.[1]

But the authority which Jesus discloses in his teaching in the Sermon on the Mount is not that of a New Moses or even the Messiah. According to the transition formula which closes the Sermon, ". . . they were astonished at his teaching, for he was teaching them as one having authority and not as their scribes" (7:29). The continuity of Moses' tradition is represented by the scholars, the scribes, who with the Pharisees are acknowledged by Jesus himself as the occupants of Moses' *cathedra* (23:2). In contrast to their practice of "erecting a fence around the Torah" in order to keep a human being far from transgression, Jesus radicalizes or overthrows Moses in order to return to the original intention of the divine will in the giving of the Law. That same authority which expresses itself in the, ". . . but I say to you" formula of the six antitheses in

5:21-47 is manifested in miraculous deeds of healing and forgiveness. Indeed, it is in his cure of the palsied man that Jesus enunciates, ". . . Son of the Human Being has *authority* on earth to forgive sins" (9:6). The authority, therefore, which he exercises, whether it is in word or in deed, is that of the Human Being, not that of a new Moses. It is also not the authority of the Messiah for in differentiating between David's Son and David's Lord in his challenge to the Pharisees, Jesus affirms the subordination of the former to the later (22:41ff.). Since the "Lord" title is linked to the Human Being, as for example in 12:8, "For the Lord of the sabbath is the Son of the Human Being," the unavoidable conclusion is that the authority which Jesus displays in his teaching as well as his conduct arises out of his identity as the Human Being who is simultaneously the Lord. His *being seated* on the mountain, a posture which reoccurs in 15:29 and 24:3 and which on the basis of 22:44, 19:28, 25:31 and especially 26:64 may be construed as an installation into office, that is, "being seated on the right hand of power," conveys the type concept of enthronement. The immediate audience is "his disciples;" Jesus' teaching is directed at them. But 7:28 indicates that the crowds are not excluded; they are to hear the demands he makes on those who would follow him.

The teaching of the Sermon is conveyed first in the more or less traditional form of the beatitude. Nine pronouncements of blessedness are introduced by the adjective *makarios* ("fortunate"). Three, possibly four, appear to have been adopted from the Q source (Lk. 6:20-2); the other five are uniquely Matthean.[2] Of the nine only the last one occurs in the second person plural; the others are in the third person plural.[3] The first eight correspond in part to the structure of the beatitudes found in Wisdom literature.[4] Certain conditions and activities are acknowledged as blessed, that is, bearing divine favor. Each, however, is accompanied by an eschatologically focused affirmation or promise which is introduced by the causal conjunction *hoti* ("because"). This form: a pronouncement of blessedness followed by an eschatological guarantee, has no parallels in the Old Testament or intertestamental Wisdom literature. It appears to be peculiar to Matthew and Luke, especially the former, for in addition to its eight occurrences in 5:3-10 it is also found in 13:16 and 16:17.

The first, 5:3 is an expanded version of Lk. 6:20. Matthew has appended the phrase *tō pneumati,* which is to be rendered as a dative of reference ("with reference to the spirit"), to the pronouncement, "Blessed are the poor." It is poverty with respect to the human, not the divine Spirit which Jesus blesses here. This kind of impoverishment may be the result of oppression: psychological, social, political or economic, by which self-identity and dignity are destroyed. It may refer to a destitution of the human spirit caused by a lack of self-esteem which in turn effects a loss of "heart" or incentive. Already now, in the present, the kingship of God belongs to all those who find themselves in this condition, regardless of its origin: ". . . theirs *is* the rule of God."

In addition to the first, only the eighth beatitude enunciates such an eschatological actuality. "Fortunate are those who are persecuted on account of justice, for theirs *is* the rule of God." Neither 5:3 or 5:10 hold out a promise or offers a reward. The copula in the clause: "theirs *is* the rule of God" is not a predicate which has future significance.[5] Both sayings pronounce a present blessedness on specific circumstances: poverty of spirit and persecution, but *only on the basis of a present possession,* namely the kingship of God.

Between these benedictions of 5:3 and 10 the evangelist has arranged a series of six affirmations upheld by promises of future realization:

5:4 Blessed are those who grieve, for they will be cheered up.

5:5 Blessed are those who are unassuming, for they will inherit the earth.

5:6 Blessed are those who hunger and thirst for

justice, for they will be satisfied.

5:7 Blessed are those who are merciful, for they will be mercied.

5:8 Blessed are the pure with reference to the heart (the seat of their motivation), for they will see God.

5:9 Blessed are the peacemakers, for they will be called the children of God.

These six are not directed at particular circumstances or conditions. Instead they affirm a present blessedness of certain activities (grieving, hungering and thirsting for justice, peace making) and attitudes (being unassuming, merciful, pure in heart) *on the basis of future fulfillment.* They are not entrance requirements into the kingdom of God;[6] for, according to the first and eighth beatitudes between which they are sandwiched, the rule of God is already a present possession. Neither are they simply a set of virtues or moral ideals which characterize the Christian life.[7] They are rather dispositions of character, pursuits of certain activities which bear promises of gratification. In spite of any and all evidence to the contrary, these are postures of authentic human existence because they have a future.

The final beatitude is spoken in the second person plural. Evidently Jesus is turning from the masses of followers to his disciples. The previous benediction on those suffering persecution for the sake of justice is expanded and applied to them. Moreover, they are charged to rejoice and exult because their reward with God is great, "for so they persecuted the prophets before you." Since Jesus has only begun his ministry and there has been no indication of persecution thus far, this pronouncement appears to reflect the life situation of the gospel. The disciples are to be identified more immediately with the Christian Jews of Matthew's church who are being persecuted by their fellow Jews.[8]

Against this background of persecution and suffering the disciples are declared to be "the salt of the earth" and "the light of the world." These metaphors have undergone such extensive editorial revision° that they express a uniquely Matthean point of view. The disciples, first of all, are to be a preservative, not merely preserved; that is, a saving instead of a saved people.[9] The peculiar notion of salt becoming "foolish" or perhaps "flat" is shared by Lk. 14:34; the consequence of such a possibility, as Matthew alone observes, is that "it has strength for nothing" and as a result is "tossed out to be trodden under foot by human beings." The continuation of the metaphor, therefore, may suggest the inclusion of other uses and functions of salt: cleansing and seasoning as well as preserving.

The second metaphor: "You are the light of the world," which is peculiar to Matthew, is interpreted by two subsequent analogies. As "the light of the world" the disciples are to be as visible as "a city located on a mountain which cannot be hidden" or as a lamp which is not placed "under a peck-measure but on a lampstand" where it can serve effectively to give illumination to those in the house. The metaphor itself is somewhat unusual, for it is traditional to think of God as the light of the world or, according to Is. 10:17 and 60:19f., "the light of Israel." The striking application of this metaphor in Matt. 5:14 does have a precedent in Is. 42:6 and 49:6 where the Servant of the Lord is appointed to be "a light of the nations." It would seem, therefore, that the disciples are nominated to fulfill this role, indeed, to function in God's stead and on his behalf as "the light of the world." For in a tradition peculiar to the gospel Jesus proceeds to exhort them: "Let your light shine before men so that they may see your good works and glorify your father in heaven."

The authority of Jesus as the lordly Human Being is perceptible in the tone and content of these beatitudes and metaphors. It is more explicit in the interpretation of various Old Testament laws to which Jesus now turns in 5:17-48. The immediate and forceful prohibition, "Do not think . . ." with its assertive use of the verb "I came," which is strikingly similar to certain later pronouncements about the Son of the Human Being,[10] reflects the self-understanding of one who is conscious of a mission and the unique authority with which it distinguishes him. Likewise, the unusual confirmation formula, "Amen I say to you . . . ,"[11] which has the character of an oath that affirms the truth of what is being said independently of external validation, conveys an almost unheard of boldness and certainty. Finally, the antithetical formula, "You have heard that it was said to the ancients . . . but I say to you . . ." (or certain variations of it), which Jesus employs six times to introduce his expositions of the law,[12] dramatically expresses a sense of independence and self-confidence.

Matt. 5:17-48 is undoubtedly the nucleus of the Sermon on the Mount; it formulates Jesus' ethics in the context of a critical exposition of the Old Testament law, the foundation stone of Judaism. The introductory statement of verses 17-20, which has the ring of a personal manifesto, serves two functions. On the one hand, it articulates the goal of Jesus' mission regarding the law; on the other hand, it epitomizes the nature of the demands which he makes on his disciples. Six concrete examples of Jesus' interpretation of the law, cast in the form of antithesis (5:21-47) subsequently clarify the meaning of this programmatic declaration.

Jesus begins by counterposing two infinite verbs: *katalysai* ("to tear down") and *plērōsai* ("to fulfill"). A similar contrast is found in Mishnaic and Talmudic tradition where the alternatives of "abolishing" (*lebateel*) and "establishing" *(leqayim)* the law are juxtaposed by the rabbis. But these terms are not necessarily equivalents of those employed in 5:17. More exact counterparts to these rabbinic expressions appear in Paul's declaration of Rom. 3:31, "Do we therefore abolish (*katargoumen*) the law through faith? By no means, but we establish (*histanomen*) the law!"[13] The opposed infinitives of 5:17, "to tear down" and "to fulfill" are a distinctive Matthean combination and cannot be clarified in the light of rabbinic terminology. Their meaning must be determined within the context of the gospel, and especially this section of the Sermon on the Mount.

The first verb, "to tear down," is quite unambiguous; yet if its meaning requires further clarification, it can be derived from 26:61, "This fellow said, 'I am able to *destroy* the temple of God and to build it after three days." Again in 27:40, "You who *destroy* the temple and rebuilds it after three days, save yourself." Additional commentary is furnished by 5:19; to relax the least commandment of the law and to teach the same is a concrete way of tearing down the law.

The second verb, "to fulfill," which is intended to be its opposite, is more difficult to define. [14] It occurs sixteen times in the gospel, chiefly in the formula which Matthew employs to note the fulfillment of prophetic utterances. The closest parallel may be in 3:15 where Jesus meets the Baptist's objection with the programmatic words, "It is fitting for us to fulfill all righteousness." But what does it mean "to fulfill?" How or in what sense does Jesus fulfill the law or the righteousness which it demands? Is it merely affirming the eternal validity of the law handed down through Moses? Is it consummating the law, which is conceived of as an empty vessel, by filling it with the content of concrete deeds? Is it perfecting the law by removing its flaws and deficiencies and thereby giving it its perfect and final form? [15] Or is there another meaning which corresponds more to the intended sense of 5:17 than any of these?

The key to unlocking the meaning of the verb "to fulfill" lies in the following verse, 5:18. [16] There Jesus connects the passing away of heaven and earth and the passing away of the law, but not in order to fix the dissolution of the one in terms of the other. That is, he is not locating the abolition of the law in the eschatological context of the end of the age. On the contrary, the link between the two "passings" has another, indeed, an opposite thrust. The law in all its parts is valid as long as heaven and earth co-exist. Not the smallest letter or the minutest particle will be abolished. Introduced by the oath-like formula, "Amen I say to you . . ." and strengthened by the use of a double negative with the subjunctive, "by no means will pass away," this saying has the force of a categorical declaration.

Yet the major emphasis is not the abiding validity of the law. For the concluding words of v. 18, ". . . until all things shall happen," bring into focus what is fundamental about Jesus' understanding of his own mission in relation to the law. "Until all things shall happen," indicates a goal: not the passing away of heaven and earth for that is not the point of Jesus' words, but rather the realization of God's will as expressed in the minutest details of the law. This final clause, therefore, does not refer back to the passing away of heaven and earth in spite of the syntactical similarity of both parts of the verse. That would be a meaningless redundancy. Instead it acknowledges a process that will reach its consummation before heaven and earth are dissolved.[17] Even Jesus' death will not alter or terminate the ultimate fulfillment of all the jots and tittles of God's will. Matthew leaves no doubt about the disciples' full participation in the mission program of fulfilling God's will and its concomitant attainability in the same measure and to the same degree as Jesus himself. Indeed, through the obedience of his disciples to the Great Commission issued on the mountain in Galilee after his resurrection, Jesus will continue his work of fulfilling the law and the prophets.

Verse 19, therefore, is a natural continuation of Jesus' programmatic statement drawing his disciples into the prospect of fulfillment: "Whoever relaxes one of the least of these commandments and teaches human beings thus will be called least in the kingship of God; but whoever *does and teaches* will be called great in the kingship of God." The phrase, "one of the least of these commandments," refers back to the unique expression, "one jot or one tittle" in the previous verse. The work of fulfillent for both Jesus and his followers is a union of doing and teaching; it involves affirming the abiding validity of the law in all its parts but a so producing the righteousness it demands in terms of concrete deeds.

The realization of this goal will demand more of the disciples than the rigorous standard of righteousness maintained by their contemporaries, the scribes and the Pharisees: "Unless your righteousness exceeds that of the scribes and Pharisees you shall by no means enter into God's kingship." Greater righteousness and entrance into God's rule are correlates; one cannot be achieved without the other. But Jesus' demand for the former in order to gain the latter must not be understood as obedience to new laws which are more absolute than those of the Old Testament or the scribes and the Pharisees.[18] Matthew does not present Jesus as a new Moses on a new Sinai handing down a new Torah in fulfillment of Deut. 18:15. Such allusions may indeed be present, but they are intended to underline contrast rather than similarity. The antitheses which follow, as will become evident, are not substitutes for old or perhaps inadequate statutes. They are examples of God's original will for human existence which in one way or another has become obscured or even reversed by later tradition. While Pharisaic or rabbinic casuistry labored to apply the ancient legislation of the Old Testament to contemporary situations in a new cultural context, Jesus' approach to the law is fundamentally different. He penetrates the civil code or its contemporary interpretations to the original divine intention behind it and thereby removes the need for casuistry and the multiplication of laws. At the same time he gives his followers the responsibility of its application to the minutest details of human life and relationships. In every situation or circumstance they must determine how God's will is to be expressed by their conduct. One ordinance may be upheld while another is annulled, yet God's will has been affirmed in both. For example, in 8:4 Jesus dismisses the cleansed leper with the command, "Go show yourself to the priest and offer up the gift which Moses prescribed for a

witness to them." Yet later in 12:9-14 Jesus breaks the sabbath
law in order to restore a human being's withered hand. Doing
good in love has precedence over the rigid observance of this
commandment. Human beings were not made for the law, but
the law for human beings; and in his interpretation of Old Testament legislation Jesus lays bare the purpose or goal for which
it was intended.

Since the starting point of Jesus' exposition is Old
Testament civil law, Matthew's rationale for the construction
of six antitheses may not be so difficult to ascertain.[19] The
number may be intended to correspond to the six books of the
Mishnah which divide civil and religious law into a corresponding number of orders.[20] As Matthew utilized the
pentateuchal pattern for the literary framework of the gospel
as a whole, he may also have considered the numerical scheme
of six to be a dramatic means of confronting his Jewish readers
with the similarity and difference between the ethical teaching
of Jesus and that of the scribes and Pharisees or their
successors, the rabbis.

The first antithesis is an exposition of the Decalogue in-
junction, "You shall not kill." Like the five which follow, it is
introduced by a formula-like acknowledgment of the
audience's familiarity with the tradition that is quoted, "You
have *heard* that it was said to the ancients . . ."[21] The auditory
experience which is presupposed here is probably based on the
continuous hearing of the law through the reading of the
Torah that takes place in the worship services and instruction
of the synagogue.[22]

An immediate concern with human relationships is
indicated by Matthew's choice of the fifth commandment as
the starting point of Jesus' interpretation of the Old Testament law. The statute itself may be derived from Ex. 20:13 or
Deut. 5:18, but the legal qualification that is appended to it,
"And whoever should kill is liable to judgment," does not
appear in either context. It may be a paraphrase of Deut. 17:8-
13 which poses the problem of different kinds of homicide

requiring appeals to a higher court. This in any case is the very nature of Jesus' antithetical response; it differentiates various kinds of killing, and it is cast in the form of a dramatic gradation of court liability: a regular court of law, the sanhedrin or supreme court, and the ultimate court of the last day, "the hell of fire." Accordingly, the meaning of the word *krisis* in 5:21b and 22a seems best rendered as "court," either local or district rather than the more general sense of judgment.[23] Thus, while the Old Testament code stipulated that ordinary homicide was to be tried in a regular court of law, Jesus declares that, "everyone who *continues* to be angry with his brother is liable" to that court. The present middle participle *orgizomenos* indicates that Jesus is not condemning the expression of anger as such but rather its continued ventilation towards a fellow human being.

"And whoever should say to his brother, *raka*, is liable to the sanhedrin." Both the origin and meaning of the singular term which Jesus cites here are uncertain. As a possible Aramaic or Hebrew derivative "*raka*" may convey the idea of empty-headedness and could be translated, "numbskull." If, however, it is a Greek word, it may be a term of contempt, a vulgar alley expression meaning "swaggerer" or "braggard."[24] Whatever the word originally meant, it is clearly understood as an expression of insult which is degrading, perhaps even devastating to a human being and, in Jesus' view, accountable to the judgment of the supreme court.

In the third and final part of his pronouncement Jesus reaches the climactic pitch of his interpretation: "And whoever should say to his brother, 'fool,' is liable to the hell of fire." As previously, a frustrating ambiguity of origin is bound up with the invective which Jesus quotes. As a transliteration from the Hebrew *mōre* would carry the sense of "godless." In Greek the word simply means "fool," and if it is to be linked to its Septuagintal use, as is often advocated, it would have a religious connotation. Either meaning essentially involves an appropriation of a divine prerogative. For only God has the right to label anyone "godless" or a religious fool.[25]

Clearly then in this first antithesis Jesus upholds the Old Testament law. But he does more: by radicalizing it he draws out its original scope and design. The prohibition of God embraces all kinds of murder, not only physical extermination but also psychological, social and religious forms of human cruelty and destruction.

Ultimately the commandment has a positive goal, as the uniquely Matthean addition of 5:23-4 shows. It can be summed up quite simply by the imperative of v. 24b, ". . . be reconciled to your brother," even to the extent of taking the initiative in those cases where "your brother has something against you." For healthy relationships with people are the precondition for a relationship with God.

The addition of a Q tradition (5:25-6) provides further commentary by posing a concrete analogy from the realm of business. It is smart to be on good terms with anyone from whom you have borrowed money, especially if the due date of the note has arrived and you are unable to make repayment. An attitude of hostility or argumentativeness will only provoke your creditor into handing you over to the judge who in turn will deliver you to the bailiff for imprisonment, and you will not get out until you have worked off the last penny of your debt.

No application is made, but the point is clear. As in the world of business, human relationships usually involve indebtedness. It is noteworthy in this respect that Matthew's formulation of the fifth petition of the Lord's Prayer expresses this idea; the word "debts" is employed instead of "sins" as in Lk. 11:4. Good will towards a neighbor or fellow human being brings certain advantages and personal gain, at the very least forgiveness and reconciliation with God: "Forgive us our debts even as we have forgiven our debtors."

The second antithesis interprets the sixth commandment: "You have heard that it was said, 'you shall not commit adultery;' but I say to you that everyone who looks at a woman in order to lust for her has already committed adultery with her in his heart." In Jesus' estimation lustful desires towards a member of the opposite sex are as much a part of God's prohibition as the act of adultery itself. For the look of lust transforms the personhood of the woman into an object of self-gratification and, even though the external act has not been committed, the "I-Thou" relationship has been broken and its accompanying regard for the integrity of personhood has been lost.

In the radicalization of this commandment Jesus again appears to have penetrated to the divine intention. Not only are his followers called to have healthy relations with their fellow human beings (5:21-6); they are also to carry on wholesome relationships with the opposite sex. Moreover, the goal is to be achieved at all costs, for its realization will mean the freedom and integrity of both parties, not only the one who is doing the lusting. "If your right eye offends you, pluck it out and toss it away, for it is better for you that one of your members should be lost and not your whole body be cast into hell . . ." Taken from Mk. 9:43-8 and utilized again as a doublet in 18:8-9, this unusual tradition supports the point the antithesis makes. Healthy relationships between the sexes is essential for human wholeness and completeness, and radical conduct may be necessary to insure attainment.

In the third antithesis Jesus focuses on the relationship between husband and wife. Accordingly his exposition of the civil code shifts from the Decalogue to another section of the Torah. The text that he cites is a somewhat distorted paraphrase of Deut. 24:1, which may reflect the practice of Matthew's time and place.[26] For while the Mosaic law treats divorce as an exception specifying certain justifiable grounds for such action, Jesus' quotation makes it appear to be a general rule: "Whoever would divorce his wife, let him give her a certificate of divorce." The same understanding of Deut. 24:1 is presupposed in 19:3-9 where the Pharisees test Jesus with the question, "Is it right to divorce one's wife for any reason?" In reply he goes all the way back to the beginning of Genesis and bases his answer on the institution of marriage which God ordained at creation, ". . . a man . . . will be joined to his wife, and the two will become one flesh." The primordial will of God is union! The Pharisees, however, seem to prefer the legislation of Deut. 24:1; and their rejoinder, "Why therefore did Moses command to give a certificate of divorce and to divorce?" expresses the same understanding of that text as that of Jesus' quotation in 5:31. Their question enables Jesus to make a basic anthropological evaluation implicit in this rendition of Deut. 24:1. Moses made concessions to the weaknesses of human beings; he legislated to them as fallen creatures. But from the beginning it was not intended to be that way (19:8b); that is, the will of God as expressed in the very beginning was not addressed to fallen creatures but to human beings made in his image and pronounced by him to be good. And Jesus refuses to regard them from any other perspective than that.

This explains his radical attitude toward divorce. Once a marriage has been constituted and the two have become one, in the light of God's plan at creation, divorce or separation cannot be justified. The one exception which Jesus allows is fornication. This is not merely an adjustment to Jewish tradition which required divorce in such a case.[27] Matthew furnishes an instance in 1:19 when Joseph, who has become aware of Mary's pregnancy, wants to separate from her because he is a "righteous, law-abiding man." Fundamentally premarital relations with someone other than the betrothed destroy the commitment to potential union promised in engagement. In fornication the will of God has already been broken, and subsequent sexual union with the betrothed would become adultery. This in turn explains the peculiar conclusion of Jesus' pronouncement in 5:32, "Whoever divorces his wife . . . commits her to adultery, and whoever marries the divorced woman commits adultery." Having been forced out of a marriage union, the divorced wife becomes a potential transgressor of the sixth commandment. She may be forced into prostitution in order to support herself. And if she is able to remarry, her new husband participates in the brokenness of the union which she has left behind.

In this exposition of the law, especially as it is developed in 19:3-9, Jesus discloses a basic hermeneutical principle, one, which in seeming contradiction to his programmatic statement of 5:17, leads him to abrogate the legislation of Moses, at least as it was interpreted at that time. A law which does not contribute to the human being's realization of union and wholeness is to be annulled. At this point the peculiar meaning of the key verb, "to fulfill," emerges more distinctly. Jesus fulfills the law by cancelling one commandment in order to uphold another. At the same time he once again confronts his disciples with the original intention of God's will.

Although the fourth antithesis deals with the matter of swearing, its basic purpose is to relate the law to the narrowest circle of human relationships, the relationship which a person has with himself or herself. Here in a uniquely Matthean tradition Jesus' exposition of God's will results in an outright cancellation of the Old Testament commandment derived from Lev. 19:12, "You have heard that it was said to the ancients, 'You shall not swear falsely, but you shall render your oaths to the Lord;' but I say to you, do not swear at all . . ." Various examples of oath formulas appealing to higher authorities or sacred institutions in order to establish truth are presented in a literary construction of progressively descending realities: heaven, earth, Jerusalem, and one's head. The last of the four, however, seems to have been appended, for the infinitive clause of 5:34a, "not to swear," is repeated in v. 36. Moreover, it is inconsistent with the previous three, for it is not a higher authority to which appeal can be made. It seems rather to be a formula by which one's own head or life is offered as a pledge of truth. Jesus' criticism of it, "You are unable to make one hair white or black," intimates that the one taking such an oath is not the ultimate giver of his own life and therefore has no final jurisdiction over it.[28]

All oaths are rejected! For their use implies a double standard: on the one hand it is presupposed that the oath-taker is generally not truthful; his testimony can be believed only in those particular instances when it is supported by the act of swearing. But what ultimately counts and simultaneously affirms the divine will is the integrity constituted in and by a simple yes or no, ". . . let your word be yes, yes, no, no; and anything beyond these is of evil."[29] Such simplicity of truthfulness is a mark of the soundness and health God wills for human beings. Jesus does not hesitate to "tear down" a statute which frustrates the realization of the divine goal.

The formulation of the fifth antithesis, like the sixth, combines a Q tradition with Matthean material. The Old Testament law cited by Jesus is an abbreviated version of one or all of three similar texts, Ex. 21:24, Lev. 24:20 and Deut. 19:21, which uphold the legal right of retribution: "An eye for an eye and a tooth for a tooth." Jesus not only opposes all forms of retaliation: "Do not withstand the evil one," thus nullifying this legislation. In his antithetical interpretation of God's will he presents four examples of responsive behavior which express "an absolute dedication to goodness in love."[30]

Firstly, "Whoever wallops you on the right cheek, turn to him also the other." In contrast to Lk. 6:29, Jesus stipulates being struck on the *right* cheek, a blow that would be more vicious because it would involve being hit by the back of the hand rather than the palm. According to 26:67 Jesus is slapped in this manner after being condemned to death by the high priest. Secondly, "to the one who wants to sue you and take your undergarment, let him also have your overcoat." According to Ex. 22:26, a creditor may claim the one but never the other, for it is needed to cover nakedness and to keep warm at night. To expose one's nakedness is indeed an extreme response, especially when there is no guarantee that it will effect any change in the attitude of "the evil one" or prevent him from taking further advantage of the situation. But it confirms the freedom of the one who acts in such a fashion, the very freedom which constitutes human existence as God the Creator intended it. The same is true of the third example: "And whoever would conscript you for one mile go with him two." Matt. 27:32 is an illustration of such an instance: the Roman execution detachment presses Simon of Cyrene into service by compelling him to carry Jesus' cross. To volunteer an additional mile is another expression of genuine freedom arising out of a devotion to goodness in love. Finally, "Give to the one who would borrow from you." In this last example Jesus upholds the commandment of Ex. 22:25 but articulates it in a more absolute manner without restrictions or limitations.

Relations with evil and evil people are not to be avoided but they must not involve reactions in kind. Neither must they be responses of submissive weakness, as Jesus' four illustrations might superficially appear to be. Bold and creative actions are called for which substantiate the very freedom and maturity out of which they arise. Their genuineness is demonstrated and perhaps even realized to a greater degree when in the face of no change in the evil of the situation or in the attitude or conduct of the evil one, there is no diminishment in the pursuit of goodness in love.

The sixth and final antithesis poses a special problem because the commandment that Jesus quotes is not found in the Old Testament. Lev. 19:18, which stipulates, "You shall love your neighbor as yourself" may have been used and expanded with the addition, "and you shall hate your enemy." On the other hand, it could be an old proverb which circulated orally as far back as 2 Sam. 19:5-6 where Joab charges David with behavior that is the very opposite of what it ought to be in this particular situation, "Then Joab came in the house of the king and said, 'Today you have covered the faces of all your servants with shame, who have saved your life . . . because you love those who hate you and hate those who love you.' " Almost two thousand years later in a book called *Mazref* by Berechia ben Natronai, who quotes Rav Nissim ha-Gaon, this quotation is found: "to love your neighbor and to hate your enemy."[31]

Yet regardless of the problem of origin, its placement alongside the previous Old Testament quotations suggests that in Matthew's community this is an ordinance that is regarded by some to be an expression of God's will handed down from the past. In contrast to the three preceding antitheses Jesus does not simply annul this tradition; he reverses the second half of it, "But I say to you, love your enemies and pray for those persecuting you . . ." Responsible relationships with enemies are characterized by love and intercessory prayer. If love cannot reach beyond those who will love in return, where is freedom? The tax collectors who are despised do as much as that. If embraces can only be extended to those who share certain beliefs, where is goodness? The Gentiles with their inferior ethical standard go at least that far. The freedom and goodness manifested in concrete deeds of love towards enemies and friends alike are god-like qualities. For in freedom God ". . . causes the sun to shine on the wicked and the good;" and in goodness God never acts according to a double standard, but "makes it rain on the just and the unjust." Where such love, goodness, freedom and wholeness are manifested, Yahweh becomes visible.

"Therefore, you shall be *teleioi* as your heavenly Father is *teleios*." With this summary command Jesus climaxes his exposition of the Old Testament civil code. Indeed, Matthew's unique formulation of this Q tradition epitomizes the ethical teaching of his six antitheses. In contrast to the version of Lk. 6:36, "Be merciful even as your Father is merciful," the evangelist appears to have constructed this saying according to the Septuagint's rendition of Lev. 19:2, "You shall be holy because I the Lord your God am holy." At the same time, however, there has been a careful avoidance of the Septuagintal adjectives, *hagioi* and *hagios* ("holy") which are the equivalents of the Hebrew originals and therefore render the meaning of the Massoretic text. Evidently these words are objectionable, for

Matthew has substituted *teleios,* which is frequently translated "perfect."

The Hebrew original, *kadosh* ("holy"), is interpreted in Tannaitic literature to mean: *perush* ("separate"), as in the Siphra's exposition of Lev. 19:2. Moreover, *perush* ("separate") may be the root from which the name "Pharisee," meaning "the separated one" is derived.[32] For Pharisaic and rabbinic Judaism holiness was realized by constructing a fence around the Torah in order to preserve its sanctity and simultaneously to keep a person far from transgression.

If the word "holy" connotes separation in the gospel's Jewish cultural milieu, Matthew has good reason to avoid adopting the Septuagint language. It stands opposed to the fundamental character of the ethical teaching of the Sermon on the Mount and therefore cannot be used in this epitomizing command.

The meaning of the evangelist's substitute adjective *teleios* is clarified by its one other use in the gospel, 19:21. In that context a rich young man has inquired about the good that he should do in order to possess eternal life. After responding with a counter question, Jesus answers, "If you want to enter into life, observe the commandments." When pressed for specific ones, he quotes five injunctions from the Decalogue and concludes with the comprehensive summary, also found in 22:39, "You shall love your neighbor as yourself." The rich man's astonishing reply, "All these things I have observed; what do I still lack?" evokes no contradiction from Jesus. He simply says, "If you want to be *teleios,* go sell your possessions and give to the poor and you will have treasure in heaven and come follow me." With these words he poses for him the radical act that is required for gaining "eternal life." By departing in sorrow, unable to surrender his riches, the young man proves his fundamental dichotomous condition: on the one hand he craves the fullness of life, on the other hand he loves his wealth and the security that it provides. "If you want to be whole . . ." — as God intended human beings

to be — is the possibility that Jesus offers him, and with it a
true fulfillment of the commandments that will enable him to
enter into the life of the kingdom of God, the very threshold of
"eternal life."

This same meaning of "whole" can be attributed to the
use of the adjective *teleios* in 5:48, "You shall be whole," —
complete, integrated! Wholeness belongs to God's being, and
from the beginning it was intended to belong to human beings
made in his/her image. The ethics of Jesus as expounded in
and through these six antitheses is directed at the realization of
the divine will.

What further clarification, then do these six antitheses
and their epitomizing conclusions make of the manifesto of
5:17-20 and particularly its opening declaration: "Do not think
I came to tear down the law or the prophets. I came not to tear
down but to fulfill?" Jesus' subsequent dissolution of four of
the six Old Testament laws (5:31, 33, 38, 43) appears to be in
flat contradiction. Yet what emerges is a basic differentiation
between the original will of God and its obfuscation and dis-
tortion through human agents who promote the law by
adjusting it to the frailities of fallen creatures.

Fundamentally and consistently Jesus upholds the law
of God. But to do that it is necessary for him in some cases to
radicalize the commandments of the civil code in order to
penetrate to their original comprehensive purpose. In other
cases it is necessary to nullify them in order to recover the
earlier will of God. Thus, fulfilling the law or the righteousness which the law demands means returning to God's design
for humanness; and heaven and earth shall not pass away until
that design has been achieved.

For Jesus, then, the law — even when it expresses God's
intention — is not an end in itself. It is a means to a divinely
appointed goal: the freedom, health, wholeness, soundness
and completeness of human beings. Jesus' mission is the realization of this human destiny both in his own life as the Son of
the Human Being — Son of God and in the divinely human

community which he is founding.

Following this progression of antitheses Matthew turns to other areas of life in which the divine qualities of wholeness and goodness can and should be manifested.

First of all a succession of three distinctively Matthean traditions, combined with Q and Marcan material, illustrate expressions of schizophrenic piety. Fulfilling the righteousness which the law demands also includes acts of love and devotion to God, such as almsgiving, prayer and fasting. But the performance of these works should be directed wholly to God. The desire for recognition which expresses itself in ostentatious display eclipses love as the motivating force and creates an unwholesome condition. "Take care not to perform your righteousness before human beings in order to be viewed by them," Jesus charges at the opening of this new section of the Sermon on the Mount. Such conduct results in the loss of the reward you have with God, at the very least a fundamental soundness of being on which healthy human life can be built.

Wholesome benevolence avoids calling attention to itself, even to the exaggerated extent of "not letting the left hand know what the right hand is doing." The giver is not to take notice of his action. Because she or he is supposed to be doing something for nothing, demonstration only distorts and destroys its purity.

Genuine prayer is offered to God, not God *and* human beings. Since there were fixed times of prayer in Jewish piety which were obligatory, prayer could be offered wherever one happened to be, for example, "standing at the corners of the main street" in a town or city. Such places, of course, provided an opportunity for show. But prayer intended for God should be addressed to him/ her with a kind of complete concentration that is possible when one locks oneself in a pantry, that is, the room that served as a storehouse for supplies, in order to be alone (6:6).

Furthermore, the length of the prayer is not important;

much talking is not required (6:7). God's attention does not have to be gained by the recitation of attributes or names which remind God of who she is and what he can do. Jesus twice (6:8, 32) emphasizes that God knows the needs of his/her children even before petitions are made.

It is in this context of instruction on prayer that the evangelist introduces the Lord's Prayer as a model to be imitated, "Therefore, pray like this." Matthew's version is longer than Luke's because of the inclusion of two extra petitions, 6:10b and 13b. The possessive pronoun "our" and a variation of one of the gospel's favorite expressions, "the one in the heavens," have been added to the opening address. Although the structure and the content are thoroughly Jewish, as the parallels of the *Shemon Esre* indicate, [33] there is a strong eschatological accent that makes Matthew's version distinctive. This is especially evident in the thrust of the first three petitions in which God is entreated to establish once and for all the holiness of his/her name, rule and will. The interpolation of the third petition, "Your will be done on earth as in heaven," and its subsequent use in Jesus' Gethsemane prayer at the beginning of the Passion (26:42) show another aspect of the evangelist's christologically and eschatologically realities of these first three petitions. His life and work fulfill the promises God made in the Old Testament. His teaching in the Sermon on the Mount recovers the original will of God. His forthcoming establishment of the community of humanness in and through the training of his disciples is directed toward the same goal of fulfillment expressed in his own ministry. Yet while Jesus and his disciples serve as bearers of God's will, rule and name, God is always regarded as the initiator of these realities.

The meaning of the fourth petition is difficult to determine because the Greek word *epiousious* has no other parallel and its origin is disputed. It may be translated "that which is coming soon" thus giving the entreaty an eschatological slant: "Give us today the bread that is coming tomorrow;" that is, the bread of the New Age or the Messianic feast.[34] It is also possible, however, that the petition may simply be a request for enough bread for daily life: "The bread that is essential for life give us today." In either case the prayer expresses a vital dependence on God.

"Do not lead us into temptation," as the sixth petition prays, does not imply that God is the author of temptation any more than a sergeant, who is leading his platoon into battle, is the originator of the war. Jesus knows the reality of evil and the danger of being overcome by it, as he admonishes Peter, James and John in 26:41, "Watch and pray that you do not enter into temptation; the spirit on the one hand is willing, but the flesh is weak." His three-fold Gethsemane prayer, "My Father, if it is possible, let this cup pass from me, but not as I will but as you (will)," expresses a similar awareness of the dangers involved in being put to the test.[35]

The addition of a Marcan fragment (11:25-6) at the conclusion of the Lord's Prayer underlines what is implied in the fifth petition; indeed, one of the central emphases of the gospel.[36] A relationship with God is horizontally rather than vertically structured and depends on the kind of relationship one has with his or her fellow creatures: "For if you forgive human beings their offenses, your heavenly Father will forgive you."

Finally, in another uniquely Matthean tradition (6:16-8), Jesus scrutinizes a third form of piety, fasting. Like benevolence and prayer it is not to be accompanied by outward show. Indeed, the very opposite appearance is to be given so that no trace of asceticism is evident: "When you fast, anoint your head and wash your face, so that you may not be manifest to human beings (as one) fasting." Be wholesome in the performance of self-denial; if it is being done for God, let it be done before God alone.

What follows in 6:19 - 7:11 are various Q traditions which Matthew seems to have assembled around the theme of God's will for human wholeness in matters of daily life and

living. The summary command of 5:48, "Be whole . . ." is
evident here in its application to the material realities of
human existence. The whole section can be divided according
to the prohibitions which Jesus lays down for his followers:
"Do not store up for yourselves treasures on earth . . ." (6:19);
"Do not worry about your life . . ." (6:25); "Do not judge . . ."
(7:1); and "Do not give the holy thing to dogs . . ." (7:6).

Human wholeness in everyday life, first of all, refrains
from the accumulation of earthly wealth. Because moths and
rust cause decay and thieves steal, preoccupation with material
possessions is basically distracting; it detracts from genuine
living and therefore reduces the quality of life. How treasures
are stored up in heaven is not immediately clear, but it is
eventually made more explicit in Jesus' final word to the rich
young man in 19:21, "If you want to be whole, go sell your
possessions and give to the poor, and you will have treasure in
heaven and come follow me." The intimation is that storing up
treasures in heaven by giving away one's material wealth
produces a singleness of orientation; one can get on with living
because the distractions have been eliminated. Where your
treasure is, the totality of the loving, desiring, willing self will
be concentrated.

This line of thought is developed by another Q tradition
drawn from a different context which contrasts two basically
opposed orientations. The single eye may imply generosity;
basically it denotes a condition of soundness out of which such
acts arise.[37] "Therefore, if your eye is single, your whole body is
full of light." "The wicked eye," on the other hand, is a traditional metaphorical expression for jealousy, avarice and
covetousness.[38] It is harmful to others and destructive to itself,
for it extinguishes the spark of life by causing the whole human
being to be dark. "If the light in you is (actually) darkness, how
great such darkness!" There is no soundness where there is no
singleness of purpose.

As a closing thought for this section another Q
tradition has been selected to stress the impossibility of two

opposed commitments. All of life has its lords and masters who claim submission and obedience. Because no one can serve two simultaneously the choice between alternatives forces itself. "For either he will hate the one and love the other... You cannot be a servant to God and capital (mammon)." The consequences of choosing or being forced into a particular choice have already been clarified in the preceding verses. Servitude to the one means freedom, health and life, to the other enslavement and emptiness.

Although the prohibition of 6:25, "Do not be anxious about your life..." begins a new section, it arises out of what already has been said in 6:19-24. Matthew expresses this connection in the opening words, "On account of this I say to you..." If God's sovereignty is to be the one and only commitment, then a fundamental attitude towards the practical matters of food and clothing is involved. "Do not worry about what you shall eat or what you shall wear." "Look at the birds... Your heavenly Father feeds them... Are you not of greater value than they?" "Consider the lilies of the field... If God so clothes the grass... how much more not you, ones of little faith?" By repeating his initial prohibition in 6:31 and again in 6:34, Jesus reinforces his call to the singleness of concentration that is to be directed to God's rule and the fulfillment of its righteousness (6:33).

The prohibition of 7:1 introduces yet another feature of daily life which destroys singleness and soundness of human existence, "Judge not so that you will not be judged." Jesus forbids his disciples to assume the role of God and hold court over their fellow human beings. "First remove the log from your own eye and then you will see clearly to remove the splinter from your brother's eye." Judging others is a distraction that diverts attention away from living one's own life. Everyone has more than enough to deal with in relation to his or her own commitment.

The final prohibition in 7:6 is the most puzzling one of all. Why Matthew inserts this distinctive tradition here and

precisely what it refers to are difficult to determine. To refrain
from giving what is holy to dogs as well as casting pearls before
pigs seems to involve the kind of judgment that is forbidden in
7:1ff. Although dogs and pigs are unclean animals in Jewish
tradition which are used metaphorically to represent the
Gentiles,[39] here they appear to refer back to various types of
people whose characterization has emerged in the teaching of
6:19 - 7:5; that is, those who pursue treasures on earth, have the
evil eye, serve mammon and are absorbed with matters of food
and drink, and perhaps also those who pronounce judgment
on others without any correlating scrutiny of their own lives.
To acknowledge their existence is an act of realism, not of
judgment. It is simply recognizing that there are such kinds of
people who have no comprehension or appreciation of
soundness, health and freedom as the goals of human
existence. In fact, Jesus warns, approaching them with these
holy things may only arouse their anger and cause them to
attack those who hold out such values.

　　The tradition of 7:7-11 which follows is used as a concluding admonition to persistence linked to a word of promise.
The concern for food in 7:9-10 ties this block of Q material into
the unity of 6:19 - 7:11 in which Jesus correlates God's will for
human wholeness to matters of everyday need and desire.
Singleness of commitment to seeking the righteousness of
God's rule includes a strong and persistent confidence in God's
motherhood and fatherhood. "Keep asking..." "Keep seeking
..." "Keep knocking..." For if it is true that a parent will not
give his or her son a stone when he asks for bread or a snake
when he asks for fish, then how much more true it is that God
will give good things to those who make petition.

　　Verse 12, which formulates the Golden Rule, is the
culmination of the Sermon on the Mount. The adverbial
particle "therefore" links it to the preceding traditions; and the
last sentence, "For this is the law and the prophets," points all
the way back to Jesus' manifesto in 5:17-20.[40] Attributed in
Jewish tradition to Hillel, although in a negative form, the

Golden Rule is employed as a recapitulation of the teaching conveyed in the body of the discourse. The intention of the law and the prophets, which Jesus came to fulfill, is authentic human relationships in which freedom and wholeness are realized by all involved. This is not a "tit for tat" affair, doing in order to receive in return. The initiative is to be taken by the disciples: "so also you do for them." The criterion is, "What you would wish from them," regardless of the initial attitude or the subsequent reaction. As Matthew uses it, the Golden Rule is another expression of Jesus' call to his disciples to follow him in an absolute dedication to goodness in love.

The remainder of Jesus' teaching in the Sermon, 7:13-27, comprising various materials of tradition derived from different sources, has the character of an epilogue conveying final admonitions and warnings. The first, 7:13-4, is an exhortation combining the Jewish teaching of the Two Ways with a Q fragment (Lk. 13:24). The disciples are reminded that there are two ways: the one is wide and "roomy,"[41] the other compact. Only the latter has a gate which corresponds in character to the way which lies beyond it; it is so narrow that "there are few who find it," especially since the former way is made so obvious by the swarms of human beings who are following it to their destruction. In the Sermon on the Mount Jesus has shown his followers the narrow gate and the compact way to which it opens. As the first of his concluding remarks he urges them to enter through and upon it.

At the same time they are to beware of false prophets who appear to be genuine members of God's flock but in actuality are ravaging predators (7:15).[42] A Q tradition provides certain criteria for their identification: "By their fruits you will recognize them . . . A good tree produces good fruit; a foul tree bad fruit." One cannot produce the other. Those who do not bear good fruit, as the use of the doublet of 7:19 stresses, will eventually be overtaken by judgment.

In this respect mere confession, according to the completely rewritten Q tradition of 7:21-3, is inadequate, "Not everyone who says to me 'Lord, Lord' will enter into God's kingship . . ." Even deeds are not enough, for there are those who acknowledge Jesus as Lord who prophecy, cast out demons and do mighty works. But because their deeds do not express God's will, they will be rejected, "I never knew you. Depart from me you workers of lawlessness."

This warning leads directly into the conclusion of the discourse. Matthew ends the Sermon on the Mount with a similitude that poses the alternative possibilities of response between which the disciples must choose. The introductory sentence of 7:24 draws the analogy between the one who *hears and does* Jesus' words and the wise builder who constructs his or her house on the rock; the outcome for the one will hold true for the other. The forces of chaos, no matter how violent, will fail to overwhelm or destroy. On the other hand, the outcome for the one who hears but does not do Jesus' words is like that of the foolish builder who erects his or her house on a foundation of sand that will be unable to withstand the chaos of storm and wind and consequently result in collapse. The hearing of Jesus' teaching is to be translated into corresponding deeds. Doing follows hearing! Any dichotomy in which one is separated from the other will have consequences as grave as the fall of the foolish builder's house or the rejection experienced by those who confess Jesus but do not do God's will. The integration of hearing and doing initiates a growth towards completeness and maturity that is promoted by the active fulfillment of God's will disclosed in Jesus' interpretation of the law and the prophets. The goal that will be realized is the goodness, wholeness and freedom that God has willed for human existence and its endurance.

The first of the gospel's five transition formulas terminates the Sermon on the Mount with an emphasis on the authority of Jesus' teaching and leads into the narrative of Book Two.

FOOTNOTES

1 A comprehensive examination of the matter has led W.D. Davies to conclude that the composite Moses typology: New Sinai, New Moses, New Torah, is deliberately equivocal. "The Sermon on the Mount is therefore ambiguous: suggestive of the Law of a New Moses, it is also the authoritative word of the Lord, the Messiah: it is the Messianic Torah." *Setting,* p. 93. Also Davies, *Torah in the Messianic Age and/or the Age to Come, JBL* Monograph Series, vol. VII (Philadelphia: *SBL,* 1952).

2 This depends on whether Lk. 6:21b corresponds to Mt. 5:4.

3 It is usually conceded that Lk. 6;20-2 retains the original form of the beatitudes except for the peculiarly Lucan use of the second person plural. See W.D. Davies, *op. cit.,* p. 382, and G. Strecker, "Die Makarismen der Bergpredigt," *NTS* (17) April, 1971, p. 257.

4 Compare with Ps. 1:1, 2:12, 31(32):1, etc. Prov. 8:32, 28:14, etc. Sir. 14:1, 25:8, 26:1, 48:11, 50:28, etc. Also Is. 30:18, 32:20. When Matthew refers to the Spirit of God, he usually does so with a preposition. See 1:18, 20; 3:11; 4:1; 12:28, 32; 22:43.

5 Against Strecker, *op. cit.,* p. 263, who surprisingly declares this as well as the other beatitudes to be aimed at a virtue to be attained in the future. See also G. Barth, *Matthew's Understanding of the Law,* p. 60, who considers the Beatitudes to be "virtues which the Christian should practise."

6 Against Hans Windisch, *The Meaning of the Sermon on the Mount,* trans. by S. Maclean Gilmour (Philadelphia: Westminster Press, 1951), pp. 26-8, 37-9.

7 Against Strecker, *op. cit.,* pp. 262, 268, 274. Placing the beatitudes opposite the sevenfold woes of the last discourse, as W. Trilling, *Wahre Israel,* p. 74 does, is a bit simplistic because there are nine, not seven, beatitudes and because the last discourse (chapter 23) does not begin with the woes.

8 See R. Hummel, *Auseinandersetzung,* pp. 28ff. and D.R.A. Hare, *Theme of Jewish Persecution,* pp. 80ff.

9 See T.W. Manson, *The Teaching of Jesus, Studies of Its Form and Content,* 2nd ed., (Cambridge: at the University Press, 1953), pp. 179ff., who expressed this very appropriately in terms of "the saving remnant" in contrast to "the saved remnant."

10 For an important parallel to 5:17 see 10:34. But see also 11:19 and especially 20:28.

11 See also 5:26; 23:36; 24:34; 25:12, 40, 45.

12 These are found in 5:21f., 27f., 31f., 33f., 38f., 43f. See J. Suggs, *Wisdom, Christology and Law in Matthew's Gospel,* pp. 110ff.

13 See also Rom. 3:3. Paul uses "to tear down" in Gal. 2:18 with what appears to be its opposite "to build." See also 2 Cor. 5:1. Above all, see H. Ljungman, *Das Gesetz Erfüllen. Matt. 5:17ff. und 3:15 Untersucht,* (Lund: C.W.K. Gleerup, 1954), pp. 53-65, for a more or less exhaustive analysis of these verbs.

14 As is obvious in Ljungman's review and discussion of various interpretations, *ibid.,* pp. 19-36.

FOOTNOTES

15 These are the three basic types of interpretation which Ljungman has synthesized in his comparison of various interpretations of 5:17.

16 Schweizer, "Matth. 5, 17-20 - Anmerkungen zum Gesetzesverständnis des Matthäus," *Theol. Literaturzeitung,* 1952, no. 8, pp. 480f. and Ljungman, *op. cit.,* pp. 36-47. Because G. Barth, *op. cit.,* p. 62 proceeds to interpret 5:18 in the light of 5:17 he ends up with an inadequate understanding of both verses.

17 Compare 24:35. E. Schweizer's exegesis of 5:17ff., as incisive as it is - and it has been very influential in almost all subsequent efforts at the interpretation of the text - does not develop this emphasis on the process of fulfillment which Jesus is inaugurating by his coming. The same is unfortunately true of Ljungman's superlative study which places the emphasis of Jesus' fulfillment of God's will and the disciples' participation in the fullness he has achieved. Ljungman of course acknowledges the doing of concrete deeds of love to which Jesus calls his disciples; but there is little stress on the disciples' obedience as the continuation of this process "until all things shall happen." See *op. cit.,* pp. 46f. and 121ff.

18 The impossibility of Jesus' ethic is more recently emphasized by John Knox in his little book, *The Ethic of Jesus in the Teaching of the Church,* (Nashville: Abingdon Press, 1961).

19 This question also raises the problem of the literary framework of the Sermon on the Mount. What model, if any, Matthew may have used or the rationale that determined this unique form of discourse has not as yet been discovered or recovered. J. Jeremias, *The Sermon on the Mount,* trans. by Norman Perrin, Facet Books #2 (Philadelphia: Fortress Press, 1963), pp. 22f., thinks that the form of the Sermon is based on the three kinds of righteousness of 5:20, "the righteousness of the theologians, of the pious laymen and of the disciples of Jesus." As will become evident, however, no such distinctions in the division of the material seem to be intended by the evangelist.

20 Davies, *Setting,* pp. 301f. and 315.

21 The full formula occurs only in 5:21 and 33; in a more or less modified form in 5:27, 31, 38, 43.

22 Lohmeyer, *Matthäus,* p. 117.

23 *Ibid.,* p. 118.

24 As Lohmeyer, *ibid.,* p. 119, prefers to think in his consideration of the question: why tradition, which generally preserves only sacred words and phrases, should hand down a vulgar alley expression.

25 See J. Schniewind, *Das Evangelium nach Matthäus, NTD,* (Göttingen: Vandenhoeck & Ruprecht, 1962), p. 59.

26 See G. Barth, *op. cit.,* p. 94.

27 Paul reflects the strength of this tradition in I Cor. 7:10f. See also W.H. Brownlee, *The Meaning of the Dead Sea Scrolls for the Bible,* p. 80, n. 33; Lohmeyer, *op. cit.,* p. 130; and Stendahl, *Matthew, Peake,* p. 777, para. 679g.

FOOTNOTES

28 See Lohmeyer, *op. cit.,* p. 134.

29 Compare with James 5:12 which, as some commentators suggest, may be an earlier and perhaps more radical version since there is only a single yes and a single no. See Strecker, *op. cit.,* p. 134. For the double yes and no, see Strack-Billerbeck, *op. cit.,* I, 337. Finally also Lohmeyer, *op. cit.*

30 This phrase is borrowed from J.A. Baker's *The Foolishness of God,* (London: Darton, Longman & Todd, 1970).

31 All of this I owe to Hans Kosmala who expounded it in a lecture on Matthew at the Swedish Theological Institute in Jerusalem, Israel. See also Lohmeyer, *op. cit.,* p. 143.

32 See T.W. Manson, *op. cit.,* p. 186f.

33 See W.D. Davies, *op. cit.,* pp. 309ff.

34 K. Stendahl, *St. Matthew,* p. 778, para. 680d.

35 Stendahl, *ibid.,* para. 680j.

36 See also Mt. 25:31-46.

37 Stendahl, *op. cit.,* p. 779, para. 681c.

38 See Mt. 20:15.

39 See Mt. 8:28-34 and 15:26-7.

40 Also G. Barth, *op. cit.,* p. 73.

41 Stendahl, *op. cit.,* p. 780, para. 681n.

42 This uniquely Matthean tradition may be indicative of a critical danger which is threatening the community to which the gospel is addressed. Comp. 24:10-2, 23:5. See G. Barth, *op. cit.,* p. 75, who identifies these false prophets as the antinomians of 7:23 against whom 5:17ff. is directed.

Chapter VI

THE NARRATIVE OF BOOK TWO: "THE CHARACTER OF JESUS' MINISTRY"

Matthew 8:1 - 9:35

The framework of the narrative section of Book Two appears to be a collection of ten mighty works of Jesus arranged in a sequence that is peculiar to the gospel:

8:2-4	Healing of the Leper	Mark 1:40-5
8:5-13	Healing of the Centurion's Servant	Q (Lk. 7:1-10)
8:14-5	Healing of Peter's Mother-in-Law	Mark 1:29-30
8:23-7	Stilling of the Storm	Mark 4:35-41
8:28-34	Healing of the Gadarene Demoniac	Mark 5:1-20
9:1-8	Healing of the Palsied Man	Mark 2:1-12
9:20-2	Healing of Woman with Flow of Blood	Mark 5:33-4
9:18-26	Raising of a Ruler's Daughter	Mark 5:21-43
9:27-31	Healing of Two Blind People	Matt. 20:29-34
9:32-3	Healing of the Dumb Demoniac	Mark 1:23 ff. and/or 7:32ff.

The first eight have been appropriated from Mark, with one exception: the Q tradition of the healing of the Centurion's servant. The ninth is a doublet of 20:29-34; the tenth is uniquely Matthean but may be a completely rewritten version of Mark 1:23ff. or Mark 7:32ff., possibly even a telescoping of both.[1] It is the addition of the last two that makes the numerical scheme of ten seem deliberate and planned. Matthew intends to assemble ten mighty works even if it means resorting to the use of a doublet and a possible telescoped adaptation of two Marcan traditions. Other "miracle stories" could have been utilized, for example, 12:9-14, 15:21-8 and 17:14-21; but evidently they were more suitable for other contexts. Or the last two could have been omitted all together without a noticeable break in the narrative, for 9:26, like 4:24 at the end of the narrative of Book One, could easily serve as a transition to the summary of 9:35. The conclusion is difficult to avoid: some kind of significance is attached to the number ten.

The Moses typology readily suggests itself, for the number parallels the ten wonders which the lawgiver performed in Egypt prior to the Exodus.[2] Like those already insinuated in different parts of Book One, this parallelism serves as a basis for contrast rather than mere similarity. There are indeed certain likenesses: both Jesus and Moses were persecuted by a king while still infants; both were recalled from exile after a king's death; both went up into the mountain in order to hand down God's law. Nevertheless, the contrasts are more significant and establish the essential difference between them: Jesus was persecuted by a king of his own people, the Jews; he was driven out of his messianic inheritance; he was forced to seek asylum in Egypt; after his return to Judaea he was compelled to move his residence to Nazareth; on the mountain in Galilee he recovered the original will of God which Moses had diluted in order to accommodate the weaknesses of human beings. Moses brought ten plagues of destruction upon Egypt; in contradistinction Jesus performs ten works of healing and restoration, even for the Gentiles. Certain facets of their careers may be similar, but Jesus is not a new Moses. In his mighty works, even as in his life and teaching, he transcends the Mosaic categories.[3]

This is immediately evident in Matthew's substitution of the cleansing of the leper (8:2-4) in place of Mark's account of an exorcism (1:23ff.) as the first episode of Jesus' healing. Moses commanded that a leper should be examined by a priest outside the community (Lev. 14:2ff.). If he was found to be

cured, he could be readmitted to society; if not he was ostracized to a "habitation outside the camp" (Lev. 13:46). Jesus
does not shrink back from contact with the leper; he touches,
heals and returns him to his community. The prescription of
Moses is not set aside, but any possibility of a Moses typology
is effectively shattered from the outset.

It is in this initial episode of healing that Jesus' identity
is confessed openly for the first time: the leper ". . . worships
him saying, 'Lord, if you wish you are able to cleanse me.' " It
may seem that this use of "Lord" is only a form of address. It is
predominantly in the vocative case that it has been edited into
the Marcan and Q traditions which have been adopted: 8:2, 6,
21, 25; 9:28; 14:28, 30; 15:22, 25; 16:22; 17:4, 15; 20:30, 31, 33;
25:11; 26:22. Yet its employment in such contexts as 8:25 and
14:30 supports its titular character and indicates that Matthew
regards the term as an appellation which Jesus shares with
Yahweh. This has already been established by the
acknowledgment of the heavenly voice at Jesus' baptism. Jesus
is God's surrogate and therefore the bearer of God's authority.
That authority was manifested in the teaching of the Sermon
on the Mount; it will now be disclosed in his mighty works by a
touch or a spoken word.

It is acknowledged by the centurion in 8:8, "Lord . . .
speak only with a word, and my servant boy will be healed." It
is accentuated by the evangelist in his summary of Jesus'
healing activity (8:16), "He cast out spirit by a word . . ." It is
implied in the revision of the fulfillment quotation of Is. 53:4,
"He *took* our sicknesses and carried the diseases." Here the
uniqueness of Jesus' lordship begins to emerge: there is no
trace of elitism in his conduct or in his exercise of his divine
office. As the Lord who "took our sicknesses" he is also the
Servant "who carries diseases." The title itself is not explicit in
this fulfillment quotation as it is in 12:18ff. It does not occur in
the original text of Is. 53:4; but perhaps the pronoun "he,"
which in Matthew's rendition refers to Jesus, can also be
understood in relation to its original antecedent, namely the

Servant.[4]

The first three works of healing which Jesus performs as the Servant-Lord include a leper, a centurion's servant boy and Peter's mother-in-law; that is, an ostracized Jew, a Gentile and a disciple's relative. A scheme is discernible here of a healing ministry that extends to three types of people who are representative of the urban community in which the gospel was composed: Jew, Gentile and Christian. By cleansing the leprous Jew and uniting him with his society Jesus uses his deeds to give expression to the original will of God which he exposited in the Sermon on the Mount: union and reunion for all human beings.

The same motive is present in the Q tradition of the healing of the centurion's servant boy. Faith is only one point, perhaps the original one, of the pericope.[5] The story also provides the occasion for an expression of the ultimate universalistic character of Jesus' mission. The reading of Jesus' interjection in 8:7 as an indignant question is probably correct: "Shall *I* come and heal him?"[6] The centurion's response evokes a declaration from Jesus which Matthew appears to have derived from another context in Q (Lk. 13:28ff.) and utilizes to present the first explicit universalistic note in the gospel: "Many will come from the East and the West and will recline at the table with Abraham . . . in the kingdom of God; but the sons of the kingdom will be thrown into the outer dark." Jesus, as he himself asserts later on in 15:24, has been sent only to the lost sheep of the house of Israel. As the dispossessed Messiah he identifies with the oppressed Jewish masses. But through the exercise of faith Gentiles begin to force him to include them in his mission of restoration and fulfillment.

The third healing is unique in as far as it is the only occasion in the gospel where Jesus takes the initiative to effect a cure. This may be due to another distinctive feature of the story: it is the only incident in which Jesus heals someone who is related to the community of his disciples. Both Matthew and Mark treat the episode as a resurrection event, but the former

relates this notion directly to the final outcome: "And the fever
left her and she was raised up *(egerthe)* and she was ministering
to *him.*" Being restored or resurrected leads directly to
ministry. According to Mark 1:31, Peter's mother-in-law
served *them,* both Jesus and his disciples. For christological
reasons, perhaps, Matthew prefers to limit her ministrations to
Jesus. No comparable response is cited in any of the other
healing stories in the gospel.

While the first three episodes underline the iconoclastic
activity of Jesus as Lord, the next two, the stilling of the storm
and the exorcism of the Gadarene demoniac, illustrate the
nature of discipleship to which Jesus calls his followers. The
theme, to which this complex of Marcan material is subordina-
ted, is introduced by the Q tradition on the two claimants to
discipleship (8:19-22) and accented by the three-fold employment of the verb *akoluthein* ("to follow") in 8:19, 22, 23. Verse
18 is the evangelist's editorial connection which provides the
transition to a new point of departure. The command to move
out "into the country beyond," a vague geographical reference
that becomes more precise in 8:28, is the immediate setting for
the two claims to discipleship that are made in 8:19 and 21.

The first would-be follower is a scribe who declares the
unqualified intention, "Teacher, I will follow you wherever
you go." Here is the first of several occasions where a distinctively sympathetic attitude toward the scribes is apparent.[7]
In his response Jesus introduces the figure of the Son of the
Human Being. It is the only title in the gospel which he alone
uses, and it is clearly a self-designation. Although it does not
occur earlier, its basis must be the distinctive origin of Jesus by
the creative activity of the holy Spirit. Nevertheless, it does not
appear to be limited to Jesus only; it reaches beyond him to
include others, specifically his disciples, who share his life
style. It is an epithet for a community as well as for an individual.[8] "The foxes have holes and the birds of the sky will
make nests, but the Son of the Human Being does not have any
place to lay his head." This, of course, contradicts Matthew's

frequent reference to Jesus' home in various places. According to 2:11, he lived in a house in Bethlehem; according to 2:23, he took up residence in Nazareth; in 4:13 he moved his home to Capernaum. How then can the Human Being be a wanderer? Or at least how can Jesus identify himself with the nomadic Human Being? According to his Son of David messiahship, "the King of the Jews" lives among his people Israel; he has a place of residence in their midst. Yet from the very beginning of his life Jesus has never remained or been permitted to remain in one place permanently, either because of persecution or by choice. Throughout his ministry the tension between these two identities and what they involve is never dissolved.

Another of his disciples, who, according to Matthew's redaction, addresses Jesus as "Lord" desires permission to return home in order to bury his father. Evidently he is ready to become a wanderer, but he feels obliged to fulfill his filial duties toward his parent. Jesus' reply, which includes the command, "Follow me . . ." edited into 8:22 by the evangelist, characterizes those who remain behind, who continue to live in one place, as dead. Let them, "the dead, bury their own dead." By contrast it is implied that the Human Being who has no place where to lay his head and therefore continuously moves forward into life, remains alive and, as Jesus states in 19:29, ". . . will inherit eternal life."[9]

Verse 23 continues where 18 left off: Jesus embarks into the boat with his disciples following him. Then ". . . a great earthquake happened in the sea so that the boat continued to be covered by waves." This description contrasts with Mark 4:37 where, "A great storm of wind happened and the waves beat into the boat so that the boat was already filling up." According to Matthew's revision, the extraordinary violence of the storm is caused by an earthquake, the first of four which the evangelist incorporates into his composition (21:10, 27:51, 28:2). Chaos threatens to overwhelm the community of Jesus and his disciples as they sail into "the country beyond." The boat, which is being enveloped by the waves is "an image of the congregation," as it is also elsewhere in the gospel.[10] The disciples' entreaty, "Lord, save!" is similar to that of Peter in 14:30. Matthew gives priority to Jesus' chiding question, "Why are you afraid, ones of little faith?" in place of the mighty work of calming the storm in order to develop his theme of discipleship.[11] The call to Jesus to exercise his lordship hardly seems to be a lack of faith; but the fear that evoked it is what underlies Jesus' rebuke. Discipleship means following Jesus into the world with full confidence that the community of the Human Being as it fulfills its mission, will survive the worst hazards of storm and earthquake.[12]

Matthew's paradigmatic treatment of discipleship culminates in the abridged and revised Marcan tradition of the Gadarene demoniacs. Upon arrival "in the country of Gadarenes,"[13] Jesus is confronted with evil in the form of *two* demon possessed human beings, who, in the evangelist's words, are "very fierce so that no one was able to pass along that way."[14]

Matthew introduces a pronounced eschatological thrust in the question placed on the lips of the demoniacs, "Did you come here before the *kairos* ("divinely appointed time") in order to torment us?" Their assumption that God will annihilate evil at the end of history corresponds to the belief of apocalyptic eschatology.[15] Jesus' action, however, is aimed at impressing upon the disciples that the overthrow of evil cannot be postponed by relegating it simply to God's sovereign intervention at the end of all things. It belongs to the establishment of God's rule in the present; and human beings, specifically members of this new community, are summoned, like Jesus, to serve as its divine agents. The destruction of the demons occurs in the drowning of the pigs "in the waters," an event which signifies the return of evil to its place of origin. Matthew omits any reference to the healed condition of the exorcised couple; in contrast to Mark, a christological motive is not the main purpose of the story. The incident closes with "the whole city" going out to meet Jesus in order to beg him to withdraw from their country. In conclusion the disciples are to know that their work for the health and restoration of human beings may result in their rejection, particularly when it interferes with the economic realities of society.

With the change in geographical location presented in 9:1 Matthew returns to the Marcan outline of events which has been suspended since the healing of the leper; but as previously, the narrative is severely abbreviated. A new aspect of Jesus' mission emerges here, which has implications for the nature and content of discipleship that the evangelist continues to develop alongside of the character of Jesus' ministry. It is important that the next events occur after Jesus has returned "to his own city," which, according to 4:13, is Capernaum "in the regions of Zebulon and Naphtali." A paralytic is brought to him for healing, but his restoration is not the point of the story. Neither is it the dispute with the scribes which is engendered by his bold pronouncement of forgiveness. It is rather the authority which Jesus exercises as the Son of the Human Being by which both forgiveness and healing are effected. The reaction of the scribes, which is quite restrained in the evangelist's redaction, serves as the point of departure for Jesus upholding the validity of his pronouncement of forgiveness by subsequently proceeding to cure the man's paralysis. Both forgiveness and healing originate from one and the same authority: "But in order that you may know that the Human Being has authority on earth to forgive sins, *then* he says to the paralytic, 'Arise, take your bed and go to your house.' " By forgiving and healing Jesus reconstitutes the individual's wholeness and opens the future to him both psychologically and physically. That the disciples are included in this prerogative, that they too bear this authority of the Human Being is indicated by the editorial revision of 9:8. "The crowds glorified God who gave *such authority to human beings;*" that is, according to Matthew, to those who participate in the community of the Human Being.[16]

The call of Matthew, the tax collector, in 9:9-13

develops this new aspect of Jesus' mission to restore human
health and freedom through forgiveness by adding the
dimension of community building as the goal to which all
reconciliation is to be directed. Matthew's discipleship,
"standing up he followed him," is another instance of the effect
of forgiveness. But it also serves as the introduction to the
subsequent dining with "many tax-collectors and sinners"
which Jesus carries on in his own house in Capernaum. This in
turn is the setting for the Pharisaic challenge to Jesus' conduct.
The scribes objected to Jesus assuming God's prerogative to
forgive sins; the Pharisees protest his association with sinners.
In response Jesus articulates his understanding of this part of
his mission: "The strong do not have need of a physician but
the ones who are sick . . . For I came not to call righteous but
sinners." Healing, forgiveness, mercy and community building
constitute the work of the Human Being.[17]

    The last of these three conflict stories involves "the
disciples of John;" the Marcan inclusion of the Pharisees in
this episode is missing. The controversy which they introduce
may arise out of Jesus' celebration with the tax collectors and
sinners; but in the light of what the Baptizer has said of the one
who would come after him (3:11ff.), they may hesitate to
criticize Jesus directly. Instead they raise a question about the
disciples' conduct which has a direct reflection on Jesus: there
is no practice of fasting. This criticism serves as the occasion
for three similitudes or analogies by which Jesus not only
defends his disciples but also enunciates the underlying
rationale for his style of life and mission.[18]

    Fasting, as carried on by John's disciples and the
Pharisees, is a form of abstinence that is an integral part of the
correct attitude of living before God. Jesus, however, rejects it
as a categorical imperative; only the immediate circumstances
authenticate such a practice of piety.[19] It is analogous to
groomsmen in the presence of the bridegroom; for the very joy
of the occasion they are unable to fast. But the situation will
change, for there will come a time when the bridegroom will be

taken from them; and then fasting will become valid.

Any attempt at applying 9:15 to the life of Jesus produces an allegorization of the similitude that distorts its meaning and intent. Matthew nowhere hints that the groom is to be identified as Jesus and that his disciples are the groomsmen. Nor is the second half of the analogy, "But the days will come when the bridegroom will be taken from them, and then they will fast;" a veiled reference to the passion or the post-Easter period when Jesus is no longer present in the church. There is no ascension in the gospel, and the evangelist presents the glorified Jesus unequivocally saying, "Look, I am with you all the days until the consummation of the age."[20]

The two similitudes which follow in vs. 16-7 are only intelligible in this context if the first analogy of 9:15 is understood in this way. New times demand new responses! Jesus as the Human Being, who is a new creation of God's Spirit and therefore has no past history, does not rely on traditions and categories of the past in order to deal with the new circumstances of the present. It will not do to mend age-old garments with new patches of unshrunken cloth! New wine requires new skins!

The reality of a new time and the need for new forms of response are dramatically accentuated by the two intertwined stories of the raising of a young girl and the healing of the hemorrhaging woman which have been adopted from a different context in Mark. The connection between the point of the three similitudes and this double tradition is established by the opening genitive absolute of 9:18, "While he continued to speak these things to them, behold one ruler having approached was worshipping him . . ." As usual, Matthew has abridged the Marcan version severely: Jesus' exhortation to the official to have faith has been deleted; neither the name of the man nor his relation to the synagogue are given. But the position of the healing of the woman with the hemorrhage in the context of the principal episode of the raising of the young girl has been retained. This seems unintelligible since the father has announced the death of his daughter at the very outset and the purpose of the healing of the hemorrhaging woman to cause the delay during which the child dies is no longer essential to the story. Matthew, however, utilizes this double tradition to present a momentous climax in his development of the character and content of Jesus' ministry and its paradigmatic instruction to the disciples.

Having been summoned to raise a young girl from the dead, Jesus — with his disciples — follows the father home. In terms of the number of mighty works assembled by the author in the narrative section of Book Two, this event that is anticipated from the very beginning as a resurrection is to be the seventh episode. But it is displaced by the interruption of the healing of the hemorrhaging woman, which in fact becomes the seventh. As a result, the raising of the official's daughter is shifted into the new position of eighth. This appears to be deliberate and to have great significance for the evangelist.

The affliction of hemorrhaging is treated in Lev. 15:25ff.[21] A woman with such a malady is ceremonially and ritually unclean. She must be kept separated from society so that the people will not be defiled by her. This means ostracism and isolation as long as the discharge continues. The woman is therefore not free to come and go as she pleases.

In this respect it is also noteworthy that she thought it would be sufficient to touch the tassels of his garment. According to Num. 15:38 and Deut. 22:12, tassels were supposed to be placed on the corners of the garments throughout all generations: ". . . and it shall be to you a tassel to look upon and remember all the commandments of the Lord to do them, not to follow after your own heart and your own eyes . . ." (Num. 15:39). In this light Matthew's interpolation of the clause, "approaching from behind she touched the tassel of his garment," is especially meaningful. The participle "approaching" is not "formalistic;"[22] it reflects a consciousness of Lev. 15:25ff., as does the adverb, "behind." Both indicate that the woman crept up behind him so that she would not be seen. She is unclean and cannot circulate freely in the community. Seeing the tassel of Jesus' garment, she should have been reminded of the "commandments of the Lord to do them." That would include the precepts of Lev. 15:25ff., to withdraw and isolate herself. Instead she commits herself to a risk: breaking the commandment, defiling Jesus and exposing herself.[23] This is the faith that saves her. Jesus intuits what has happened and declares her to be set free. The verb "to save" has been derived from Mark's account, but the evangelist has also edited it into his summary statement of the immediate effect of Jesus' power. It implies a genuine redemption that is not simply limited to a physical cure. She has deliberately perpetrated what the law of Moses forbade and has been delivered. The healing of the hemorrhaging woman may be symbolic of Israel's delivery from the tyranny of the law and the bondage and separation it often imposes. As the seventh work of Jesus it expresses the eschatological realization of Israel's anticipated sabbath age: a new time of freedom and wholeness inaugurated by God's kingship through the agency of the Son of the Human Being.

What was anticipated as the seventh mighty work becomes the eighth. The raising of the young girl from the dead serves as the culminating feature of the character and content of Jesus' mission.[24] As the eighth episode it parallels certain expectations of apocalyptic eschatology. In the Apocalypse of Weeks, I Enoch 93:1-10 and 91:12-7, the eighth week signals a new beginning, an age of righteousness, which continues for the final three weeks of time. At the very end the great judgment occurs and a new creation comes into existence. A somewhat similar interpretation of history is found in II Enoch 24:1-33:1. The world continues for 7000 years; the seventh millenial period is the great Sabbath Age of rest and blessedness. An eighth millenium follows which will be an endless time of a new creation.[25]

Jesus' eighth work, a resurrection event, expresses a new beginning, a new period of activity analogous to the commencement of a new week. It is not the *terminus ad quem* of life but rather the point from which life begins anew. The ninth and tenth works of healing, a doublet and what appears to be a fabricated incident which conclude the evangelist's selection and arrangement of ten mighty deeds, unfold this eschatological reality. The restoration of seeing, speaking and hearing establishes the possibility of communication and therefore also of community in which human health and freedom are gained through union and unity. This is essentially the result of God's kingship, and Matthew illustrates it by placing these two final healing episodes immediately after the resurrection of the official's daughter.

The first of the two is a restoration of vision. As in the more original form of the story in 20:29-34, there are two blind people; but the evangelist has reversed their employment of the two christological titles: "Son of David" and "Lord." In 9:27 "Son of David" is spoken first as a part of the plea for mercy. The difference appears to be linked to the question of faith. Jesus' query, "Do you believe that I am able to do this?" is not found in 20:29ff. There is no need for him to raise that question because their faith is obvious in their persistence and in their use of the "Lord" title. The same is true of the Canaanite woman in 15:21ff. It is when the blind men affirm their faith in 9:28 that they utilize the "Lord" appellation. Jesus responds immediately by touching their eyes and declaring, "According to your faith let it be to you."[26] In this manner Matthew dramatizes the connection between faith and Jesus' lordship: for the restoration of sight there must be a manifestation of faith conveyed through the confession of Jesus as "Lord." The Son of David christology, as will become more apparent, is ultimately inadequate.

In contrast to the two blind men healed in 20:34, who subsequently follow Jesus, the two of 9:31 leave his house and spread his fame throughout the land. This is in direct disobedience to the command not to report what they have experienced to anyone, the only such command found in the gospel. Jesus' attempt to impose silence may be in preparation for the fulfillment quotation of Is. 42:1-4 in 12:18ff. where his unassuming style of ministry is underlined by the evangelist. In any case, as a result of his deeds, his reputation and popularity, contrary to his own intention, are growing. In the same proportion the hostility and rejection of the religious leaders increase as they become more aware of the crowd's attraction to Jesus.

The tenth and final work of Jesus is particularly instructive in this respect. It is presented with utmost brevity.[27] Jesus heals a demoniac who is unable to speak and perhaps also, if the meaning of *kōphoi* in 11:5 can be utilized here, to hear. As at the end of the Sermon on the Mount in 7:28, here at the conclusion of the narrative of Book Two the reaction of the crowds is observed by Matthew. Their former astonishment has turned to wonder, "Never was anything like this manifested in Israel." The Pharisees, however, begin to reveal their animosity with the vilifying judgment, "By the chief of the demons he casts out demons," which they will repeat in 12:24 in order to contradict once more the amazement of the masses.

The narrative of Book Two is terminated by a revised Marcan tradition taken out of another context and used to summarize Jesus' ministry of teaching and healing. As such 9:35 is parallel to 4:23ff., the summary conclusion of the narrative of Book One.

FOOTNOTES

1 B.H. Streeter, *The Four Gospels,* (London: Macmillan, 1926), pp. 169f.
2 See Pir. Ab. 5:1-6 for a rabbinic parallel to the use of the number ten.
3 Also W.D. Davies, *Setting,* pp. 93f.

FOOTNOTES

4 F.V. Filson, *Matthew*, p. 112.

5 Compare Held, *Matthew as Interpreter of Miracle Stories*, pp. 193-4.

6 According to Zahn, *Matthäus*, p. 338; Lohmeyer, *Matthäus*, p. 157, and Held, *op. cit.*, pp. 194ff. See also 15:24ff.

7 See Mt. 13:53. Compare 22:34 with Mk. 12:28. Also Hummel, *op. cit.*, pp. 17f.

8 As Matthew makes more explicit in 9:6, 8. Compare Dan. 7:13-8, 26-7.

9 Compare with Matthew Black's attempt to recover the Aramaic original of this saying in *An Aramaic Approach to the Gospels and Acts,* (Oxford: at the Clarendon Press, 3rd ed., 1967), pp. 207f.

10 See Held, *op. cit.*, p. 266. Also Bornkamm, "The Stilling of the Storm," *Tradition and Interpretation in Matthew*, p. 55. Comp. Mt. 14:23.

11 Contrast Mk. 4:39f.

12 Compare an unusual parallel to this story in Test. of Naph. 6:1-6.

13 Matthew appears to be correcting Mark's geography here, perhaps finding it difficult to imagine pigs running about 25 miles to drown in the Sea of Galilee.

14 A contrast with Moses may be present in the evangelist's editing of the clause: "anyone to pass along the way," which is strikingly similar to LXX Num. 20:21, "to pass along through his regions." Moses and Israel retreated before Edom on the way to the Promised Land. Num. 24:18 reflects on this lack of "strength" and asserts that the Star of Jacob will work "with strength."

15 See the Apocalypse of Weeks in 1 Enoch 93-91 and 2 Bar. 53-74. Comp. Held, *op. cit.*, p. 269, and Strecker, *Weg*, p. 88.

16 Also Held, *op. cit.*, pp. 273f.; Hummel, *Auseinandersetzung*, pp. 36-7; Strecker, *op. cit.*, pp. 220f. And not the least, R. Bultmann, *Synoptic Tradition*, p. 16.

17 It is worth repeating that there is a close structural similarity between the "I came . . ." sayings and "The Son of Man came . . ." sayings of Jesus. Compare with Mt. 11:19 and 20:28.

18 E. Linnemann, *Jesus of the Parables*, pp. 3f., who defines a similitude as "a typical situation or a typical or regular event." "The similitude appeals to what is universally valid . . ." Also see J. Jeremias, *The Parables of Jesus*, p. 92.

19 That Jesus recognizes the validity of fasting is evident in Mt. 6:16-8.

20 Jeremias, *op. cit.*, p. 52, n. 14, makes the contention, which is shared by many, that a distinction should be made between Mk. 2:19 and 2:20, the sources for Mt. 9:15. The former is an authentic saying of Jesus, while the latter is a product of the early church. There is no more reason to separate the two parts of the analogy in Mark than there is in Matthew. See also Lohmeyer, *op. cit.*, p. 175; Stendahl, *Matthew*, p. 782, para. 682n.

FOOTNOTES

21 In Mt. 9:20 the verb "to hemorrhage" is used; in Mk. 5:25 the phrase: "with a flow of blood."

22 Held, *op. cit.,* p. 217.

23 In Lk. 8:45 the woman "trembles," not as Klostermann and Held think, because "she has taken advantage of the miraculous power of Jesus without his consent;" but because she knows the O.T. law applying to herself in Lev. 15:25 and Num. 15:38.

24 The verb, "she was raised," in 9:25 is derived from Mk. 5:41, but in place of Mark's original imperative, Matthew has substituted an aorist passive indicative which corresponds to the usage in 27:52 and 28:7.

25 See especially 2 Enoch 33:1. Compare with A. Farrer, *A Rebirth of Images,* (Glasgow: Dacre Press, 1949), pp. 36-90.

26 Thus, Held, *op. cit.,* p. 224, is right in affirming that ". . . the whole pericope is planned around" Jesus' saying of 9:29. Compare Strecker, *op. cit.,* pp. 209, 212f.

27 Held, *op. cit.,* p. 247, is wrong to reject 9:33f. as an independent miracle on the same level with the others.

Chapter VII

THE DISCOURSE OF BOOK TWO: "ON MISSION"
Matthew 9:36 - 10:42

The second of the gospel's five discourses begins in 9:36 with an adopted Marcan text carefully edited to correspond in structure to the beginning of the Sermon on the Mount in 5:1. "Seeing the crowds he was moved with compassion for them because they were harrassed and oppressed as sheep without a shepherd. Then he says to his disciples, 'The harvest is great, but the workers are few . . .' "

The narrative of Book Two has illuminated the content and character of Jesus' ministry and simultaneously revealed a basic correspondence with the objective of his ethical teaching in the Sermon on the Mount. In word and in deed the goal of Jesus' mission is health and freedom for human beings, above all the Jewish masses whom he wishes to serve. Having been dispossessed of his messianic heritage in Judaea, Jesus, the Son of David and the Son of the Human Being, has labored as the shepherd of God's people in Galilee identifying with them because they too are disenfranchised, having compassion for them because they are harrassed and oppressed. He is determined to fulfill his destiny as "the ruling one who will shepherd my people Israel" (2:6), but, in spite of his ceaseless activity on their behalf, much work remains to be done. He not only urges his followers to pray for more laborers; he establishes his mission on a broader basis by appointing twelve disciples to carry out the work of restoring the twelve tribes of Israel.[1] Their ministry is to parallel his; they are to follow his example. The imminence of the kingdom of God is to be proclaimed, and they are to manifest it concretely by healing the sick, raising the dead, cleansing lepers and casting out demons (10:8).

To the Twelve who are specifically chosen and named to be apostles (10:2-4) Jesus addresses his missionary charge. Its content consists of various edited materials of tradition derived from Mark and Q as well as oral sources and arranged by Matthew to furnish his church with a brief manual on mission conduct.[2] That it is for his church, however, is not immediately apparent. The very reverse seems to be true. For the opening words, "Do not go away to the Gentiles, and do not enter into a city of the Samaritans; but go rather to the lost sheep of the house of Israel!" contradict the gospel's climactic mandate: to make disciples of all nations. The exclusivism of these initial commands of the second discourse appear to be historically bound to Jesus' ministry; they are directed at the twelve who have been called to be apostles (10:2).[3] Judas has not yet betrayed Jesus and hanged himself. Furthermore, this limitation of the disciples' mission to Israel corresponds to the nationalistic orientation of Jesus' messiahship.[4] It also accords with his advice in 10:23.

Nevertheless, in spite of these historically determined features of the discourse, Jesus' charge on mission is intended for the gospel's audience. Because it is placed in the context of Jesus' career, it must be consistent with the character and thrust of his ministry and therefore also addressed to the Twelve who are designated to be the patriarchs of the new Israel which he is founding. They are being trained for a mission that is strictly nationalistic, but there is no indication in the gospel that they ever fulfilled it. That it should not simply be presupposed is evinced by the contrast that Mark poses: according to 6:12-3, "Going out they preached . . . and cast out many demons;" and subsequently according to 6:30, ". . . the apostles gathered together with Jesus and reported to him all such things as they did . . ." Neither of these passages has been adopted by Matthew; and nowhere in the gospel is there a corresponding mission of the disciples.

The mission charge of 10:5-42 remains in effect, but its nationalistic limitations are cancelled by Jesus' death and the universalistic mandate of 28:18-20 which supercedes it. The new mission is completely inclusive: all are to be evangelized, both Jews and Greeks. Jesus' warning of 10:17-8 anticipates this universalism: "Beware of human beings; for they will hand you over to supreme courts, and they will scourge you in their synagogues. And you will be led before governors and kings on account of me for a witness to them and the Gentiles." This notice suggests that in spite of the eventual cancellation of nationalistic exclusiveness, Matthew regards the Jews to have a certain priority in the mission activity of the church.

The life style which Jesus urges in verses 9-10 is consistent with his teaching in the Sermon on the Mount and upholds its emphasis on singleness and soundness, wholeness and freedom in living as well as relating to other human beings. Nothing is to distract them from the purpose of their mission. They are not to take gold or silver; they are not even to have any copper money in their belt. They are not to carry a knapsack or traveler's bag in which an extra undershirt or other needs might be kept. They are to go without sandals on their feet and without a staff in hand. While they are not to be anxious about what they shall eat or wear, they are to identify as closely as possible with the masses of the lost sheep of the house of Israel to whom they are being sent. For if "the worker is worthy of his food" and clothing, then the disciples should be as poor as the people they are serving from whom they will receive the basic necessities of life.

Jesus then proceeds to prescribe the manner in which they are to enter a community. They are not to select a home or household at random: "Into whichever city or village you should go, inquire as to who is worthy in it" (10:11). No criteria for determining what makes a household worthy are given. Jesus may simply be designating a home that is charitable, open in hospitality to strangers. This will become apparent in the response of the household to the greeting that is pronounced: "If the home is worthy, let your peace come upon it, and if it is not worthy, let your peace return to you." The apostles are surrogates or representatives of God. In a worthy home the greeting which they verbalize will become effective as the word of God. The open household that receives them will experience the eschatological benefits of their word and work; a dynamic peace will be established by which the individual members will gain new health and freedom from the wholesome relationships that will arise between them as well as between themselves and the apostles.

In the case of rejection they are not to waste time making appeals or arguments. They are to leave the house or city and shake off the dust from their feet.[5] No dust from that place is to cling to them by which they could be identified with the judgment that is to fall; ". . . it will be more bearable for the land of Sodom and Gomorrah on the day of judgement than for that city." Verse 15 is repeated in 11:24 where Jesus condemns Chorazin and Capernaum for not having responded to the mighty works of health and restoration that had been performed in those cities.

Their mission requires alert sensibilities and purity of motives: "Therefore," Jesus exhorts, "be wise as snakes and innocent as doves." They will be like sheep among wolves, for they will be facing human beings at their very worst, who because of their vested interests in the political, economic and social *status quo* will not hesitate to deliver them up to supreme courts for trial or the synagogue for scourging.[6] What will make their mission work heartrending is betrayal by members of their own family even to the point of death (10:21). There will be very few people they can turn to for help or support; indeed, they will be hated by everyone. What is required is courageous endurance and steadfastness.

Even as they are not to remain in a city or a household where they are not welcome, so they are not to continue in a situation of persecution at all costs, including death itself. Matt. 10:23 corresponds in structure to verse 19; the pronoun "they" of both these verses refers back to "human beings" in verse 17.

"When they hand you over, do not be anxious about how or what you shall speak . . ."

When they persecute you in this city, flee to another. Their mission to their fellow Jews will not be accomplished even when the coming of the Human Being takes place. The words of verse 23b, "For amen I say to you, you will by no means have completed the cities of Israel until the Son of the Human Being comes!" appear to refer to the Parousia at the end of history.[7] But in view of Jesus' confession before the High Priest in 26:64, "From now you will see the Son of the Human Being seated on the right hand of power and coming on the clouds of heaven," the coming that Jesus is speaking of seems to be a more ambiguous reality. Both *seated* and *coming* are simultaneously true of Jesus' death and resurrection which consummate the third epoch. He is enthroned in his crucifixion, and yet he is only coming to enthronement; he is enthroned in the resurrection, and yet he is only coming to enthronement. His coming to enthronement will finally be consummated at the end of the fourth age in the reconstitution of all things: when a new heaven and a new earth will be created and the community of the Human Being will be gathered together to form the kind of society which God originally willed.

As the disciples go about their mission during this fourth age they can expect no other treatment than that which their teacher has already received and will receive (10:24-5). "If they call the master of the house Beelzebub, how much more his servants." In this reference to 9:34, there is an anticipation of 12:24 and perhaps also what lies beyond.[8]

In spite of all the possible consequences which they may have to endure, the apostles are to be committed to open proclamation. "Therefore do not fear them . . ." The accusative pronoun "them" undoubtedly refers back to the "human beings" of 10:17. Fear is not to drive them into a secretive or secluded ministry; nothing about their work is to be concealed. "What I say to you in the darkness, speak in the light; and that which you hear in your ears, proclaim from the rooftops." Because life as well as light are the supreme realities in the universe, the apostles are also not to be afraid of those who kill to protect their vested interests. The destruction of their bodily existence does not mean the extinction of their essential life: "Fear not those who kill the *sōma* ("body") but are not able to kill the *psychēn* ("life"); but fear rather the one who is able to destroy both *psychēn* and *sōma* in hell." As in 6:25 and 26:38, *psychē* means the essential life of a human being, that which is divinely inbreathed and therefore originates from God. The *sōma* on the other hand, is the bearer or the vehicle of this life. According to 6:25, it can be clothed; as in 27:58 it dies and is buried. Moreover, according to 27:52, it can also be resurrected. Together "life" and "body" constitute the totality of the human being.[9] While people can destroy the one, the other, since it originates from God, is completely under divine jurisdiction.

The divine jurisdiction cannot prevent sparrows from falling to the earth or the apostles from being killed. But it includes an awareness or a knowledge of such events: "Are not *two* sparrows sold for a penny? and *one* of them does not fall to the ground without your Father. And all the hairs of your head are numbered; therefore, do not fear, you are worth more than *many* sparrows." Jesus' concept of providence, which is communicated for comfort and encouragement in a context of persecution and martyrdom, involves a God who sees and knows, not one who controls the events of human lives and determines when and how they happen.

In view of these things, confessing Jesus is to be fearless. Whatever its immediate consequences, it will ultimately result in being confessed by Jesus: "I will confess him before my Father in heaven." Denial, on the other hand, has its own effect:

it brings about repudiation.

The climax of the second discourse occurs in 10:34. It is a Q tradition adopted from the general but not immediate context out of which verses 26-33 have been taken. It has been structured by the evangelist to parallel the manifesto declaration of 5:17. Jesus came to reconstitute the original will of God in the law and the prophets and thereby to begin to restore the health and freedom of human beings. Nevertheless, his mission and ministry have also produced offense and alienation; and Jesus takes responsibility for them: "Think not that I came to cast peace on earth; I came not to cast peace but a sword." This, of course, appears to contradict the content and character of his works of healing or his response in 11:4-6 to John the Baptist's uncertainty about his identity in the light of the absence of the work of separation and division in his messianic activity.[10] Nevertheless, it is the necessary concomitant of his words and deeds. The sword that Jesus wields severs the bonds of enslavement and oppression. For one it means freedom, for the other the loss of power and profit. It begins with the many forms of bondage which exist within a family and ultimately extends to all relationships in society: "For I came to divide a man against his father and a daughter against her mother and a bride against her mother-in-law."

Those who put their parents or siblings above following Jesus in order to avoid this division or separation are not worthy of him (10:37). The condition for discipleship is nothing less than taking up the cross and losing one's essential life on account of him. Yet that is the very way that leads to authentic life and freedom.

The mission charge ends with a tradition peculiar to Matthew (10:40-2) which is addressed to those who receive these apostles Jesus sends forth. In their charitable response they will be welcoming God. Furthermore, they will have a share in the reward of these ministers, whether they are "prophets" or "righteous," for without their support these could not carry out their mission. However, if there is no opportunity to welcome such high emissaries as apostles, a cup of cold water offered to a "little one," that is, an ordinary follower of Jesus who can claim to be nothing special, yet whose angels always behold the face of God (18:10), will have its own reward. Indeed, so that there will be no elitism in Christian hospitality Jesus concludes this brief section and the entire discourse with a vigorous affirmation followed by a forceful double negative, "Amen, I say to you, he (she) will by no means lose his (her) reward."

By means of the formula transition of 11:1, the second in the gospel, the author closes Book Two.

FOOTNOTES

1 Schniewind, *Matthäus,* p. 127.

2 Compare with the Didache 11-3.

3 In contrast to the Great Commission which is given on the cosmic mountain in Galilee to eleven disciples, 28:18-20.

4 See 15:24 and 2:6.

5 Compare Acts 13:51 and 18:6.

6 See 2 Cor. 11:24. Compare D.R.A. Hare, *The Theme of Jewish Persecution,* pp. 48-62, pp. 105-6.

7 Compare Schniewind, *op. cit.,* p. 131, and H.E. Tödt, *The Son of Man in the Synoptic Tradition,* trans. from the German, 2nd ed., by Dorothea M. Barton, (London: SCM Press, 1965), pp. 90-1.

8 Trilling, *Das Wahre Israel,* pp. 64-5.

9 Matthew's anthropology seems to be similar to Paul's. Compare 2 Cor. 5:1-5.

10 See Mt. 3:11-2.

Chapter VIII

THE NARRATIVE OF BOOK THREE: "CONTROVERSY AND CONFLICT"

Matthew 11:2 - 12:50

Jesus' messianic works have begun to elicit different reactions. At the conclusion of the narrative of Book Two the crowds marveled at the healing of the dumb demoniac (9:33). The Pharisees, on the other hand, attributed the deed to the agency of "the chief of the demons" (9:34). Matthew continues his narration of Jesus' career by introducing the reaction of the imprisoned John the Baptizer at the beginning of Book Three: "Having heard about . . . the works of the Messiah, John sending through his disciples said to him, 'Are you the Coming One or do we await another?'" "The works of the Messiah" are the basis for evaluating his person and identity. The masses wonder, the Pharisees malevolently associate Jesus with the forces of evil, and John the Baptizer has misgivings: "Are you really the Messiah?" His uncertainty must be understood in the light of his original eschatological expectation: "The Coming One . . . will thoroughly sweep his threshing floor. He will gather his grain into the barn, but the chaff he will burn with inextinguishable fire" (3:11-2).[1] John anticipated his successor to be the great separator and assumed that his mission consisted essentially in exercising judgment. Comprehending the person and work of the Messiah in the traditional categories of apocalyptic eschatology, it is no wonder that he is troubled about the inconsistency between his prediction of 3:11-2 and the subsequent "works of the Messiah."

Jesus, who has just declared, "I came not to cast peace

on earth but a sword" (10:34), responds to John's christological inquiry by referring to the works of healing and renewal he has performed. "The blind see again and the lame walk, the lepers are cleansed and the deaf hear and the dead are raised and the poor are evangelized." Although separation and division belong to his messianic activity, they are not to be considered as his primary objective. They are necessary concomitants of his works of reunion and restoration.

In a continued utilization of this Q tradition (Lk. 7:18-28) Matthew shifts the focus from the respondent to the inquirer. An evaluation of the Baptizer's person and work by Jesus himself discloses his equally ambiguous identity. John is not simply an ordinary prophet; he is the fulfillment of Mal. 3:1 and therefore the promised Elijah who has returned for his second career.[2] It is this identity that establishes his peculiar eschatological position. For although he stands in the new age which Jesus inaugurated at his birth and therefore also proclaims the same good news as Jesus and his disciples,[3] his office as the eschatological prophet, the last prophet in the continuity of Old Testament history, places him in the time of "the prophets and the law."[4] Jesus' ambiguous evaluation of John corresponds to his distinctive position of having one foot in each age, the new and the old: "Amen, I say to you, he has not been born . . . who is greater than John; but the least in the kingdom of God is greater than he."

Since those days of the Baptizer "until now," according to Matthew's editing of a newly introduced Q tradition (11:12/Lk. 16:16), that is, during the overlapping of the old and the new ages, there are those who have attempted to gain a forceful entry into God's kingdom. By insisting on continuity and correspondence with revered ancient patterns and precedents, these impetuous human beings have violated this emerging eschatological reality. Jesus compares them to children playing games in the marketplace who are offended because they fail to evoke the appropriate response from their fellows. When they pipe, they expect others to dance; when they sing a dirge, they look for mourning. Their insistence on corresponding reactions is a demand for continuity. Disjunction and difference are offensive to them. The Baptizer who stands at the end of the Old Testament is condemned because he lived ascetically; Jesus the Human Being is vilified because he celebrates life with tax collectors and sinners. The tragedy is that they do not comprehend that the activity and movement of God are visible precisely in this exasperating discontinuity.

Thus, it is not simply a lack of response which drives Jesus to denounce the cities of Galilee: Chorazin, Bethsaida and Capernaum. It is this categorical insistence on continuity which has blinded them to that which is actually taking place and so leaves them unchanged. The prophets threatened Tyre and Sidon with divine retribution for their great iniquity and unrighteousness.[5] For its wickedness Sodom was obliterated by "brimstone and fire from the Lord out of heaven" (Gen. 19:24). Transgression and sin are evidently countered with divine vengeance.

But this pattern has now been reversed in the ministry of Jesus. Instead of requiting evil with punishment, Jesus meets it with mighty deeds of healing and restoration. Such a divine visitation would have moved Tyre and Sidon to repent in sackcloth and ashes, and Sodom would have survived to the present day. Indeed, they will rise up in judgment and condemn those cities of Galilee because Jesus' works of renewal have effected no change. They have not been moved to repentance.

Matthew continues with yet another incongruity expressed in a thanksgiving which Jesus voices to the "Father" (11:25ff.). The wise and the knowledgeable in their dependence on categories and classifications have been blinded while infants have been blessed with a marvelous capacity to grasp the discontinuities of life and of the divine movements in history. It is the Son of the Human Being-Son of God who displays these irregularities and incongruities and thereby reveals God (11:27). Thus it is not so much knowledge about God as it is knowing God through a recognition of his/her *modus operandi* or style of activity in the life of Jesus and his disciples.[6]

Matthew follows this series of Q traditions with a brief saying peculiar to his gospel. (11:28f.). Originating in Jewish wisdom and adopted for this particular context by the evangelist, its original form is no longer determinable.[7] Its meaning is linked to both the previous and subsequent materials of tradition. Although Jesus may have replaced Wisdom as the one who extends this invitation to rest, there is no justification in ascribing a Wisdom christology to Matthew.[8] Jesus is simply inviting the belabored and the burdened to enjoy his rest. The style of life which he expresses as the Son of the Human Being-Son of God, by which the activity of the Father is unveiled, involves a yoke; but in contrast to others it is easy and light. The subsequent narrative (12:1ff.) clearly shows this. Jesus, unlike the scribes and Pharisees who sit in Moses' chair (23:4), does not bind heavy burdens on people's shoulders. In offering his followers the eschatological gift of rest he invites them to participate in his identity which has no past, they can confront life freely and openly according to the context of each situation and the destiny of the Human Being.

Both 12:8 and 9:14 serve as paradigmatic examples of release from the burdensome yoke of the law. For this narrative material the evangelist has returned to the Marcan outline which had been temporarily abandoned at 9:17. The interpolated reference to hunger in 12:1, which may only be intimated in Mark 2:23, makes the reason for the violation of the Sabbath very explicit. Since the example of David is not immediately appropriate because there is no indication that his act was perpetrated on the Sabbath, the evangelist adds verses 5-7 which offer a more parallel instance of Sabbath defilement: "Do you not know that on the Sabbath the priests in the Temple desecrate the Sabbath and are blameless?" But there may also be another reason for this insertion. Verse 6, "And I say to you something greater than the Temple is here!" implies a rabbinic inference from a minor premise to a major premise.[9] If the Temple annuls the Sabbath law, how much more that which is greater than the Temple! And what is that? By quoting the declared will of God in Hos. 6:6 — indeed for a second time in the gospel (9:13) — Jesus asserts it to be "mercy." The irony of this pronouncement must have been plain to Matthew's original readers, for the new Judaism that was being con- solidated by the rabbis under the leadership of Rabban Jochanan ben Zakkai after the destruction of the Temple in A.D. 70 was founded on the word of God in Hos. 6:6.[10] Verse 7 quotes Hos. 6:6 but in the context of a conditional sentence which is simultaneously a polemical charge against the forerunners of the rabbis, the Pharisees, "If you knew what it is, 'I wish mercy and not sacrifice,' you would not condemn the innocent." Thus, a slight gradation is present here. Hos. 6:6 had been spoken to the same people in 9:13 as an exhortation. It now becomes manifest that they have left Jesus' admonition unheeded; they still have not comprehended the divine will. The insertion of the adverbial conjunction "for" in 12:8 connects this Marcan tradition to the inserted material of verses 5-7. Mark 2:27 has been omitted, not because it ". . . might lend countenance to a laxer attitude to the Law,"[11] or because the Sabbath commandment has been relativized but is still presupposed.[12] It is simply a redundancy; what it says is contained and epitomized in 12:8, the climax of the pericope. Because the Human Being is Lord of the Sabbath he determines his ethical conduct on the Sabbath in the light of the uniqueness of each situation. Human hunger justifies the abrogation of the principles of Sabbath observance. Since it is the disciples' conduct which is being exonerated by Jesus, the declaration of 12:8 also applies to them. The Human Being is also a community which Jesus, the individual Human Being, is establishing in which the lordship that is his is shared and exercised by all its members.

In the second episode Jesus invalidates the Sabbath law

for the sake of healing an individual with a withered hand. The insertion of the phrase, "whole as the other," in 12:13 indicates that the wholeness of the human being is the motivation for this teleological suspension of the Sabbath commandment. Verses 11-12, uniquely Matthean, provide the rational justification for Jesus' action, in terms of the rabbinic principle of inference from a minor to a major premise. It is often noted that Jesus' reply to the question of 12:10 reflects an ignorance of rabbinic casuistry.[13] However, the major premise of 12:12 may determine the formulation of the minor premise in the previous verse. In 12:1-8 the ethical problem concerned the individual's adherence to the law in the face of his or her own needs and predicaments. Here the focus is the individual's obedience to the law in view of the needs and predicaments of others. The simple criterion of 12:12 is recapitulated in 22:39-40.

For the first time, by means of a tradition borrowed from Mark 3:2, the author observes that "they" — the Pharisees, according to 12:14 — sought an opportunity to accuse Jesus. In fact, in contrast to Mark 3:4, it is the Pharisees, not Jesus, who raise the provocative question whether it is right to heal on the Sabbath. Jesus' act crystallizes their alienation which expresses itself for the first time in their wish for his destruction. From this point onward Matthew will unfold the gradual rejection of Jesus that culminates in his crucifixion.

In the face of this new threat Jesus withdraws and simultaneously admonishes the crowd following him not to reveal his whereabouts (12:15f.). No geographical references accompany this retreat in contrast to such previous incidents in 2:14, 22 and 4:12. But like the former instances this is an inconsistency in the conduct of Jesus as the Human Being and the Messiah. As on each previous occasion, Matthew interrupts his narration with an edited fulfillment quotation; 12:18-21 is taken from Is. 42:1-4. The correlation of this text with the life of Jesus permits the explicit identification of Jesus

as "my Servant" or the Servant of the Lord, something that
was only implicit in 8:17. The present retreat corresponds to
the character of the Servant who ". . . will not contend nor cry
out, neither will anyone hear his voice in the streets." Verse 20
echoes Jesus' works of restoration and contemplates his eradi-
cation of judgment and condemnation for the establishment of
true freedom and wholeness.[14] Verse 21 anticipates the
climactic universalism of the gospel.

The evangelist moves on to Mark 3:20f. omitting 3:13-9
because of its earlier use in chapter 10. Verses 22-23 bear a
resemblance to Luke 11:14 and may be designated as Q, while
verse 24 is Marcan. The demon possessed individual of 12:22 is
dumb as well as blind; by adding "blind" Matthew expresses
anew his interest in the healing activity of Jesus which, like
9:27-33, is focused on the organs of sense that enable
communication and community. The interpolation of the
crowd's question in 12:23 is particularly noteworthy, "Is this
the Son of David?" The interrogative particle *mēti,* which need
not be translated, expects a negative answer or at least conveys
a marked hesitance or uncertainty. Matthew has already
observed the surprise of the masses in 7:28-9, their inquisitive
wonder in 9:33. This continued astonishment gradually
engenders christological speculation. For the first time there is
an effort on their part, although very reluctant, to christo-
logize Jesus.

The Pharisees, who have been edited into this pericope
in place of "the scribes from Jerusalem" in Mark 3:22,
immediately contradict this with the same hostile charge they
made in 9:34, "He casts out demons by Beelzebub." Jesus has
made a retreat in accordance with his character as the Servant
of the Lord. But the Pharisees now begin to show signs of
determined pursuit and persecution.

This, then, is the setting for the following redaction of
Marcan and Q traditions which constitute the complex
pericope of 12:25-37 in which Jesus replies to the invective of
the Pharisees. After exposing the foolishness of their

assessment (12:25-7), he raises the possibility of another evaluation, "If I by the Spirit of God cast out demons, then the rule of God has settled over you."[15] Indeed, Jesus is the one who ravages the house of evil by subduing "the strong one," Satan himself.

Therefore, to attribute this eschatological work ultimately to Satan is a sin against the holy Spirit. Human beings will be forgiven all kinds of offenses and blasphemies, even those spoken against the Son of the Human Being (12:32). But blasphemy against the holy Spirit will never be forgiven, "neither in this age nor in the one to come." This eschatological differentiation between two ages appears to refer to the third epoch of Israel's history, as structured by Matthew in 1:17, which is terminated by Jesus' death, and the fourth and final period in which his followers who constitute the church, are engaged in mission.[16] For as long as the activity of the holy Spirit in the ministry of Jesus — and the Community of the Human Being — is evaluated as the work of Beelzebub, there is no possibility of repentance. It is an eternal offense. Only a complete change of mind which recognizes the creative and recreative action of God's Spirit in the mighty deeds of Jesus will reverse this condemnation and open up the possibility of divine forgiveness.

Verse 34 echoes the Baptizer's excoriation of the Pharisees and Sadducees in 3:7, but here the demonstration is limited to the former who are implicated by their own words to be like bad trees producing bad fruit or those who "out of evil treasure throw out evil works."

In conclusion Jesus promises a final accounting for every careless word spoken. This summary tradition, 12:36-7, is peculiar to the gospel and is most likely the evangelist's formulation. Its eschatological delineation, "in the day of judgment" followed by the pronouncement of verse 37 corresponds to the final separation effected by the verdict of the Human Being in 25:31-46. The judicial sentence there is based on the performance or non-performance of concrete deeds of mercy; here the alternatives of justification or condemnation are determined by the use of speech. In the light of Jesus' first antithesis in the Sermon on the Mount, vitriolic words can be as effective in destroying human beings as deeds of physical violence and oppression. Conversely, words of love and reconciliation can restore freedom and health.

For the validation of such harsh yet authoritative words "some of the scribes and Pharisees" solicit a sign. This is an ironic request for those who have observed Jesus healing the dumb and the blind and have discredited these acts as operations of Satan. For Jesus' response Matthew draws a tradition out of another context of Q (Lk. 11:29-32). The Lucan version draws an analogy between the appearance of Jonah as a signal to the Ninevites and the phenomenon of the Son of the Human Being as a sign to his contemporaries on the basis of their common eschatological preaching of repentance. Matthew, on the other hand, is preoccupied with the event of Jonah's burial in the belly of the great sea monster for three days and three nights and offers it as an analogy of the Human Being's forthcoming burial "in the heart of the earth for three days and three nights." As a sign, however, it is a riddle; for the the similarity between Jonah and Jesus is not merely intended to point out to the scribes and Pharisees that Jesus is a prophet and messenger of God. To establish a solid identity between them the evangelist employs the time designation, "three days and three nights," which contrasts with the phrase, "on the third day," that is used without exception throughout the gospel.[17] Once the two are linked together by a common bond, the sign then points beyond itself to another reality. What lies beyond Jonah's burial is a resurrection; and if Jonah and the Son of the Human Being are linked together by the former, the implicit deduction is that what is subsequently true for the one will also be true for the other.[18] That is, the sign of Jonah implies Jesus' resurrection from the dead. And if the scribes and Pharisees can "see" that in this enigmatic sign which Jesus offers, then they will begin to comprehend his person and work. But if they do not, then the foreign people of Nineveh will stand up and condemn them for they repented at the preaching of Jonah, a nationalistically oriented prophet, while the Jews, God's own people, reject the words and deeds of the one who is greater than Jonah, Jesus the Son of the Human Being-Son of God. In the same vein, the foreign Queen of Sheba will condemn them, for she journeyed from the end of the earth to hear the wisdom of Solomon, while in their very midst one greater than Solomon is present, the Messiah, the shepherd of Israel; and they refuse to listen to him.

Matt. 12:43-5 is a slightly edited Q tradition that may be more correctly located in its Lucan context.[19] Matthew, however, has reversed its position in relation to the previous pericope and skillfully utilized it as a diagnosis of a potential predicament. The editorial addition of 12:45c, "Thus it will be with respect to this wicked generation," is a warning of what can develop in a sterile law and order society such as that which is being fostered by the scribes and Pharisees. The demons may be banished temporarily and a rigorous legalism with its emphasis on the continuity of tradition may be effective in ordering life for a while. But the exorcized demons will return in greater force, and when they take up residence, ". . . the final state of things . . . will be worse than the first."

In the climactic conclusion of the narrative of Book Three, the Marcan tradition of 12:46-50, Jesus offers another solution in place of the tradition based society advocated by the religious leaders of Judaism. It is essentially the pro-grammatic declaration of 10:34-5, which he has begun to put into effect in the narrative of Book Three: "Think not that I came to cast peace on earth; I came not to cast peace but a sword. For I came to divide a man against his father, a daughter against her mother and a bride against her mother-in-law." Jesus is working for a radical disjunction in traditional human relationships. While addressing the crowds he receives word that his mother and brothers are standing outside to speak with him. His response, according to the editorial insertion of verse 49, is to point to his disciples and to designate them as his family. The sword of division which Jesus is wielding is very conspicuous. Human relationships are being transformed. The family, society, the nation, in as far as they are based on blood ties and supported by genealogical tables, are now superceded by a new community in which the unifying bond is generated by participation and cooperation in doing "the will of my Father in Heaven," which Jesus has already exposited in the Sermon on the Mount. By doing the will of God this new family, which Jesus is forming and which adumbrates the culminating universalism of the gospel (28:16-20), becomes the bearer of God's kingdom and the vehicle for extending his rule.

FOOTNOTES

1 On "the Coming One" see O. Cullmann, *The Christology of the New Testament,* (London: SCM Press, 1959), pp. 26, 36-7, and F. Hahn, *Titles of Jesus in Christology,* (Cleveland: World Publishing Co., 1972), pp. 389ff.

2 See Mt. 11:14 and 17:12.

3 Compare 3:2 with 4:17 and 10:7.

4 While Jesus fulfills "the laws and the prophets," John the Baptist stands in the continuity of "the prophets and the law." But compare Strecker, *Der Weg,* pp. 186-7, who considers John only from the standpoint of one side of this ambiguity, namely his participation in the new time of the gospel. Contrast Hummel, *Auseinandersetzung,* p. 134.

5 See Am. 1:9ff., Is. 23:1ff., Ezek. 26:1ff.

6 W.D. Davies, " 'Knowledge' in the Dead Sea Scrolls and Matthew 11:25-30," *Harvard Theological Review,* XLVI (1953), pp. 113-39, seems predisposed to assign the type of knowledge hinted at in this passage simply to Judaism. H.D. Betz may be far more accurate in attributing it to "a Hellenistic-Jewish syncretism." See "The Logion of the Easy Yoke and of Rest," JBL, LXXXVI (1967), p. 19. But he has not delineated the unique character Matthew has stamped on this gnostic-like tradition and the use of the concept "knowledge" in the evangelist's redaction.

FOOTNOTES

7 Betz, *ibid.*, pp. 17-20, links this saying to the concluding Great Commission of the gospel in terms of a contrast. See especially pp. 23-4. The idea is interesting but somewhat contrived. The meaning of 11:28ff. must be sought in its immediate context, and that includes what follows, 12:1ff. as well as what precedes it.

8 See M.J. Suggs, *Wisdom, Christology, and Law in Matthew's Gospel.*

9 See J.W. Doeve, *Jewish Hermeneutics in the Synoptic Gospels and Acts,* (Assen: Van Gorcum and Company, 1954), pp. 52-90 for an explanation of this interpretive principle.

10 J. Neusner, *From Politics to Piety. The Emergence of Pharisaic Judaism,* p. 98. Also Hummel, *op. cit.,* pp. 98ff.

11 Thus, Bornkamm, "End-Expectation and Church in Matthew," p. 31, n. 2.

12 Strecker, *op. cit.,* p. 33, n. 1.

13 Compare Strack-Billerbeck, *Matthäus, I, p. 629.*

14 Against G. Barth, *Matthew's Understanding of the Law,* p. 141, who translates *ekballō* as "establish" and renders the thought of the text as "the complete establishing of the will of God, of the judgment of God." But the verb means "to drive out, to expel." The law brings "judgment," but Jesus transforms it into victory by expelling it through his death and resurrection.

15 See R.G. Hamerton-Kelly, "A note on Matthew xii. 28 Par. Luke xi. 20," *NTS,* Vol. II (1965), p. 169. Matthew may have substituted "Spirit" for "finger" in order to avoid the hint that Jesus is Moses *redivivus,* as the parallel in Ex. 8:19 might suggest. On the eschatology of ". . . the kingship of God has settled over you." see Strecker, *op. cit.,* p. 169, who rightly emphasized its present reality in the intended understanding of the evangelist.

16 See Bornkamm, *op. cit.,* p. 34.

17 Tödt, *The Son of Man,* p. 214, recognizes this, but does not seem to know what to make of it. See his discussion of the text, pp. 211ff., which unfortunately sheds little light on the meaning of the pericope, except for p. 213 where he begins to sense Matthew's intention. See also Strecker, *op. cit.,* pp. 103f. Suggs, *op. cit.,* pp. 51f.

18 Since 12:40 is so important for the analogy, it is hard to agree with Stendahl, *School,* p. 132, that verse 40 is foreign to Matthew's original text.

19 So Stendahl, *Matthew, Peake,* p. 785, para. 684u.

Chapter IX

THE DISCOURSE OF BOOK THREE: "PARABLES OF THE KINGDOM"

Matthew 13:1 - 52

But there are also the great crowds (13:2). They are attracted to Jesus, astonished at his words and deeds and curious about his identity. Conscious of his responsibilities as the Son of David sent to the lost sheep of Israel, he is concerned about them and filled with compassion for them. Like him they too have been disinherited, and he would begin to restore their lost franchise on life by drawing them into the new community he is building where God's rule is actualized.

While the Sermon on the Mount was addressed primarily to the disciples and the teaching on mission (10:5-42) only to them, the third discourse, at least a large part of it, is spoken to the Jewish masses. Similitudes and parables are the means Jesus utilizes, and four of the seven which comprise the discourse are intended for them.[1] It is not until 13:36 that he "leaves the crowds" and returns to his house followed by the disciples.

The setting corresponds to the audience. Jesus leaves the privacy of his house (13:1) and speaks to the multitudes of people out in the open at the shore of the sea or more precisely from a boat on the sea. As in 5:1 and 24:3, he is seated; it is a posture that Matthew uses to underline the authority of the one who is teaching.[2] Seated on the mountain in 5:1, Jesus addressed his followers as the lordly Son of the Human Being-Son of God. His being seated in a boat as he speaks to the masses may be intended to convey the same image, for it was in a boat that Jesus arose as Lord to calm the wind and the sea (8:23-7).

The similitude of the sower introduces the discourse.[3] Except for a few incidental changes it is substantially taken over from Mark 4:3-9. Jesus dramatizes the risky but rich prospects of farming in Palestine. A sower broadcasts his seeds generously without prejudging the soil in terms of its potentiality for growth and harvest. Some seeds fall on a well-trodden path and are immediately devoured by the birds. Some fall on rocky earth and, because good rootage is not possible, the sprouts that spring up are soon scorched by the sun. Some fall among thorns by which the growing grain is eventually choked so that there is no production of fruit. But seeds also fall on good soil, and there is healthy growth that results in an abundant harvest with a return of one hundred, sixty and thirty percent.

Before Jesus offers an interpretation of this analogy, the basic question of why he employs "parables" to teach the crowds is raised by his disciples (13:10). Here there is considerable revision of the Marcan material that is adopted in order to enable Jesus to demonstrate his concern for the masses and their continuing impoverishment. For unlike Mark, who employs the parables as enigmatic analogies which are not self-evident to the hearers and which require especially sensitive ears to discern their truth, Matthew presents them as vehicles of illumination or windows of light intended for those who have not had the benefit of some instruction or education. There is no need to speak in parables to the disciples because they have been taught by Jesus: "because to you has been given the mysteries of God's kingship." Indeed, they are in the fortunate position of: "Whoever has, it will be given to him, and he will abound." That is, the richness of their knowledge and insight will produce further dividends.[4] But to the crowds this has not been given. Their plight corresponds to the other half of the proverb which Jesus employs in verse 12, a proverb the evangelist has derived from Mark 4:25, ". . . and whoever

does not have, even that which he has will be taken from him."
This predicament is fostered by a certain blindness and
deafness: "Seeing they do not see and hearing they neither hear
nor understand." Speaking in analogies in view of this
condition is not intended to insure a greater judgment on the
masses by preventing them from seeing and hearing. On the
contrary, because of their plight Jesus uses parables in order to
facilitate understanding and promote enlightenment.[5]

The quotation of Is. 6:9-10 in verses 14-5, therefore, is
not only incongruent with Jesus' understanding of his mission
to the lost sheep of Israel; it also contradicts his rationale for
using parables. It is very likely a gloss possibly appropriated
from Acts 28:26f. and interpolated by a scribe who interpreted
13:10-3 in the light of Mark 4:10-2. The smooth transition
from verse 13 to verse 16 lends support to this. Jesus moves
from the misfortune of the multitudes to the good fortune of
his disciples, "But blessed are your eyes because they see and
your ears because they hear. Amen I say to you, many prophets
and righteous longed eagerly to see the things you see and they
did not see and to hear the things you hear and they did not
hear." Because of their fortunate eyes and ears, they are
commanded to hear the analogy of the sower (13:18). The
interpretation which Jesus offers in verses 19-23, however, is
more than an explanation; it is an allegorical development of
the similitude in a particular direction for their benefit.

The story itself as it was addressed to the masses accentuated the bold, venturesome sowing of a farmer which, in
spite of heavy losses due to various contingencies, gained a rich
harvest. The people are to know that Jesus' messianic activity
is like that: he does not foreclose his ministry and the community of humanness he is forming to any kind of human
being. No one is prejudged or automatically excluded. There
will be repeated failure but the fullness of the final harvest will
justify all the risks that are taken.[6]

The interpretation of the story, on the other hand,
which is given exclusively to the disciples, concentrates on the

various types of soil on which the seeds are sown and compares them to different kinds of responses to the broadcasted "word of the kingdom." Evidently Jesus wishes to confront his followers with the question of their own response. As they hear they are to evaluate their discipleship critically and honestly: to which of these types of soil do their lives compare? The characterization of each may reflect conditions within the community to which Matthew is addressing his gospel.[7] The harvest that is eventually realized comes from the seeds that have fallen on good soil, that is, from those who hear the word and do it. In Matthew's version of the interpretation of the similitude Jesus stresses the degree and quality of the response, not the number of respondents.

In place of Mark's similitude of the seed growing secretly (4:26-9) the evangelist substitutes the parable of the tares which is introduced by the clause, "The kingdom of God has become like . . ." The peculiar use of the verb *hōmoiōthē* is most likely to be interpreted as an ingressive aorist denoting a point of entrance in the past and may be rendered in English by the perfect tense, "it has become like."[8] The story is told to the Jewish masses but not as an apologetic against unbelieving Israel nor as a message of judgment and condemnation.[9] Quite the reverse is true! The analogy is intended to assure the multitudes of another aspect of Jesus' messianic activity which stands in sharp contrast to the ideology of their religious leaders. The farmer who discovers that an enemy has sown darnels in his field of good grain does not permit his servants to do any weeding because of the difficulty in differentiating the one from the other. Both are to grow side by side until harvest time and then the separation will be made.

In the same manner Jesus, who does not foreclose his mission to any types of human beings, postpones any and every attempt to separate the bad from the good, since it is difficult if not impossible to differentiate between the two and, as a result, the good may be uprooted with the bad. In the present, therefore, both are to exist side by side.

Like the interpretation of the similitude of the sower, Jesus' exposition of this analogy in 13:36ff. is limited to the disciples. It is a thorough-going allegorization of each aspect of the story: the sower is the Human Being, the field is the world, the children of the kingdom are the good seed, the offspring of the wicked one are the bad seed, the enemy who sows the darnels is the devil, the harvest is the consummation of the age and the harvesters are the angels. The original emphasis on no separation is ignored. The point of departure is the parable's conclusion, that is, the separation which is effected at harvest time which is eschatologized to refer to the close of the age and its concomitant judgment: "Even as they gather together the darnels and burn them up with fire, so will it be at the consummation of the age." Obviously Jesus' purpose is to provide the disciples with special instruction in eschatology and perhaps simultaneously to anticipate the gospel's concluding discourse.[10] The concept of *synteleia aiōnos* ("the consummation of the age"), which is introduced in 13:39-40 receives fuller treatment in chapters 24-5. Especially significant is the distinction made in 13:41ff. between the kingdom of the Human Being in which the good and the bad exist side by side and the kingdom of the Father where "the righteous shine as the sun" and where Jesus, according to his words at the institution of the Lord's Supper, will drink the fruit of the vine anew with his disciples.[11]

The third and fourth analogies, the similitude of the mustard seed, a Marcan tradition, and the similitude of the leaven, a Q tradition, are also spoken to the great crowds. Like the remaining three stories in the discourse, both are introduced by the clause, "The kingdom of God is like . . ." Both make essentially the same point. The Jewish masses ought not to misjudge the insignificant beginnings of God's rule. It may appear as small as a tiny mustard seed or a handful of yeast buried in 50 pounds of flour. But even as the mustard seed grows into a huge shrub in which birds nest, or as a little yeast produces a mass of dough large enough to make bread for 100 persons, so the phenomenal growth and the marvelous outcome of God's rule are a guaranteed certainty.[12]

Matt. 13:34-5 closes the section of the discourse that is addressed to the masses by repeating Jesus' intention of communicating his teaching to the people by utilizing analogies. "All these things Jesus spoke in parables to the crowds, and without parables he was saying nothing to them." For Matthew this corresponds to the word of promise spoken by the prophet in Ps. 77:2, "I will open my mouth in parables, I will utter things hidden from the foundation (of the world);" and he pauses to pronounce fulfillment.[13] Revelation, not separation or division is the purpose of Jesus' stories. As analogies they do not conceal or disguise but rather elucidate his teaching: the secrets that have been hidden from the beginning, as his exposition of the Old Testament law in the antitheses of the Sermon on the Mount has disclosed.

The last three analogies which follow the interpretation of the parable of the weeds are spoken in the context of the setting specified in 13:36, namely Jesus' house and the company of his disciples. The first two are a pair, the similitude of the hidden treasure and the similitude of the pearl of great price — both peculiar to Matthew — which make the same point. God's kingdom is that kind of reality which demands single-minded commitment like that of a human being who discovers a treasure in a field and "from his joy goes forth and sells such things as he has and purchases that field." Again, its character is such that the only genuine response to it is like that of a merchant searching for beautiful pearls, who, when he finds one of especially great value, goes away to sell all his possessions in order to buy it. It is this absolute dedication to God's rule and its justice that Jesus urged on his disciples in his teaching of the Sermon on the Mount in order to attain to the wholeness and soundness which the Creator intends for his creatures.

The final story Jesus tells his disciples is a brief similitude which seems intended for concluding emphasis. For its key note is similar to that of the parable of the weeds: separation is reserved for the future; the present is the time for gathering. God's rule is analogous to the activity of fishermen working a dragnet to catch fish. When it is filled, it is brought to shore for the sorting of its content: the eatable fish are collected into vessels, and the worthless or unclean ones are thrown away.[14] While the main thrust of the analogy is the activity of gathering in the present, Jesus uses the conclusion of the story, as previously in the case of the parable of the tares, as a point of departure for his eschatological allegorization. The sorting of the fish is like the judgment that occurs at the consummation of the age; the angels will come and separate the wicked from the righteous and cast them into the furnace of fire (13:50).

The discourse of Book Three is drawn to a close with an editorially inserted question which Jesus asks his disciples, "Have you understood all these things?" Their affirmative reply confirms them as ideal disciples and serves as the basis for one more analogy: "*On account of this* every scribe having been taught with respect to the kingdom of heaven is like a housemaster who tosses out of his treasure new things and old things." These disciples who have eyes that see and ears that hear those things which many prophets and righteous longed to see and hear and who understand the instruction they have received are intimated to be scribes who function as housemasters of God's word. They are authoritative interpreters of the Old Testament who do not simply hand down the old and relate it to the new; nor do they discard the old in favor of the new. Rather out of their rich resources they bring forward things that are both new and old. Simon Peter will eventually be named the prototype of those who receive "the keys of the kingdom of God" (16:19) and serve as its authorized treasure masters in "binding and loosing," that is, in determining how the new and the old are to be integrated in order to make a creative response to the new circumstances of the present.[15]

The transition formula in 13:53 concludes Book Three

and introduces the narrative of Book Four.

FOOTNOTES

1 For the structure of Mt. 13, see J. Kingsbury, *The Parables of Jesus in Matthew 13,* (London: S.P.C.K., 1969), pp. 12ff.

2 See also Kingsbury, *ibid.,* p. 23, who finds the scene to be very much like apocalyptic vision of God seated on his throne while his worshippers are standing before him in Rev. of John 7:9-12.

3 Although it is usually called a parable, it may be more technically correct to designate it a similitude, if the generous sowing of the seed without prejudicing the soil is typical farming technique in Palestine. See E. Linnemann, *Jesus of the Parables,* pp. 3ff.

4 Although "the mysteries of the Kingdom of God" is an eschatological idea, that is no reason to interpret 13:12 eschatologically, especially in terms of Mt. 25:14-30, as Kingsbury does, *op. cit.,* p. 46.

5 Against Kingsbury, *ibid.,* pp. 47ff., who lumps together the Jewish masses and their religious leaders with whom Jesus has entered into conflict in chapters 11-2. Compare with Strecker, *op. cit.,* pp. 106-7 who also views this discourse as a punishment of the masses for not hearing Jesus' proclamation.

6 Jeremias, *Parables of Jesus,* p. 150.

7 See Kingsbury, *op. cit.,* pp. 57ff. for his views.

8 C.F.D. Moule, *Idiom Book of New Testament Greek,* pp. 10-1. Kingsbury, *op. cit.,* p. 67, rightly claims that from Matthew's viewpoint the kingdom "is a present reality and already has a certain history behind it."

9 Against Kingsbury, *ibid.,* pp. 64-5, 75-6.

10 Kingsbury, *ibid.,* does not make a careful distinction between the one point of the analogy: no separation in the present, and the eschatological character of the allegorized interpretation. As a result, he reads the former in the light of the latter. See also Jeremias, *op. cit.,* pp. 224f. and 81ff.

11 The righteous who "shine as the sun in the kingdom of their father" reflect the destiny of the transfigured Son of the Human Being foreshadowed in 17:2.

12 See Jeremias, *op. cit.,* pp. 147ff. Kingsbury, *op. cit.,* pp. 76-88, continues to understand these analogies as an apologetic addressed to unbelieving Jews, the masses as well as the religious leaders, and therefore continues to misunderstand their intention.

13 Kingsbury, *ibid.,* p. 89, senses a contradiction between the fulfillment quotation and his understanding of Jesus' use of parables, but proceeds to dismiss it as "apparent."

14 Jeremias, *op. cit.,* pp. 225f. Also Kingsbury, *op. cit.,* pp. 119ff.

15 Matthew himself is such a scribe who in his fulfillment quotations as well as his rewriting of Mark's gospel does this very thing.

Chapter X

THE NARRATIVE OF BOOK FOUR: "PREPARING AND TRAINING THE DISCIPLES FOR THE FUTURE"

Matthew 13:54 - 17:27

Since the content of Mark 4 and 5 has already been utilized in chapters 13, 8, 9 and 10, Matthew resumes his narrative with the adoption of Mark 6:1ff. The continuity between the final scene of the narrative of Book Three and the opening incident of Book Four is natural and smooth. Jesus who has enunciated the establishment of a new community transcending the bond of blood relationships (12:46-50) now returns to his hometown and teaches in the synagogue. The reaction which he evokes is a mixture of astonishment and critical scrutiny: what is the origin of his wisdom and mighty works? The people of Nazareth remember him as the carpenter's son; and they are acquainted with the immediate members of his family: Mary, his mother, his brothers, James and Joseph, Simon and Judah, as well as his sisters. But a knowledge of genealogical relationships resolves nothing; the continuity of his family history provides no explanation for the anomaly that confronts them in his life and work. To emphasize their perplexity Matthew repeats their question: "Where does he get all these things?" But they cannot find an answer. Jesus remains inexplicable to them, and they are scandalized. The incident ends with the evangelist's observation, "He did not do many mighty works there because of their unbelief."

While Jesus is being rejected, John the Baptizer is being martyred. The added phrase in 14:1, "in that season," indicates that the evangelist wants these two events to be understood as simultaneous occurrences. Although they have exhibited different styles of life (11:18-9), there is an indissoluble link between them, a link that binds them together in life and in death. Moreover, their careers are so identical that it is difficult to distinguish them from each other. Both proclaimed the same good news to the people and called for their repentance; both are acknowledged by the masses to be prophets (14:4, 21:11). Their likeness is the point of Matthew's formulation of Herod's statement to his servants in 14:2, "This (Jesus) is John the Baptizer; the same was raised from the dead and on account of this the mighty deeds are effective in him." That is to say, the two are one and the same person; Jesus is John the Baptizer who through resurrection has returned for a second career. Matthew uses this identity between them to hint that the martyrdom of the one forbodes the fate of the other, who "in that season" is being rejected by his hometown people. With this bleak set of events the author commences the narrative of Book Four.

The link between John and Jesus continues to be manifested in different ways. Herod wants to kill John but hesitates because he fears the masses. The Jewish religious leaders wish for Jesus' destruction, "but not on the feast so that there will be an uproar among the people" (26:5). Herod finally succeeds but only because he has sworn to give Herodias' daughter who has gratified his pleasure with a dance anything she requests; prompted by her mother she asks for John's head. The high priests also succeed but only because Judas approaches them with the question, "What will you give me if I betray him to you?"[1]

The relationship between the two is not dissolved by John's death. The addition of the concluding sentence in 14:12, ". . . and coming they (the disciples of John) reported to him;" provides the motivation for Jesus' subsequent withdrawal into the wilderness. Once more the destiny of John has immediate consequences for the one whose way he prepares. Upon his im-

prisonment Jesus returned to Galilee (4:13). Now at his
martyrdom, in view of the threat that it imposes on his own
life, he crosses the Sea of Galilee and *anechōrēsen* ("he
withdrew") into the desert.[2]

The crowds, however, continue to pursue Jesus
wherever he goes; they even follow him into the wilderness on
foot. As previously (9:36), Jesus is moved to compassion for
them and, according to an editorial expansion in 14:14, he
heals their sick. He also feeds them, ". . . about 5000 apart from
the women and children," by multiplying five loaves and two
fish.

However, the disciples are now drawn into an active
participation in his mission to the masses. To some extent this
is also true of the Marcan account, but its emphasis lies on the
disciples' lack of faith and understanding. Matthew's revision
accentuates a new resolution on the part of Jesus — in the light
of his rejection in Nazareth and the martyrdom of John — to
equip his disciples for ministry. In 10:5-42 Jesus instructed
them in the techniques of mission work among the lost sheep of
the house of Israel. Here, in anticipation of his own forthcoming rejection and death as foreshadowed by John, he sets
them an example that they are to emulate in their future
ministry. At the very outset he contradicts their proposal to
dismiss the crowds, "They have no need to go away; you give
them to eat." For them, however, that appears to be
impossible; the resources at hand are too meager: "We have
only five loaves and two fish."[3] Without hesitation Jesus shows
them a new possibility: using such resources as there are and in
faith and thanksgiving proceeding to distribute them to the
masses. "Taking the five loaves and two fish, looking up into
heaven he blessed and breaking he gave the bread to the
disciples and the disciples to the crowds" (14:19).

This action bears a significant resemblance to the institution of the Lord's Supper in 26:14, "And while they were
eating Jesus taking bread and blessing (it) broke and giving to
his disciples he said, 'Take eat; this is my body.'" At the feeding

of the five thousand they had taken the bread which Jesus multiplied and distributed it to the masses. Now they themselves are commanded to take and eat the bread which Jesus is giving them: it is his body! What is unspoken but nevertheless implied is that they are to do as they did earlier, to distribute this bread of life to the multitudes. But because they have become joined to him by partaking of his life, they too — like Jesus — are bound to offer themselves as bread that is to be broken and partaken of by others.

This paradigmatic character of Jesus' acts is continued — indeed, it is even more pronounced — in Matthew's redaction of Mark 6:45-52. After the feeding of more than five thousand people, Jesus urges his disciples to embark and "to go before him into the country beyond." This is almost a repetition of an earlier event (8:18), but here they are to venture forth alone unaccompanied by Jesus. Mark's specific geographical reference to "Bethsaida" has been omitted, perhaps because of the condemnation which Jesus pronounced on that city in 11:21. After dismissing the crowds, he ascends *eis to oros* ("into the mountain") alone in order to pray. For Matthew Jesus' work as the sovereign Human Being includes the messianic work of praying. Since all of the other mountain episodes in Galilee involve activity for the benefit of others, it is probable that Jesus' prayer is intercessory.

During the fourth watch of the night while the boat, "the little ship of the Church,"[4] continues to be tormented by the waves and the wind, Jesus approaches walking on the sea. He who multiplied the loaves and fish in the wilderness now unveils another facet of his sovereignty as the divine Human Being in this epiphany to his disciples. He displays his authority over the forces of chaos as they are represented by "the sea" and "the waters," two images that have already expressed this reality in 8:24 and 32. In spite of the mighty work of feeding a multitude which the disciples have witnessed and participated in, the last thing they expect to see is Jesus walking on the waters. The spectacle is overwhelming; thinking it is an apparition they cry out for fear. Jesus responds immediately with the encouraging identification, "Be confident, I am." This word is not simply intended to reassure them; it is also the climactic moment of the epiphany, for it is a startling self-disclosure of his identity with God.[5]

Peter, however, comprehends what Jesus has intimated and, according to the distinctive tradition of 14:28-31, which the evangelist has added to this Marcan story, he replies, "Lord, if you are (what you say, namely, "I am"), command me to come to you on the waters." Acknowledging Jesus' lordship Peter challenges him to prove his identification with God by permitting him to participate in this act of walking on the sea. Without hesitation he is invited to come: "And descending from the boat he walked on the waters and came to Jesus." Peter succeeds in imitating Jesus in doing that which, according to Job 9:8 and 38:16, only God is capable of.[6] Jesus' epiphany becomes a moment of apotheosis for Peter. For the first time in his life he begins to exceed the self-appointed or society-decreed limitations of his creaturehood. Because he is ready to leave "the little ship of the Church" and to join Jesus in his sovereignty over chaos, he becomes the ideal disciple. Both he and all the disciples are to know that they have a share in the destiny of the Human Being that is being disclosed by Jesus, a destiny involving nothing less than deification.[7]

But Peter also succumbs to fear "when he sees the wind," that is when he becomes overwhelmed by the chaos around him; and beginning to drown, he cries out, as all the disciples did in 8:25, "Lord, save me." Jesus exercises his lordship in another way by stretching out his hand to grasp him, while reproving him with the same epithet that he addressed to all the disciples in 8:26, "One of little faith, why did you doubt?"

When they return to "the little ship of the Church" the wind ceases. Perhaps the disciples are to catch an eschatological glimpse of that time when Jesus will come out of the future as the Son of the Human Being and reconstitute his community in the new age when the forces of chaos will finally be subdued. The response of those in the boat, including Peter, according to Matthew's editorial work in 14:32, is worship and confession, "Truly you are God's son." Although they have addressed Jesus as "Lord," as 8:27 shows, they have not been aware of his true character. Now, however, in view of this epiphany and its accompanying experience of deliverance they all acknowledge his godness. This united profession of faith not only stands in contrast to that of Peter in Mark 8:29; more significantly it displaces the confession that Peter will eventually make in 16:16 as the very first creedal affirmation in the gospel.

They disembark at Gennesaret. There, according to Matthew's abridgement of Mark 6:53-6, Jesus is recognized, and "the men of that place send (word) into the surrounding countryside, and they brought all the sick to him . . . and as many as touched (the tassels of his garment) were completely cured." Jesus continues to extend his ministry throughout Galilee,[8] and wherever he goes he is able to fulfill his messianic mission to the lost sheep of Israel, especially by continuing to "take their sicknesses and carry their diseases." It is in this context that the following encounter with the Pharisees and scribes takes place.

Matt. 15:1-20 is a revision of Mk. 7:1-23 which has been carried out chiefly by transposition. By placing Mk. 7:9-13 before 15:7ff. the evangelist has produced a more compact and lively dialogue out of materials that seem to be loosely joined together. Mark's reference to the origin of these religious leaders has been omitted; as far as Matthew is concerned, it is not until chapters 21-3 that the Pharisees and scribes of Jerusalem will confront Jesus. Unlike the previous situations of 9:9ff. and 12:1ff, Jesus is immediately challenged with a polemical question, "Why do your disciples transgress the tradition of the elders? For they do not wash their hands when they eat bread." Since Mk. 7:2 has been deleted, there is no record of such conduct on their part. The accusation may or

may not be unfounded, but that is not the point. The purpose
behind Matthew's use of the story is revealed as Jesus counters
with another question that challenges the entire legal tradition
of these representatives of Mosaic authority, "And why do you
transgress the commandment of God through your tradition?"
In contrast to Mk. 7:10 it is not Moses but God who said,
"Honor your father and your mother . . ."[9] This substitution
heightens the tension between the commandment and the
tradition of the elders and renders the latter indefensible. For if
God said it, any alleviation or accommodation of his word is
invalid on any grounds. "But you say, 'Whoever states once
and for all to his father or mother: that which you should
benefit from me is a gift (to God), he shall by no means honor
his father or his mother;' and you invalidate the word of God
through your tradition." Of course, obedience to God is ultimately more important than love and devotion to parents, as
Jesus has already asserted in 10:37. But that is not the point
here. Nor is it a question of the equal validity of both the
written law and the oral tradition of the elders. Jesus is not
interested in establishing the superiority of the one over the
other, for he has already abrogated certain injunctions of the
written code in 5:31-47 and transgressed the sabbath law in
12:1-13. What he is objecting to here is the annulment of the
divine will for human health and freedom. The dedication of a
gift to God which might be used to support parents in their old
age is an attempt to establish a vertical connection with the
Creator which is essentially unaffected by human
relationships. It is another form of separation or divorce which
is contrary to the will of God. Jesus has already rejected this
kind of religion in his teaching of the Sermon on the Mount:
"If therefore you bring your gift before the altar and there
remember that your brother has something against you; leave
your gift before the altar and go back, first be reconciled to
your brother and then coming offer your gift." Serving and
obeying God are always done in the horizontal context of
human need. Pharisaic piety which severs this union is a

religious way of life that fosters a basic dichotomous condition in human existence, and it evokes a bitter denunciation
from Jesus, "Hypocrites, well did Isaiah prophecy of you, 'This
people honors me with their hands but their hearts are distant
from me. In vain do they worship me teaching as instruction
commandments of human beings" (15:7f.).[10]

For a reply to the original charge, "Why do your
disciples transgress the tradition of the elders, for they do not
wash their hands when they eat bread?" Jesus turns to the ever
present crowd. They especially must hear the liberating word
which he is going to speak, because their own lack of
observance makes them despised in the eyes of their religious
leaders: "Not that which goes into the stomach defiles a human
being but that which comes out of the mouth." The disciples, in
a tradition peculiar to the gospel (15:12-4), report that the
Pharisees have been offended by this pronouncement. Jesus'
reply is a mixed analogy which differentiates between two
kinds of human beings. There are those which "my heavenly
Father planted;" and the implication is that they will be
healthy, attain to full maturity and bear fruit. On the other
hand, there are also those whose life and religion discloses that
they have not been planted by God; they are not whole and
therefore they will not mature and produce fruit. Indeed, they
will eventually be rooted up and perhaps, if Jesus' earlier
warning of 7:19 may be included, ". . . cast into fire." "Let them
be!" is his advice. Judgment will come soon enough, for as
"blind leaders of the blind," a charge that will be elaborated in
23:16ff., they along with those who follow them will fall into a
pit.

Peter, according to Matthew's revision of Mk. 7:17,
begs an explanation of the "parable" spoken to the crowd in
15:11. Evidently because of his participation in Jesus' lordship
in walking on the Sea of Galilee, he begins to emerge as the
spokesman of the disciples. Although he has manifested ideal
discipleship for a fleeting moment, he and the disciples for
whom he speaks lack understanding. Jesus can only wonder,

"Are you even yet still senseless?" They have been "planted" by God, but they are in need of growth and maturity. Nevertheless his request provides an opportunity for further explication: it is not the neglect of washing hands which defiles a human being, but the thoughts and actions that are harmful to others. All the uncleanness which Jesus enumerates, "wicked schemings, murders, adulteries, fornications, thefts, false testimonies, blasphemies, are horizontally oriented sins which destroy the personhood of other human beings.[11]

In view of this open contradiction of these religious leaders Jesus is obliged to withdraw from the scene. Once again, *anechōrēsen* ("he retreated"), this time "into the regions of Tyre and Sidon," and there he is immediately confronted by a woman who poses a startling contrast to "the masters" of the law, the Pharisees and scribes who sit in Moses' seat. In Mk. 7:26 she is a "Greek, a Syro-phoenician by birth." Matthew, however, alters her identity; she is a Canaanite and therefore a descendant of the people who were dispossessed of their land and enslaved by the conquering Israelites under Joshua. Since there probably were no longer any Canaanites living in this time, the evangelist's change can only be meaningful in the light of the Old Testament accounts of the relations between the Israelites and the Canaanites.[12]

She appears before Jesus with the unexpected confessional cry, "Mercy me, Lord, Son of David." This is Matthew's insertion, and it is somewhat similar to the invocation of the two blind men in 9:27-8. The "Lord" epithet is appropriately placed before the Son of David title, for it belongs to Jesus' primary identity as the Son of the Human Being-Son of God. The editorial addition of verses 23-4 is another expression of the nationalistic thrust of the gospel's presentation of Jesus' messianic mission. At first "he did not answer her a word." When the disciples urge him to dismiss her, apparently suggesting that he take heed to her plea, he replies in terms of the circumscribed commitment which he laid on them in 10:5-6, "I have not been sent except to the lost sheep of the house of Israel." As the Son of David he has been called to shepherd God's own people; this automatically excludes the Canaanite woman.

But she persists. According to the redaction of 15:25, "she worships him and says, 'Lord, help me.' " The Son of David title is dropped; now she appeals to him only on the basis of his universally oriented Son of the Human Being lordship. Jesus not only remains adamant in his refusal but even degrades her with the racist pronouncement, "It is not right to take the bread of children and throw it to the dogs." The woman does not disagree but goes on to observe that ". . . the dogs eat of the crumbs falling from *their master's table.*" In this edited statement, Matthew has the Canaanite woman acknowledge her Old Testament destiny of enslavement under the Israelites and yet for that very reason to have a tiny share of the benefits of his ministry. Jesus surrenders to her eloquent and persistent faith and heals her daughter. The evangelist notes that "she was cured from that hour." This is the second healing at a distance in the gospel and like the first (8:5-13) involves someone who is outside the community of God's elect people. It is another step in the movement from nationalism to universalism which the author is tracing in the life of Jesus.

Matthew follows his Marcan source (7:31) in returning Jesus to the countryside of the Sea of Galilee, but by eliminating the references to various geographical regions through which he passed, his reentry is made direct and deliberate. The redaction of 15:29 indicates that his destination is the mountain, the very one on which he taught his disciples (5:1), on which he also prayed (14:23). His being seated, as in the first instance, denotes his enthronement as the lordly Human Being. This is the christological identity that prevailed in his encounter with the Canaanite woman, and as in her case it is to be expressed in and through the works of healing. But it is as though, in the light of this previous episode, he is more determined than ever to minister to the lost sheep of Israel, the Jewish masses: "Great crowds came to him having with them

their lame, crippled, blind, dumb and many others, and they
lay them down at his feet, and he healed them." For the very
first time there is a positive response to his messianic work: ". . .
and they glorified the God of Israel."[13]

Because Matthew has omitted the time reference in Mk.
8:1 and has inserted the adversative conjunction *de* ("and" or
"now") in 15:32, the healing of the crowds and the feeding of
the four thousand are linked together as one continuous event.
The setting, therefore, remains the same; like the preceding
works of healing the meal occurs on the mountain. In contrast
to 14:14 Jesus articulates his concern for the masses and takes
the initiative to feed them, "I have compassion for the crowd
because they are continuing with me already three days and
they have nothing to eat, and I do not want to send them away
fasting lest they should give out on the way." The disciples
seem to have learned nothing from the previous feeding and
wonder where so much bread can be acquired to feed such a
multitude. Jesus, however, commands them all to recline on
the ground, and taking the resources at hand, seven loaves and
a few fish, he gives thanks, breaks and gives to his disciples who
as before distribute to the people.[14] This language, as in the
case of the previous feeding, points forward to the institution
of the Lord's Supper. At the same time, however, in spite of the
parallel features of both feedings, the notable differences, the
setting of the mountain, the seven loaves, the seven basketfuls
of leftovers and the more than four thousand people, will not
permit the two to be identified and merged into one meal.[15]
With Jesus as the lordly Son of the Human Being-Son of God
conducting the meal on the mountain, the feeding of more than
four thousand men, women and children takes on the
character of a messianic banquet and marks a climactic
moment in his mission to the lost sheep of Israel.[16] The
symbolism of the seven loaves and seven basketfuls may be
eschatological — not ecclesiological! — pointing forward to
that new time when "the Human Being comes into his
kingdom" (16:28). For on the one hand the number seven

denotes a week and is used in apocalypticism as a measure or division of time in relation to the end of the age; on the other hand it also designates the last day of the week, the time when the week reaches its climax in the celebration of the Sabbath and correspondingly when history arrives at its culmination in the new age.[17]

After dismissing the people Jesus embarks "in the boat" and, according to Matthew's redaction, sails across the Sea of Galilee to "the mountain regions of Magadan." No motivation for this movement is given. Perhaps Jesus wishes to continue his ministry to the Jewish masses in that area. In any case, it becomes the setting for another encounter with the religious leaders. Once again the Pharisees seek out Jesus; on this occasion, however, their accomplices are the Sadducees (16:1). Their intention is similar to their earlier approach in 12:38; they want Jesus to give them a sign from heaven for his authentication. But this time, in contrast to 12:38, their alienation is more pronounced: their objective is to tempt him.

The authenticity of 16:2b-3 is questionable. Not only are these verses missing in such prominent manuscripts as the Vaticanus, the Sinaiticus, the Ferrar group, the Sinaitic and Curetonian Syriac and the Sahidic Coptic, the similarity with Luke 12:54-5 suggests a scribal effort at harmonization. Most telling is the contradiction between the sign which Jesus verbalizes in verses 2b-3 and his subsequent censure of these tempters with his refusal of any sign except the one he has already offered in 12:39ff., the sign of Jonah.

Taking leave of them Jesus departs and with his disciples moves, according to Matthew's distinctively vague geographical reference, "into the country beyond."[18] The latter forget to take along bread; and when Jesus warns them to beware of "the yeast of the Pharisees and Sadducees" who have just tempted him to give them a sign, they can only conclude that he is reprimanding them for their forgetfulness. Using the epithet that he has applied to them before, "Ones of little faith," Jesus rebukes them on two counts: they have not grasped the significance of the two feedings, and they have misunderstood "yeast" to refer to bread. While the Marcan version (8:14-21) presents a sharp reprimand of the disciples, Matthew's revision is primarily a disparagement of the religious leaders.[19] The Old Testament quotation of Jer. 5:21 and Ezek. 12:2, which Jesus aims at his disciples in Mk. 8:18, has been omitted; it contradicts what he has said to them in 13:16-7. Accordingly, the incident ends on the positive note, "Then they understood that he did not say to beware of the yeast of the bread but of the teaching of the Pharisees and the Sadducees."

Omitting the Marcan story of the blind man of Bethsaida (8:22-6), the evangelist moves on to a drastic revision of the pericope of Peter's confession at Caesarea Philippi.[20] The disciples, who finally have comprehended Jesus' warning against the teaching of the religious leaders, are now questioned by him about the people's identification of "the Son of the Human Being." This title has been substituted in place of Mark's use of the personal pronoun "I," and it indicates that Jesus' inquiry about popular opinion is, for Matthew at least, only a pretext for the more important question that is to follow: "Who do you say that I am?" This self-expression of his fundamental christological identity in the gospel vitiates the various possibilities that are cited.[21] Moreover, in view of its omission in 16:21, the first suffering Son of the Human Being prediction taken from Mk. 8:31, it avoids a possible one-sided emphasis on suffering and places the following complexes of tradition, especially Peter's confession, under its comprehensive implications.

It is Simon Peter, who has emerged as the ideal disciple and at the same time the spokesman of all the disciples, who answers the second and more substantial question Jesus has raised: "You are the Messiah, the Son of the living God." The use of the Son of God title is a repetition of the creedal affirmation made earlier by all the disciples in 14:31; the participle "living" is also Matthean and will be edited into the

High Priest's adjuration in 26:63. What is distinctive about Peter's confession is his designation of Jesus as the Messiah. Although Jesus accepts it and pronounces a beatitude on Peter for it — in contrast to Mk. 8:30 — it will become evident in 16:22f., that the two of them have a mutually opposed understanding of it.

Verses 17-9, a uniquely Matthean insert, conveys Jesus' immediate rejoinder: "Simon, son of Jonah, you are fortunate because flesh and blood have not disclosed (this) to you but my Father in heaven." The insight that Simon has articulated, as inadequate as it may prove to be, is nevertheless an indication that God has been at work in his life. That became apparent already in his fearless challenge to Jesus to be permitted to join him in his lordship over chaos. His faith, small though it was, enabled him to climb out of the boat and to walk on the sea; that experience, including his subsequent rescue, opened up a new way of viewing Jesus.

Because of this profession of faith, Jesus introduces a new way of viewing this ideal disciple. Simon has bestowed a title on him; he in turn awards him an epithet that becomes a new name: "You are *Petros* and on this rock I will build my church, and the gates of death will not be dominant over it." He is "the Rock *Man*" — in contrast to the feminine gender of the Greek word *petra* ("rock") — and on him and his style of discipleship, which includes his confession of faith, Jesus will consolidate his church. His role will be similar to that of Abraham, the grand patriarch of Israel, who, according to Deutero - Isaiah's analogy (51:1-2) is "the quarry from which you (Israel) were digged."[22] As Abraham gave up the security of the walled city of Ur and wandered about as a nomad for the rest of his life, never settling down anywhere permanently, so Peter, who left the security of "the little ship of the Church" for a moment in order to participate in Jesus' sovereignty over chaos, will become a wanderer, a "rolling stone."[23] Accordingly he will join Jesus in manifesting the life style that the Creator intended for authentic humanity: he will become identified with the Human Being who has no place to lay his head. And the Church, quarried from this rock, consolidated with it and therefore manifesting all of its qualities of nomadic existence, faith, solidity, strength and endurance, will never be vanquished by the power of death; in moving into the open future it will continuously be rejuvenated by the supreme reality of life.

Jesus furthermore entrusts Peter with "the keys of the kingdom of God." As the bearer of the keys he holds a unique office. He is like Eliakim in Is. 22:20ff. who was called to "shoulder the key of the house of David" and given the authority to "open and none shall shut and . . . (to) shut and none shall open." Peter, therefore, has access to God's house and simultaneously the authority to dispense its treasures: "And whatever you bind on earth will be bound in heaven, and whatever you loose on earth will be loosed in heaven." This is not to determine the destiny of others by locking or unlocking the gates of God's kingdom. The gender of the relative pronoun is neuter: "Whatever you bind . . . whatever you loose . . ." Peter is granted the privilege of determining ethical conduct and ecclesiological practice as well as establishing or dissolving institutions, precedents and programs. His freedom in the exercise of this office is unqualified; his decisions are acknowledged by the Lord God.[24]

In view of the benediction which Jesus pronounced on Peter for his creedal affirmation, the vigorous rebuke of the disciples that follows that confession in Mk. 8:30 is modified to a charge to silence. Messiahship, as Peter himself will subsequently show, can easily be misinterpreted; it is therefore not to be disclosed to anyone. Matthew proceeds to adopt the Marcan tradition of Jesus making known for the first time his anticipated death and resurrection (16:21), but several significant changes are introduced. The Son of the Human Being title is deleted; it was used earlier in 16:13 by Jesus himself and stands as the governing christological identity for the entire episode. Concomitantly the Christ title is inserted immediately after the name Jesus and as a result becomes a surname. This seems to be the evangelist's way of indicating where the epithet belongs. Perhaps the most significant is the appending of the phrase, *apo tote* to the beginning of 16:21, "*From then* Jesus Christ began to show his disciples that it is necessary for him to go away to Jerusalem and to suffer many things from the elders and chief priests and scribes and to be killed and to be raised on the third day."

This time reference, "from then," was used earlier in 4:17 to accentuate a critical turning point in Jesus' career: the commencement of his ministry in Galilee after being forced on three different occasions to withdraw from his homeland Judaea. In the present context this phrase denotes another juncture in Jesus' life. A momentary climax occurred in Peter's confession: "You are the Christ, the Son of the living God." Although Jesus acknowledged this identification and the evangelist has indicated its significance by attaching it to him as his surname, a new time now begins in Jesus' career as well as in the disciples' instruction.[25]

They are to learn about the culminating character and content of his messiahship: suffering, death and resurrection. Peter, however, who has emerged as the ideal disciple is not ready for this turning point. Taking Jesus aside, he censures him for this surprise announcement; and Matthew, in contrast to this Marcan source, quotes the words on his lips, "God be gracious to you, Lord! By no means will this be for you!" Evidently Peter has begun to exercise his authority as the bearer of the keys of God's rule. Jesus responds with a stinging rebuke denouncing him as Satan. Suddenly the "Rockman" has become a stumbling block, a rock of offense: "You are my scandal, for you do not think the things of God but of human beings." Nevertheless, in spite of his lack of understanding as well as his forthcoming denial — which pale the luster of his new identity — Peter continues to be representative of ideal discipleship, not as a static condition but rather as a constant movement toward new growth and greater maturity.

For Jesus this is an occasion requiring further instruction aimed at producing such growth and maturity. The evangelist's use of the particle "then" is indicative of the connection intended between Peter's lack of comprehension and the teaching which is to follow. Ideal discipleship is not only participation in the Human Being's messianic mission to heal people's lives and to restore their communion with each other. It also involves a correspondence with the life style of the Human Being that includes suffering and death: "If anyone wants to come after me, let them deny themselves and lift up their cross and follow me. For whoever would save their life will lose it and whoever would lose their life on account of me will find it."

Instead of adopting Mk. 8:38ab, the author expands the final clause of the verse (8:38c) into an eschatological glimpse of the lordly Human Being who will come at the end of the age "in the glory of his father with his angels" for a final reckoning. "And then he will render to each according to his or her activity."[26] As elsewhere in the gospel, especially 25:31ff., the final judgment is based on works. Since it is Jesus who formulates the character of the Human Being in and through his own life, it is also he as the Human Being who will judge who expresses it through words and deeds. Those who are "workers of lawlessness" (7:23), like the weeds growing in the field of good grain, will be eliminated from the kingdom of the Human Being at the consummation of the age (13:41). Those whose deeds correspond to the character of the Human Being will constitute the community of authentic humanity and, according to 25:34, will inherit "the kingdom prepared from the foundation of the world."

In this context of eschatological judgment Jesus' affirmation in 16:28 that some of his disciples will live to experience the Human Being "coming in his kingdom" appears to refer to the Parousia.

According to 24:29-30, this takes place in conjunction with the cosmic reconstitution of all things: in terms of

Matthew's fourfold scheme of Israel's history conveyed by the introductory genealogy, at the end of the fourth age. But there is another possibility. The Human Being also comes at the end of the third epoch and, according to Jesus' confession before the High Priest, "From now on you will see the Son of the Human Being seated at the right hand of power and coming on the clouds of heaven." This is Jesus coming into or entering upon his kingship at the beginning of his passion. Thus, when the disciples encounter the resurrected Jesus on the mountain in Galilee declaring, "All authority in heaven and on earth was given me;" they see the Human Being coming *in* his kingdom.[27] Not all of them have survived. Only eleven ascend the mountain; Judas has died by his own hand. Thus it would seem that 16:28 can *also* refer to the culminating event of the gospel.

Of these two alternative ways of interpreting 16:28 Matthew intends both to be understood at the same time.[28] On the one hand, the coming of the Human Being to his passion concludes the third age; and his resurrection from the dead, which is also his enthronement, inaugurates the fourth and final epoch of Israel's history. On the other hand, this fourth and final epoch is consummated by the Parousia of the Human Being who comes "in the glory of the Father with his holy angels" for judgment (24:30, 25:31) and whose kingdom, purified of all evil, subsequently merges with the everlasting kingdom of the Father prepared from the foundation of the world (13:42, 25:34). Even as the former is preceded by Jesus' suffering and death, the latter occurs when "the birthpangs" are at their very worst, when there will be "great affliction such as has not happened from the beginning of the cosmos until now . . ." (24:21). Matt. 16:28 is Jesus' final response to Peter's rejection of his announcement of his forthcoming passion: it is necessary that these things happen, for only then will they see the Human Being coming in his kingdom.

The story of the transfiguration conveys this very same eschatological ambiguity as it elucidates the words of 16:28. The time reference of Mark 9:2, "after six days . . ." has been retained and, it can be assumed, with a consciousness of its underlying eschatological symbolism.[29] The seventh day or the end of the week implies the culmination of the present age. According to the numerical structuring of Israel's history in the opening genealogy this can be the end that occurs at the termination of the third period or the end at the termination of the fourth period. In relation to the first Jesus represents both the thirteenth and fourteenth generations. As the thirteenth he brings about the consummation of history: at his death the earth is shaken, the rocks are split and the creation returns to its primeval state of chaos. As the fourteenth he, the enthroned Human Being along with the holy ones who have been resurrected with him, initiates a new creation. An ambiguity, however, lies in the twofold significance of the number fourteen. Not only is it the beginning of a new creation; it is a transition, like the events of David - the king and the Babylonian Captivity, to another era: the fourth and last of Israel's history. This in turn will be terminated by the cosmic collapse into darkness and chaos (24:29-30). The Human Being will then appear for the final judgment, the great separation will be effected and the community of the Human Being which has been constituted will enter into the kingdom of God forever. The transfiguration of Jesus foreshadows both of these consummations.

Jesus leads Peter, James and John "into a high mountain." The prepositional phrase is similar to the one which was used in 4:8 and may be intended to pose a parallel situation.[30] In Judaea on a very high mountain Jesus was tempted to worship Satan in order to receive "all the kingdoms of the world." In Galilee on a (very) high mountain the transfiguration adumbrates Jesus' apotheosis by his resurrection from the dead and concomitantly the kingdom which he receives as the Human Being who is seated on the right hand of power.

The high mountain, therefore, is another architectonic center or navel which is the dwelling place of God as well as the point from which a new creation originates. In place of Mark's description of the metamorphosis, "And his garments became exceedingly white such as a bleacher on earth is unable to whiten;" the evangelist substitutes the language of an apocalyptic theophany: "His face shone as the sun and his garments became as white as the light."[31] Jesus is being disclosed to his disciples as God! Moses and Elijah, the Old Testament representatives of the law and the prophets, make their appearance; and Jesus, the culmination of Israel's history, the fulfillment and the fulfiller of the law and the prophets, gives them an audience. "They were seen speaking with him." Undoubtedly they are acknowledging his work as well as what his work will ultimately realize.

For Peter this appears to be a moment of glory that he does not want to relinquish too quickly, "Lord, it is good for us to be here." In contrast to Mark's version, he announces his willingness to construct three tabernacles only "if you wish." Matthew has deleted the comment on Peter's ignorance and fear in Mk. 8:6. Instead, "while he was still speaking a voice from the cloud says, 'This is my beloved Son in whom I am very pleased. Hear him.' " The reality of Jesus' metamorphosis is acknowledged by the Lord God. In a reaction typical of theophanies the disciples fall on their faces in great fear.[32] Touched by Jesus and bidden to "be resurrected and stop fearing," they lift their eyes and see no one except Jesus. He alone, without Moses and Elijah and independent of their authority, voices this Easter oriented command.

Jesus' transfiguration looks beyond his forthcoming suffering and death to the moment of his apotheosis and enthronement on the right hand of power as the Human Being by his resurrection from the dead. It is therefore an eschatological anticipation of the new creation which Jesus inaugurates after his death and its accompanying collapse of the old creation. At the same time Jesus' transfiguration adumbrates the ultimate destiny of the Human Being that is realized at the Parousia: the constitution of the Human Community and its consolidation with "the kingdom of the Father" in which "the righteous ones will shine as the sun" (13:43). The metamorphosis of Jesus the Human Being into God is therefore a corporate reality, for it includes the disciples, indeed, all those who are drawn into the Human Community and who therefore participate in its destiny.

While descending from the mountain Jesus adds some instruction to this experience which Peter, James and John have shared with him. The epiphany is not to be communicated to anyone until after "the Son of the Human Being was raised from the dead," for, as has become evident, that is the time when the Human Being will come in his kingdom. For the disciples this raises the question of the scribe's teaching of Elijah's return for a second career. If Jesus' death and resurrection will establish the new age and the kingdom of the Human Being, "Why do the scribes say that Elijah must first come?" Jesus upholds the eschatology of the scribes but insists that "Elijah already came, and they did not recognize him but did to him such things as they wished." To take into account John the Baptizer's recent martyrdom, the tense of the verb, "to come," has been altered by substituting the aorist for Mark's use of the present perfect. In a tradition peculiar to the gospel, Jesus links his own suffering as the Human Being to the rejection of John, a conjunction which the evangelist intimated earlier in 14:1-13. Matthew pauses to note another instance of ideal discipleship, "Then the disciples understood that he spoke to them about John the Baptizer."

Matthew adheres to the Marcan sequence of events in his narration of the healing of the epileptic child (17:14-21). The story, however, has been drastically abbreviated.[33] The setting of the disciples' argument with the scribes has been omitted; Jesus returns to the crowd, not to the disciples. The subsequent entreaty to heal the epileptic boy in the light of the disciples' ineffectiveness becomes the basis for instruction on the nature of faith. The conversation between Jesus and the father (Mk. 9:21-4) has been stricken from the narrative. The latter, whose trembling faith is so eloquently expressed in Mk. 9:24, has been transformed into a suppliant who has no doubts about Jesus' ability to heal his child. Matthew presents him falling on his knees, addressing Jesus as "Lord" and begging for mercy. For some reason the diagnosis given in Mk. 9:17-8 has been revised: instead of "having a dumb spirit," the lad is "moonstruck." Such an editorial change defies explanation; yet it should be noted that this peculiar condition is included among the sicknesses which Jesus heals in the evangelist's first summary of his ministry in 4:24.

Jesus orders the boy to be brought to him and cures him by rebuking "the demon" (17:18). Mark's description of the evil spirit rending the child as he is presented to Jesus is also missing. The restoration is effected effortlessly and immediately — in contrast to the disciples' failure. Once again Jesus reveals his authority as the lordly Son of the Human Being-Son of God. The culminating instruction which he gives his disciples discloses the motive behind Matthew's revision.[34] Chiding his disciples for their "little faith" Jesus teaches them that faith is the basis for the authority he has exercised, the power he has displayed: "If you have faith as (small as) a seed of mustard, you will say to this mountain, 'Be moved from here to there,' and it will be moved and nothing will be impossible to you." Once again the horizontal relationship between the actual sovereignty of Jesus as the Human Being and the potential participation of the disciples in that sovereignty is affirmed.[35]

Verse 21 is another instance of a later scribal interpolation influenced by and derived from Mk. 9:29 and perhaps motivated by the later obsession for gospel harmony. It is omitted by some of the more reliable witnesses of the text: the Vaticanus, the Sinaiticus, the Koridethi, the Sinaitic and the Curetonian Syriac and a few others.

When they have returned to Galilee, Jesus again announces his forthcoming death and resurrection to the disciples (17:22-3). This is the second prediction, made after his

authoritative healing of the moonstruck boy and his teaching
on the remarkable possibilities of faith. The third will be enunciated when Jesus is on his way up to Jerusalem to make his
messianic claims (20:17-9). In this way, it would appear, the
evangelist illuminates the paradox of the Human Being: by
juxtaposing his sovereignty and its glory over against his
humiliation and death.

The narrative of Book Four closes with Jesus' return to
Capernaum and to his own house (17:24ff.). The final episode
of his Galilean ministry is the question of paying the double
drachma, a coin that seems to have been used for the Temple
tax. The tradition, which is peculiar to the gospel, is neither
polemical nor apologetic. It serves rather as a transition to the
discourse on church conduct which follows, while it also
elaborates upon the nature of the authority and freedom which
Peter has received as the bearer of the keys of the kingdom of
God.[36]

Peter, the ideal disciple and the spokesperson of all the
disciples, is approached by tax collectors with the question,
"Does your teacher not pay the double drachma?" The use of
the negative particle *ou* ("not") in this query anticipates an
affirmative reply which Peter unhesitantingly gives, "Yes."
When he joins Jesus in his home, he is addressed by his former
name, "Simon," and interrogated regarding his thoughtless
response to the tax collectors: "From whom do the kings of the
earth take tribute and toll? From their sons (citizens) or from
foreigners?" Simon, in accordance with those times, correctly
answers, "From foreigners." Jesus' deduction, "Consequently
the citizens are free;" shows up the foolishness of his hasty
reply to the tax collectors. For if the sons or citizens are free,
then by analogy the citizens of that rule which transcends the
kings of the earth, the kingdom of God, are not obliged to pay
taxes. Whether this means the Temple tax which all Jews were
required to pay to the Temple during Jesus' lifetime or the tax
which the Romans collected from the Jews after the
destruction of the Temple is irrelevant. What is at stake is the

church's relations to Judaism as well as to the Roman government. The decisions that are made on how to relate to these religious and political realities belong to the exercise of the keys of the kingdom of God. Whatever is bound or loosed, established or revoked, will be acknowledged by God. There is to be no absolute commitment to anything except God's rule; and it is this very rule which liberates its citizens to determine for themselves what their relations to these entities will be from one moment to the next. The apriori starting point for their ethical conduct is freedom.

"But in order that we do not offend them, go to the sea cast a hook and take the first fish coming up, and opening its mouth you will find a silver coin; taking that give to them for me and you."[37] Although fundamentally and initially the children of the kingdom of God are free, there is one limitation imposed on that freedom: "So that we do not offend . . ." That is to say, love is the sole criterion by which the exercise of freedom and authority is to be determined.

FOOTNOTES

1 Mt. 26:14.

2 For the use of the same verb, see 2:13, 14, 22; 4:12; 12:15; 15:21. The gradation is especially noteworthy; 15:21 is Gentile country.

3 There is no need to assume that because Jesus does not ask how many loaves there are that he already knows. Nothing in the text indicates such a christological motive. See 15:34.

4 From Bornkamm, "Stilling of the Storm," *op. cit.,* p. 55.

5 See especially the Test. of Naph. 6:1-6 where the chaos of wind and sea smashes the ship of Jacob and scatters the twelve patriarchs to the farthest corners of the earth. Also Job 3:8, 26:12; Ps. 74:13f., 89:9f.; Is. 27:1, 51:9, where Leviathan and Rahab are the chaos monsters of the sea.

6 The "I am" of Mk. 6:50 and Mt. 14:27 is generally not acknowledged to carry such christological significance by those who hold the story to be an epiphany. This is surprising because in view of Jesus' unusual feat of walking on the sea, which the O.T. ascribes to God, what else can *egō eimi* mean? See D. Daube, *The New Testament and Rabbinic Judaism,* (London: Athlone Press, 1956), pp. 325ff.

7 Also Held, *Matthew as Interpreter of Miracle Stories,* p. 206, "The whole

FOOTNOTES

scene of Peter walking on the sea . . . presents a disciple on the way to discipleship." This is another way of understanding this climactic episode. In addition see p. 272, "Christ is not only the deliverer of his own from need and danger; rather, he gives his disciple a share in his power to walk on the water." This is an aspect of the story which Bultmann, *History of Synoptic Tradition*, p. 216, does not seem to have appreciated. See also A. Schlatter, *Matthäus*, p. 471.

8 According to Lohmeyer, *Matthäus*, p. 243, a topographical plan reveals itself, which begins in 9:35 and continues into 14:36, including the regions around the Sea of Galilee, Nazareth and Gennesaret. Such expressions as "the people of that area" indicate, however, that the author is far removed from this territory.

9 Matthew's attitude towards Moses is more explicit in 19:8. Moses relaxed the commandments in order to accommodate them to the weaknesses of human beings. See also Matthew's deletion of Moses in his reproduction of Mk. 12:26 and 22:31.

10 Hummel, *Auseinandersetzung*, pp. 46ff., does not get to the heart of the matter. Neither the scribal tradition nor the written code has authority for Matthew's church if it does not correspond to the fundamental will of God.

11 Matthew has reduced Mark's catalog of vices to the commandments of the Decalogue. Compare 15:21-47, 19:17ff. and 22:36ff.

12 See Gen. 9:20-7.

13 Compare Lohmeyer, *op. cit.*, pp. 257f., who is convinced that these crowds should be identified as strangers and heathen. So also Stendahl, *Matthew*, p. 787, para. 6861.

14 Lohmeyer's surmise, *op. cit.*, p. 258, that the seven loaves and seven baskets of leftovers point to the seven deacons of Acts 6 and intimate the identity of these people as the Gentiles of Galilee is an attractive idea. But in view of 15:24 they can only be the Jewish masses. Trilling, *Das Wahre Israel*, pp. 109f. recognizes that the "great crowds" of 15:30 are the same as the more than four thousand of the feeding and has difficulty in identifying them as Gentiles.

15 Against Held, *op. cit.*, pp. 186-7.

16 See Is. 25:6-10.

17 See I Enoch 93:3b, 5, 7, 8. Also Rev. 8:1. Contrast Rev. 16:17ff.

18 See 8:18, 14:22.

19 Strecker, *Der Weg*, p. 16, maintains that 16:11-2 contradicts 23:2ff. Not necessarily so. The evangelist has already focused on the discrepancy between the word of God and the tradition of the elders in 15:1-20. The words of 23:2ff. are limited to the historical situation of Jesus and his disciples who have entered Jerusalem to take up Jesus' messianic claims. His recognition of their Mosaic authority belongs to the end of the third age that is rapidly drawing to a close; it is an authority that will be cancelled by his death and resurrection.

20 In the light of 11:21-2 the setting of this story in Bethsaida would seem to

FOOTNOTES

be inappropriate. Perhaps the healing was not eliminated altogether but added to the Marcan account of blind Bartimaeus in 20:29-34. See B.H. Streeter's discussion of this problem, *The Four Gospels,* pp. 169ff. H.J. Held, *op. cit.,* pp. 208ff. rejects such an explanation and contends that since neither the theme of christology nor that of faith nor that of discipleship is contained in these two miracle stories (Mk. 7:32ff. and 8:22ff.), Matthew would have no interest in them.

21 Jeremiah has been added to the list by Matthew most likely because of the parallel features that will emerge in 27:3-10.

22 See John Lowe, *Saint Peter,* (Oxford: At the University Press, 1956), pp. 56f. Trilling, *op. cit.,* pp. 132ff. Compare Suggs, *op. cit.,* pp. 120ff.

23 Compare I Cor. 10:4.

24 But see Mt. 17:24-7. Also Hummel's discussion, *op. cit.,* pp. 61ff., and especially A. Schlatter, *op. cit.,* p. 511.

25 See Strecker, *op. cit.,* p. 92, on the time differentiation Matthew wishes to introduce through the use of the phrase, "from then."

26 This addition seems to have been derived from Ps. 62:12 (61:13) or Prov. 24:12. It is probably not a pre-Matthean expansion originating in apocalyptic tradition, as Strecker, *op. cit.,* pp. 27f., insists.

27 The preposition "in" denotes a state or condition. See Blass, Debrunner, Funk. *Grammar,* p. 110.

28 Against Strecker, *op. cit.,* p. 42.

29 See the discussion on Mk. 9:2 in E. Schweizer, *The Good News according to Mark,* (Atlanta: John Knox Press, 1970), pp.

30 As suggested above, the phrase *kat idian* ("alone") which follows may be a later scribal emendation based on Mk. 9:2 which replaced the word *lian* ("exceedingly"). Both the Codex Bezae and Eusebius have the reading *lian.*

31 Compare Test. of Lev. 18:3-4, Rev. 1:16.

32 See Rev. 1:17; Dan. 5:6. Also D.S. Russell, *The Method and Message of Jewish Apocalyptic,* pp. 161ff.

33 See Held's analysis, *op. cit.,* pp. 187ff.

34 Held's estimate is correct that "the concluding conversation is no longer an appendage but the real goal of the pericope." *Ibid.,* p. 189.

35 Also Held, *ibid.,* p. 271.

36 Strecker, *op. cit.,* p. 31, n. 1, may be right when he says that in its cultic meaning this tradition is bound to the existence of the Temple and that Matthew could not have taken over this pericope in its original sense. But did this legend ever have an original cultic sense? Did it arise before A.D. 70? And does it necessarily presuppose the existence of the Temple? Perhaps it was created to make a point about the exercise of freedom by the ideal disciple. See Hummel's discussion, *op. cit.,* pp. 103ff.

37 The Syrian stater has approximately the value of two double drachmas; so that Peter can pay Jesus' taxes and his own.

Chapter XI

THE DISCOURSE OF BOOK FOUR: "ON COMMUNITY CONDUCT AND DISCIPLINE"

Matthew 18:1 - 35

The discourse of Book Four is composed of various units of tradition: 1-5, 6-9, 10-14, 15-17, 18, 19-20, 21-22 and 23-35, from different sources, which have been compiled by the evangelist in order to elucidate matters of church conduct and discipline. In one way or another the issues that are raised are related to the authority of the keys granted to Peter as the ideal disciple in 16:19 and its concomitant problems of freedom which emerged in 17:24-7. Mark's setting has been revised; the question: "Who, then, is greater in the kingdom of God?" does not arise out of a dispute among the disciples. It is presented as emerging from the preceding conversation between Jesus and Peter. The use of the comparative degree in the question implies a comparison of two entities. These are not named, but in the light of the editorially inserted time reference, "in that hour," and the adverbial particle *ara* ("consequently") which link the discourse to the preceding pericope, they must be the two groups implied in 17:26-7. That is, those who are free and those who restrict their freedom for the sake of their fellow human beings.

Jesus answers by drawing a child into their midst and speaking a logion that has been taken from Mk. 10:15, "Amen I say to you, unless you turn and become as children, you will by no means enter into the kingdom of God." Thus, judging between those who are free and those who limit their freedom in love, the one who is greater in the kingdom is the one who, like a child, adapts himself or herself to each situation by a new response. By means of the evangelist's interpolation of 18:4 Jesus clarifies what he means: "*Therefore,* whoever will humble himself as this child, he will be greater in the kingdom of God." To be great, as Jesus tells his disciples in 20:26ff., is to be a servant; to be first is to be a slave: "Even as the Human Being came not to be ministered to but to minister and to give his life a ransom for many." Drawing upon his Marcan source again Matthew has Jesus add, "And whoever receives one such child in my name receives me. That is to say, whoever gives hospitality to a child of the kingdom who restricts his own freedom by serving others, he or she is entertaining Jesus himself.[1]

Mark 9:38-41 is passed over; it has no relevance for this discourse on community conduct and discipline. Instead Matthew moves on to an appropriation of Mark 9:42-8 which is easily related to the initial question that the disciples have raised and especially to the thought of the previous verse: "But whoever scandalizes one of these little ones who believe into me, it is profitable to him that a millstone were hung around his throat and he were drowned in the depths of the sea." The phrase, "one of these little ones," denotes the humble disciple who serves and adjusts her or his freedom to the needs of others. Giving offense to such persons has grave consequences, as Jesus warns in the evangelist's insertion of 18:7, "Woe to the world for its temptations to sin, for it is necessary that temptations to sin come; however, woe to the human being through whom they come." Freedom all too easily leads to a new bondage, for there are "the little ones" who freely offer themselves to serve others, and there are those who take advantage of them. There are also those who proclaim freedom as a license to do all things and lead many "little ones" astray. To avoid exploiting other human beings within the community, especially those who limit their freedom for the sake of others, may require action as radical as that proposed by Jesus in verses 8-9, "If your hand or your foot causes you to sin, cut it off and throw (it) away; it is better for you to enter life crippled or lame than to be cast into eternal fire having two hands and two feet. And if your eye causes you to sin, pluck it out and throw (it) away, for it is better for you to enter life one-eyed than to be cast into the hell of fire having two eyes."

Mark's saying on salt (9:49-50) is excluded; 5:13 may be a complete revision of it. The remainder of the discourse contains Q traditions and special materials peculiar to the gospel which have been revised extensively by the creative handiwork of the evangelist. Verse 10 is an editorial construction that continues the theme of "the little ones" and serves as a transition to the thought of the subsequent Q tradition of the parable of the "misled" sheep. The value of these little ones, Jesus asserts, may be measured by the fact that their guardian angels continually look upon the face of "my Father in heaven." They have God's full and immediate attention. Indeed, God's concern for them is analogous to a shepherd who "leaves 99 sheep on the mountains" in order to seek the one that was led astray. Significant in Matthew's revision of the parable is the use of the passive forms: "it was led astray," "the one continuing to be led astray" and "those having been led astray" in place of the verb "to lose" in the Lucan text. The sheep, or analogously "the little one," is not simply lost; it has been deceived or misled. It is not a matter of willful disobedience but of being led astray. That is why the shepherd is so happy and relieved to recover it. As Jesus says, according to the redaction of verse 14, "And if he should happen to find it, Amen I say to you, he rejoices over it more than the 99 sheep which have not been deceived." The conclusion of the analogy in verse 14, another Matthean construction, returns to the introductory note of verse 10. Because they have God's full and immediate attention, ". . . it is not the will in front of your Father in heaven that one of these little ones should be lost."

The tradition on excommunication that follows (18:15ff.) is related to the parable and its application by the adversative particle *de* ("and"). Thus the procedure of dealing with a fellow member of the community who has sinned or been misled must be linked to and interpreted in the light of the analogy of the good shepherd. An erring brother or sister is to be sought out and reproved privately. If there is no repentance, a second approach is to be made with two or three other members of the community present as witnesses. If there is a continuous refusal to be corrected, the matter is to be laid before the entire assembly of the church: "If he does not listen to the church, let him be to you as a Gentile and a tax collector" (18:17). This final step in the orderly course of discipline which has been outlined has generally been interpreted to mean exclusion or ostracism from the community.[2] But the fact of the matter is that the one who refuses to listen to the assembly of the church withdraws himself or herself from their communion. Such a one, therefore, is to be pursued in the same way the shepherd searches for the sheep that has been led astray.[3] He or she is to be the object of the same mission activity that is directed toward pagans and tax collectors. For, as Jesus has stated in verse 14, "It is not your Father's will that one of these little ones should be lost."

By repeating the logion of 16:19 Matthew applies the authority of the keys of the kingdom to this issue of church discipline: "Amen I say to you, whatever things you bind on earth will be bound in heaven, and whatever things you loose on earth will be loosed in heaven." As previously — but now to the community as a whole — Jesus grants the authority to determine all matters of ecclesiological practice and ethical conduct. The keys are not to be used to include or exclude human beings; they are rather the means by which such a procedure of dealing with an erring member of the community is to be established or cancelled.[4]

Verses 19-20, which form a unit and are distinctively Matthean, set forth the extraordinary effects of unity in community prayer: "Again amen I say to you, if two of you agree on earth concerning a matter, whatever you ask will be done to you from my Father in heaven. For where two or three are gathered together in my name, there I am in the midst of them." Mutual concern for wholeness and freedom establishes genuine community; this is what is involved in "two or three being gathered together in my name." In such a context Jesus himself is present. Prayer which arises out of the emerging unity has the unqualified promise that whatever is agreed upon by those who constitute it will be granted by God.[5]

Peter, the initial recipient of the keys of the kingdom, is reintroduced in the revised Q tradition of verse 21. The question which is placed on his lips is another aspect of church conduct relating to the reproval of a fellow member of the community: "How often shall my brother sin against me and I shall forgive him? Seven times?" Jesus' answer, "Not seven but seventy-seven times;" may have been drawn from Gen. 4:24, but in contrast to its original source it maintains the principle of unlimited forgiveness as opposed to unlimited revenge.[6]

The discourse ends with an oriental tale that illustrates as well as climaxes this teaching on forgiveness and love.[7] The prepositional phrase "on account of this" provides the connecting link with Jesus' pronouncement in the previous verse. Like the parables in 13:24ff., 31f., 33, 44, 45f., 47f., the story is introduced by the clause, "The kingdom of God is analogous to . . ." A servant owed a king the enormous sum of "myriads of talents," perhaps an amount beyond reckoning,[8] When the latter expressed his intention to sell the man, his family and all his possessions for partial repayment of the debt, the servant fell on his knees begging, "Have patience with me and I will repay you everything." Moved with compassion and perhaps amused by the absurd promise of total repayment, the king cancelled the entire debt. Moments later, however, the forgiven servant seized a fellow servant by the throat and demanded immediate repayment of a debt of 100 *denarii,* a sum equivalent to $20. In spite of his appeal for patience, the debtor was thrown into prison until the amount was repaid. When the matter was reported to the king, he summoned the unmerciful servant before him and handed him over to the jailors until he repaid the entire debt. For immediate application to the reply which Jesus' made to Peter's inquiry Matthew appends the concluding warning of verse 34, "And so my heavenly Father will do to you if you do not forgive your brother from your heart." God's rule, on the one hand, is that kind of reality in which enormous debts are forgiven. But where there is no horizontal extension of this forgiveness to other human beings, it is also that kind of reality in which forgiveness is denied. In the Sermon on the Mount Jesus expressed this in terms of an antithetic parallelism: "For if you forgive human beings their offenses, your heavenly Father will also forgive you; and if you do not forgive human beings, neither will your Father forgive your offenses."

Jesus' teaching is brought to a close by the evangelist's transition formula (19:1) which, as in the previous instances, also introduces the narrative of a new section.

FOOTNOTES

1 See Mt. 10:42 and 25:34ff.

2 See Trilling's discussion on the problems of this tradition, *Das Wahre Israel,* pp. 92ff. Many of his conclusions are shared by others: Stendahl, *School,* p. 138. O. Michel, "Polemik und Scheidung," *Judaica* 15 (1959), pp. 193-212. Hummel, *Auseinandersetzung,* pp. 23, 28. Strecker, *Der Weg,* pp. 222ff. The tradition is most likely to be ascribed to the Palestinian Jewish Christian church, but simply because Matthew had adopted it is no indication that he agrees wth it. See also G. Barth, *Matthew's Understanding of the Law,* p. 84, who alone has realized that Matthew works against its obvious meaning through the immediate framework.

3 See Stendahl, *Matthew* in Peake, p. 789, para. 688f., who is troubled about the usual interpretation of 18:17.

4 Compare Strecker, *op. cit.,* pp. 224f.; Trilling, *op. cit.,* p. 98, and Hummel, *op. cit.,* pp. 25f.

5 Barth's interpretation of these words, *op. cit.,* pp. 136f., are too colored by Bultmannian theology. The presence of Christ is not merely the result of the proclamation of the word; it is more especially the result of concrete deeds of love and forgiveness which foster wholeness. See also Trilling, *op. cit.,* p. 27.

6 *Ibid.,* p. 99.

7 See Jeremias, *The Parables of Jesus,* pp. 210ff.

FOOTNOTES

8 If a Syrian talent — a talent being the largest currency unit in the Middle East — was worth approximately $250, it would be the equivalent of $2,500,000. But Matthew reads, "myriads of talents;" therefore it may not be intended to be limited to 10,000, "the highest number used in reckoning." See Jeremias, *ibid.* .

Chapter XII

THE NARRATIVE OF BOOK FIVE: "RETURN TO JUDAEA AND REJECTION IN JERUSALEM"

Matthew 19:2 - 22:46

After this fourth and final discourse of his Galilean ministry Jesus "departed from Galilee and came into the regions of Judaea on the other side of the Jordan." Judaea, of course, is his homeland, the land of his inheritance as the messianic Son of David. This is his third return since he was forced to seek safety in Egypt as a child; his first since he withdrew at the time of John's imprisonment.

Except for the tradition of 20:1-16 the evangelist follows the Marcan sequence of events; 19:2 - 20:33 consists of a series of episodes which take place in Judaea on the way to Jerusalem. As throughout his Galilean ministry "large crowds followed him," and, according to Matthew's editorial edition, "he healed them" (19:2). Except for the cure of the two blind men beyond Jericho on the way up to Jerusalem (20:29), no further healing incidents are recounted by the evangelist. Judaea is like Nazareth, a place of unbelief and offense.

This is immediately evident in the encounter which Jesus has with the Pharisees while still on the borders of Judaea and ministering to the needs of the masses. Their hostility, open and aggressive, is an indication of what awaits Jesus in Jerusalem. "And the Pharisees approached him tempting him . . ." The question which they pose, "Is it right to divorce one's wife for any reason?" enables him to treat the basic problem of Mosaic legislation. Jesus' counter question in Mark 10:13, "What did Moses command you?" is omitted.

What concerns him, as has already become apparent in the
antitheses of the Sermon on the Mount, is God's law, not that
of Moses. His immediate quotation of Gen. 2:24, God's first
commandment to Adam after he presented him with a
helpmeet, hints at such a distinction: "On account of this a man
will leave his father and his mother and will be joined to his
wife and the two will become one flesh, so that they are no
longer two but one flesh." Verse 8 with its editorial revisions
makes this more explicit: "Moses for your hard-heartedness
permitted you to divorce your wives; but from the beginning it
was not so." The word of God and the law of Moses are not
always commensurate entities; indeed, Moses compromised
the will of God by making concessions to the weaknesses of
human beings. His laws were consciously formulated to
correspond to the fallen condition of men and women. The
Pharisees, as the representatives of the Mosaic heritage, continue this anthropological orientation and, as a result, as Jesus
has shown in 15:3ff., promote this dichotomy between the law
of Moses and the word of God, "You transgress the commandment of God for the sake of your traditions." Jesus rejects this
cleavage even as he refuses to deal with human beings on the
grounds of the Fall. His ministry of healing and teaching which
constitutes God's rule is directed at restoring the lost sheep of
Israel to their original, divinely intended health and integrity.
The fundamental will of God for union and wholeness cannot
be promulgated by accommodations and concessions which
foster separation and which simultaneously produce an elitist
condescension and patronization by those who make them.
Jesus, therefore, rejects both divorce and that Mosaic legislation which institutionalizes separation in all of its forms and
levels of human society.[1]

From the very outset as he returns to Judaea, the land
which is representative of separation and elitism, Jesus enunciates his understanding of God's will in relation to the Old
Testament. His hermeneutical principle stands opposed to
those who separate themselves from the masses in order to

attain to God's holiness and who for their own benefit erect a fence around the Torah to keep themselves far from transgression. The gulf between them will widen in Jerusalem as the different groups of religious leaders seek to ensnare him in his teaching.

Matthew has added verses 10-2 to this Marcan tradition in order to allow Jesus to put forward celibacy as a valid expression of God's will alongside the fundamental movement towards union as it is manifested in marriage. For celibacy must appear as a contradiction of the divine commandment, as Jesus has articulated it with his quotation of Gen. 1:27 and 2:24 in response to the Pharisees.[2] The disciples' reaction to the enormous burden of responsibilities which marriage imposes "If such is the case of the man with his wife, it is not profitable to marry," permits him to elucidate the matter. He cautiously asserts that marriage must not be embraced as an absolute; it is not the only way to fulfill God's will for union and wholeness. Celibacy, however it may originate, is a valid possibility, for it does not exclude wholesome relationships with others: "Not all (will) grasp this word, but to whom it has been given. For there are eunuchs who have been so from birth, and there are eunuchs who were castrated by human beings and there are eunuchs who emasculated themselves for the sake of the kingdom of God. He who is able to grasp, let him grasp."

Celibates, like Jesus, can have wholesome relationships as Matthew's use of the Marcan tradition of Jesus blessing the children in 19:13-5 shows. To indicate a continuation of thought between verses 11-2 and 13-5 the evangelist inserts his favorite particle *tote* ("then"). The noun "children" which is the direct object of the verb, "they were bringing," in Mk. 10:13 has been made the subject of the sentence; and the verb has been changed from the imperfect active indicative to the aorist passive indicative, "(they) were brought." As a result the censure of the disciples is directed at the children themselves and not, as in the case of Mark, at those who were bringing

them. Matthew eliminated Mark's reference to Jesus' dis-
pleasure and simply has him respond, "Let the children, and do
not prevent them to come to me, for of such is the kingdom of
God." Although he is unmarried and has no children of his
own, Jesus, who lives before God as a child, is able to relate to
these human beings and to enjoy a mutuality with them that is
the very nature of God's rule.[3]

A vague change of location closes this first episode of
Jesus' entrance into the regions of Judaea: "And having placed
his hands on them, he departed from there." Where he went is
not indicated; no setting is provided for the narrative that
follows. Only after this lengthy incident ends in 20:16 is it
specified that Jesus is going up to Jerusalem. Because this new
encounter has no new location accompanying it, its significance may be related to the story that has just been concluded.
The confrontation with the Pharisees over the question of
divorce revealed fundamental opposition between the law of
Moses and the will of God. It also displayed Jesus' authority in
setting aside the one in favor of the other. God's will is absolute in its precedence, and the criterion by which it is
ascertained is the health and freedom of human beings in
relation to each other. Matthew now has Jesus turn to the concomitant question of true obedience to God's will. In an
encounter with a rich Jew — somewhere in Judaea — he
discloses how the law of God is to be observed.

In Mark's narrative the identity of the inquirer who
approaches Jesus is vague. He is rich "having many possessions;" but since he claims to have observed the commandments
"from my youth," his age is indeterminable. Matthew also
characterizes him as one "having many possessions" but identifies him in verse 22 as a "youth," one who still has his whole
life before him and therefore is rightly concerned about how he
in the present might "have eternal life." The adjective "good" in
the Marcan form of the salutation (10:17) has been transferred
to the question that is being asked, "What good shall I do in
order that I might have eternal life?" This enables the

evangelist to place a startling counter-question on Jesus' lips: "Why do you ask me about the good? One there is who is good." Jesus does not consider himself qualified to give an answer. Only the one who is good —God! — is able to define goodness; and he has conveyed his will in the commandments. "If you want to enter into life, observe the commandments." Whether this is the answer to the youth's question, whether "eternal life" is synonymous with "life" and will be gained by obedience to God's will is not immediately clear. Nevertheless, no objection is made over the substitution of the one for the other. The new question that is raised in reply, "Which ones?" evokes from Jesus a recitation of five individual commandments of the Decalogue all of which are directed at human relationships: "You shall not kill; You shall not commit adultery; You shall not steal; You shall not bear false witness; Honor your father and mother." As a conclusion he adds the comprehensive summary, "You shall love your neighbor as yourself!" which according to 22:40 is one of the two great commandments on which the law and the prophets depend.

Not satisfied with this answer and convinced that there must be more that is required, the young man presses Jesus, "All these things I have entered into observing. What do I still lack?" Within the borders of Judaea Jesus meets a rich Jew who is searching for "eternal life" and at the same time claims to be engaged in observing all the commandments of the Decalogue that have to do with human relationships. Either obedience to God's will does not satisfy the hunger for "eternal life" or the youth has no comprehension of what obedience involves or how God's commandments are to be kept. Without disputing the claim that has been made, Jesus replies in the form of a condition similar to 19:17, "If you want to be *teleios* ("whole"), sell your possessions and give to the poor and you will have treasure in heaven and come follow me." This new possibility of gaining life is the very test of the young man's contention to have entered into observing all these commandments. His departure in sorrow upon hearing Jesus' condition reveals the

tragic double-bind of his existence: he craves "eternal life" yet
he is unable to surrender his riches. He cannot shed the
protection and comfort of his wealth in order to expose himself
to the insecurities of human existence and therefore also to
God's coming in love and care. But even more than that, his
withdrawal proves the faultiness and inadequacy of his understanding of observing the commandments. For in not being
able to sell his possessions and to give the money to the poor in
order to follow Jesus in ministering to the needs of others he
demonstrates that his concept of keeping the law is vertically
oriented towards God and by-passes his fellow human beings.[4]
The commandments of the One who is good are to be observed
horizontally in relation to others. Obedience, as Jesus has
shown in the antitheses of the Sermon on the Mount, involves
the disciples in an absolute commitment to goodness in love
that reaches out to all human beings, good and evil. In living to
bring health and freedom to others on all levels of life,
economic, political, social, psychological and religious, the individual will gain them for himself and thus have "life," the
qualitative life of the kingdom of God. The link between the
two, "life" and "the kingdom of God", is implicit in Jesus'
observation to his disciples at the departure of the distressed
rich youth, "Amen I say to you, the rich will enter into the kingdom of God with difficulty." And to dramatize that he adds,
"It is easier for a camel to go through the eye of a needle than a
rich person (to enter) into the kingdom of God." Astonished at
this analogy the disciples wonder, "Who then can be saved?"
Their question insinuates an existential uneasiness about the
inadequacy of their own obedience to God's will. Aware of
their anxiety Jesus fixing his gaze on them said, "With human
beings this is impossible, but with God all things are possible"
(19:26).

    In response Peter introduces a new subject by calling
Jesus' attention to the ideal discipleship which he and his
fellow disciples have manifested, "Look, we have left all things
and entered upon following you." Into this Marcan tradition

Matthew injects the question, "What will there be for us?" Jesus' immediate reply to Peter appears to be a revised Q tradition, "Amen I say to you, you who follow me once and for all, in the *paliggenesia* ("regeneration") when the Son of the Human Being shall sit on a throne of his glory, you yourselves will sit on twelve thrones judging the twelve tribes of Israel." The noun *paliggenesia* is a *hapax legomenon* which is defined by the qualifying clause that follows, "when the Son of the Human Being shall sit on a throne of his glory . . ." It corresponds to 25:31 and anticipates the scene of the great judgment portrayed in 25:31-46. The twelve disciples who stand at the forefront of those who have followed Jesus will sit in judgment of their fellow Jews. This prerogative is limited to the twelve who have participated in his mission to the lost sheep of Israel or more precisely, in the light of what is to come, to the eleven who remain after Judas' self-exclusion from the circle and Jesus, the Human Being who at the conclusion of the gospel joins himself to the eleven and so re-establishes the original number of the twelve.

Verses 29-30, drawn from Mark, move beyond the immediate twelve and in answer to Peter's question speak universally to all who have left everything and followed Jesus: "And *everyone* who has left home or brothers or sisters or father or mother or children or fields on account of my name will receive many times as much and will inherit eternal life." With this promise the episode introduced by a rich young man searching for "eternal life" reaches its climax. True discipleship, which radically uproots a human being from the soil of heritage and family and exposes him or her to the uncertainties and contingencies of existence is the entrance into life and the very threshhold of "everlasting life."

No one will have an advantage, not even the original twelve who will judge the tribes of Israel. Discipleship in God's kingdom is not measured by seniority or length of service. No form of elitism can develop because ". . . the first will be last and the last first."

Jesus illustrates this with a concluding parable which, like the previous ones, is introduced by the formula, "For the kingdom of God is analogous to . . ." A housemaster went to the marketplace at dawn to hire laborers for his vineyard. Those whom he found agreed to a wage of one denarius and set to work. At nine o'clock he went out and hired others: "Go into the vineyard and whatever is just I will pay you." Again at noon and at three o'clock in the afternoon he repeated his trip in order to hire still others. The last group of workers was sent into the vineyard at five o'clock. At dusk the housemaster ordered his steward to pay everyone one denarius "beginning with the last up to the first." The latter who were the first to be hired and are now the last to receive their wage expect to be paid more than the others, for if those who worked only a few hours were given one denarius, fairness dictated that those who had labored from sunrise to sunset through the fierce heat of the day should earn more. But they too are paid one denarius. Indignant about this seemingly gross injustice they complain to the housemaster. "And answering one of them he said, 'Dear friend, I do you no wrong. Did you not agree to a denarius with me? Take what is yours and go. But I wish to give to this last (group) as (I gave) to you. Is it not right for me to do what I want with what is mine? Is your eye wicked because I am good?"[5] "So," Jesus repeats once more, "the last will be first and the first last." In God's kingdom whoever is called first and therefore works the longest and perhaps the hardest has no advantage over latecomers. Rewards for service are not measured out according to human standards of fair play. God is good in his/her freedom and free in his/her goodness.[6]

At this point Matthew, returning to his use of Mark, indicates for the first time that Jesus, now in Judaea, is planning to go up to Jerusalem. It is the destination that was designated in his first passion prediction of 16:21; and the transfiguration has hinted that it involves receiving a kingdom by enthronement. While alone with the twelve and "on the way," according to the evangelist's redaction, Jesus announces his forthcoming passion for a third time (20:18-9).

Against this background the mother of the two sons of Zebedee appears before him. According to Mk. 10:32, James and John themselves approached Jesus; but since their petition does not correspond to his ideal portrayal of the disciples, Matthew substitutes their mother. Worshipping him she solicits for them co-enthronement with him: ". . . one on your right and one on your left in your kingdom." In his response, however, Jesus turns directly to the two brothers, "You (plural) do not know what you ask. Are you able to drink the cup that I am going to drink?" Without hesitation they boldly affirm, "We are able;" and Jesus does not hesitate to concur, "On the one hand you will drink my cup." Discipleship will cost them suffering and death, even as it involves them in taking up the cross and following him (16:24). "But to be seated on my right and on my left, this is not mine to give, but for whom it has been prepared by my Father." Jesus does not reject their co-enthronement with him; it is something, however, that does not lie under his jurisdiction. It is a matter of God's appointment. What he does object to is their desire for an elite position in the kingdom he is going to gain through suffering, death and resurrection. Even if they are willing and able to join him in drinking that cup, that will not qualify them for privileged places in his kingdom.

The indignation of the other disicples at the hierarchical appointments which these two brothers have sought for themselves is the setting for the climactic teaching with which Jesus concludes the episode: "You know that the rulers of the nations are lords over them and the great ones exercise authority over them, but it is not so among you. But whoever among you wishes to be great will be your servant, and whoever among you wishes to be first will be your slave." By means of the interpolated *hōsper* ("even as") the evangelist links this teaching to the exemplary conduct of the Human Being who "came not to be ministered to but to minister and give his life as a release price for many."

As Jesus continues his journey to Jerusalem and moves beyond Jericho, Matthew observes that he is followed by a great crowd (20:29). Two blind men who are sitting by the roadside cry out for mercy when they hear that he is passing by. Mark's account names only one, "Bartimaeus, the son of Timaeus" (10:46). The evangelist expunges his name and adds a second blind man to the incident. Except for a few details the story parallels the healing of the two blind men in the distinctively Matthean tradition of 9:27-31 and may be the original version of the doublet. The addition of the second blind man may be based on the legal requirements to establish testimony by two or three witnesses or the significance of two as the beginning of community. But it is curious and can hardly be accidental that two blind human beings appear on Jesus' way up to Jerusalem immediately after two disciples have sought for elite status in his kingdom.

Their entreaty, "Lord, mercy us, Son of David," approximates that of the Canaanite woman in 15:22. When the crowd attempts to silence them, they cry out their prayer all the more. The "Lord" epithet which acknowledges Jesus' authority as the Human Being has been edited into the text both times as the opening form of address. The accompanying christological title, "Son of David," expresses his nationalistic messiahship. It is in terms of both of these identities that Jesus will enter Jerusalem riding on two donkeys.

It is strange that when he calls them he asks what they wish he should do for them; that should be quite obvious. Yet they must have an opportunity to articulate precisely what they want from him, for it is this final petition that brings the story to its climax: "Lord," — this is their third use of the title — "that our eyes might be opened." This final prayer replaces the formulation in Mk. 10:51, "Rabbouni, that I might see again."[7] While two disciples are concerned about seeking a privileged place for themselves, two blind persons refuse to be stifled in their passionate desire to see. As Jesus goes up to Jerusalem to receive his kingdom, it is this intense need for opened eyes that expresses true discipleship. In conclusion it is noted that, "immediately they saw again and followed him."

When Jesus arrives at the outskirts of Jerusalem, he proceeds "into the Mount of Olives." This is the only one of the many mountains in the gospel which is named. Like the others it is a center of the earth and therefore a reference point for Jesus' messianic career, but in its own distinctive way. For in contrast to the others the Mount of Olives has apocalyptic significance.[8] It is the site of Jesus' eschatological discourse (chapters 24-5) as well as his declaration of the beginning of judgment and its resulting exodus (26:31f.). More immediately it is the mountain from which Jesus makes his triumphal entry into Jerusalem, an event that is apocalyptic in character, for according to Matthew's redaction it causes a "city-quake:" *eseisthe he pasa he polis* ("and the whole city was shaken.").[9]

Upon his arrival on this mountain, he sends two disciples to procure two animals for him. Can they be the two blind men whose eyes were opened and who therefore followed him? Are they James and John whose mother requested special places for them in his coming kingdom? Either possibility is tantalizing, but their identity is not disclosed. More significant is the evangelist's introduction of a second animal, an *onos* ("donkey") in 21:2. Both it and the *pōlos* ("colt"), derived from Mk. 11:2, are edited into the fulfillment quotation of 21:5, where the latter is further identified as a *huios hypozygiou* ("son of a pack animal"). Both are to serve Jesus' purpose. The substitution of the plural pronoun "them" in 21:3 and again in 21:7 in place of Mark's use of the singular "him" suggests that the evangelist's deliberate intention is to present Jesus entering Jerusalem riding on two beasts simultaneously: *epekathisen epanō autōn* ("he sat over them"). The donkey, on the one hand, employed by Old Testament kings to ride to their coronation, represents his Son of David messiahship.[10] As the legal heir of David through Joseph's adoption Jesus enters the city on a coronation animal to claim his royal inheritance. Ironically he will be crowned in his crucifixion as "the king of the Jews." On the other hand, "the colt of a pack animal" is a young beast of burden which symbolizes his identity as the Human Being-Servant of the Lord who "took our weaknesses and *carried* our diseases" and, according to 12:19ff., ". . . will not contend or cry out in the broad streets" but will nevertheless "cast out judgment for victory." More immediately, however, he exercises judgment in the Temple as the lordly *Human Being*.

Jesus is welcomed by the largest crowd of his messianic career. For the first and only time the evangelist utilizes the superlative degree "very great" in order to indicate the size of the throng. They honor him by casting clothing and branches in the way and by acknowledging him jubilantly as the Son of David: "Hosanna to the Son of David, blessed is the one who comes in the name of the Lord, hosanna in the highest."[11]

The whole city quakes and reacts with the question, "Who is this?" Matthew's interpolation of verse 11 sets forth the response of the masses accompanying Jesus: "This is the prophet Jesus from Nazareth of Galilee." The very people who have been welcoming him as the Son of David now introduce him as the prophet from Nazareth. This is the paradox of Jesus' life. The evangelist referred to it in 2:23. Although he was born in Bethlehem and adopted by Joseph to become the legal heir of David's throne, he was forced to withdraw to Nazareth, and as a result he has become known as "the prophet Jesus from Nazareth of Galilee."[12] Here both viewpoints stand side by side showing perhaps the difficulty which the masses are having in grasping Jesus' christological identity. Their vacillation continues until at the end they join the chief priests and elders in apprehending Jesus (26:47-55) and clamoring for his execution (27:20).

The goal of Jesus' entry into Jerusalem is the Temple (21:12). There without hesitation or warning he commences to drive out those who are selling and buying and to overturn the tables of the moneychangers and the stools of those selling doves. This is not an act of cleansing or reformation. It is rather the enactment of judgment by the sovereign Human Being who has come down from the Mount of Olives riding on a pack animal as well as a donkey. His condemnation is pronounced in the form of a composite Old Testament quotation taken from Is. 56:7 and Jer. 7:11, "My house shall be called a house of prayer, but you are making it a den of thieves." It is reminiscent of the verdict that Jeremiah issued prior to the first destruction of the Temple:

> Has this house, which is called by my name, become a den of robbers in your eyes? Behold, I myself have seen it, says the Lord ... and now because you have done all these things ... and when I spoke to you persistently, you did not listen and when I called you, you did not answer; therefore I will do to the house which is called by my name, and in which you trust, and to the place which I gave to you and to your fathers, as I did to Shiloh. And I will cast you out of my sight, as I cast out all your kinsmen, all the offspring of Ephraim.[13]

Restoration, however, follows judgment. According to the distinctively Matthean tradition of 21:14-6, Jesus proceeds to heal the blind and the lame in the Temple. Yet ironically at this point the two christological identities which he bears clash with each other. For in as far as he restores the blind and the lame, he acts as the Human Being-Servant of the Lord who "takes our frailities and carries our diseases." But at the same time he contradicts the typology of his Son of David messiahship, as it is defined in 2 Sam. 5:6-8:

> And the king and his men went to Jerusalem against the Jebusites, the inhabitants of the land, who said to David, "You will not come in here, but the blind and the lame will ward you off"— thinking, "David cannot come in here." Nevertheless, David took the stronghold of Zion, that is, the city of David. And David said

on that day, "Whoever would smite the
Jebusites, let him get up the water shaft to
attack the lame and the blind, who are *hated* by
David's soul." Therefore it is said, "The blind
and the lame shall not come into the house."

Instead of expelling the lame and the blind whom David hated
and who were refused entrance to the House of the Lord, Jesus
permits them to approach him in the Temple; and he heals
them. At the very moment the children are crying, "Hosanna
to the Son of David" (21:15), Jesus is acting contrary to the
Son of David character.[14] Sensing this discrepancy between
what he has done and the adulation of these young people, the
chief priests and the scribes protest, "Do you hear what they
are saying?" But Jesus makes no effort to prohibit or correct
them; instead he points out, "Did you never know: 'Out of the
mouth of infants and sucklings I will create praise?' " These
children may not grasp the inconsistency of what they are
singing in the light of what he has done, yet their adoration —
which stands in contrast to the vacillating crowds — belongs to
the creative work of God.

After spending the night in Bethany Jesus returns to
Jerusalem early the next morning (21:18). On the way he seeks
fruit from a fig tree. When he finds only leaves, he curses it; and
it withers immediately. In astonishment the disciples inquire
about its instantaneous dessication. He replies by pointing to
faith as the source of this mighty deed: "Amen I say to you, if
you have faith and do not waver, not only will you do the thing
of the fig tree but you will say to this mountain (Mount Zion),
'Be raised and cast into the sea,' and it shall be so." While the
original incident in Mark is divided into two parts, the cursing
of the fig tree and the teaching of faith, which are separated
from each other by the "cleansing" of the Temple,[15] Matthew
consolidates both into a single episode. As a result the wilting
of the fig tree, which must of course be instantaneous, becomes
a more impressive basis for Jesus' teaching on faith. The omission of the remark in Mk. 11:13, ". . . for it was not the season

of figs," disposes of the problem of unreasonableness.[16] The absence of fruit at a time when it evidently could be expected has dire consequences.[17] In view of its placement immediately after Jesus' judgmental visit to the Temple, the episode intimates the result of Jesus' condemnation of the Temple institution: like the fig tree it too has withered and dried up. At the same time, however, Jesus' pronouncement on faith, which is the point of the story, indicates a substitute for the sacred Center which the Temple represents.[18] Faith is a way of life which surrenders reliance on all fixed points, centers and absolutes for confrontation with chaos and "the terrors of history."

Jesus, however, does not avoid the Temple; he returns to it as a place for his teaching activity. In this setting the chief priests and the elders of the people confront him with the question: "By what authority do you do these things? And who gave you the authority?"[19] This is the first time he encounters these religious leaders of Jerusalem and the Temple. Their challenge may refer more immediately to his teaching in the Temple, but it must especially relate to his judgmental act of the previous day. In return Jesus poses a counterquestion: "I also will ask you one thing which if you answer me, I will tell you by what authority I do these things. The baptism of John, from where was it? From God or from human beings?" Since he is linked to the Baptizer eschatologically, their answer to his question will test the motive of theirs. If they are willing to acknowledge the divine origin of John's baptism, they should have no difficulty in recognizing the source of Jesus' authority. "But they reasoned among themselves, 'If we should say from God, he will say to us, "Why therefore did you not believe him?" and if we should say from human beings, we fear the people for they hold John as a prophet.' And answering Jesus they said, 'We do not know.' " Their refusal reveals their lack of integrity and sincerity. On that basis Jesus turns aside their original question and instead proceeds to characterize their schizophrenic mentality by a parable.

The analogy of the two sons, which is uniquely Matthean, is the first of three stories which Jesus addresses to these religious leaders. A farmer who had two sons said to the first, "Go and work in the vineyard today." He refused but later relented and went. The second son who was also ordered to work in the vineyard consented but did not go. "Which of these two sons," Jesus asks, "did the will of the father?" In answering the question correctly, "The first one," the chief priests and the elders of the people are confronted with the correspondence between the second son's lack of integrity and their own. They too know "the will of the father" but desist from doing it. The tax collectors and prostitutes will enter into God's kingdom before them because, although they first declined, like the other sons, they repented and did the father's will (21:31b). Verse 32 echoes 11:18 and serves to connect the parable to the religious leaders' refusal to acknowledge the divine origin of John's ministry: "For John came to you on the way of righteousness, and you did not believe him. The tax collectors and prostitutes believed him. And when you saw later you did not change your mind in order to believe him." They have no excuse, for if they did not know before, they "saw later" that John had come on the way of righteousness.[20] If they had responded to him, they would have been open to Jesus' ministry and message, and the question of his authority would have resolved itself.

The second story is Mark's allegory of the evil tenant farmers in which Jesus focuses on the history of Israel's repudiation of God's servants culminating in the rejection of Jesus. Mark's version cites three sendings arranged in a graduated sequence: the first is beaten, the second is wounded in the head, the third is killed. Any effectiveness which this order might have is minimized by the subsequent reference to additional missions which end in similar fashion (12:15b). When the last one, the beloved son of the owner, is sent, he is killed and cast out of the vineyard.

Matthew also differentiates three sendings but the

details are more highly allegorized in order to connect the story to its context and its sequence of events. A landlord planted a vineyard and leased it to tenant farmers in order to receive his fruits" (21:34).[21] Some are beaten, some are killed, some are stoned. A second group of servants, "more than the first," is sent, "and they did to them similarly." These two missions may denote the earlier and later prophets.[22] The third sending is limited to the son who — in contrast to Mark's version — is first cast out of the vineyard and then murdered by the tenant farmers in order to seize his inheritance. The story, like the preceding one, is concluded with a question: "When therefore the lord of the vineyard comes, what will he do to those tenant farmers?" As previously, the chief priests and the elders supply the answer: "He will annihilate them and he will lease out the vineyard to other tenant farmers who will pay him the fruits in their season." Thus by their own words they pronounce judgment on themselves.[23] The irony, as Jesus points out by his quotation of Ps. 117:22f., which anticipates the conclusion of the gospel, is that "the stone (or the killed son of the vineyard landlord) which the builders rejected has been made the cornerstone . . ." of God's new community.

The evangelist's interpolation of verse 43 draws the final and culminating inference from the allegory by applying the answer given by the religious leaders in 21:41 to the consequences of their rejection of all of God's servants and especially Jesus, "On account of this I say to you: the kingdom of God will be taken from you and given to a people producing its fruits."[24] Verse 44 corresponds to Luke 20:18 and is probably the result of a later scribal effort at harmonization.[25] Matthew, in contrast to Mark, observes that the priests and the newly introduced Pharisees are aware that Jesus has been speaking about them (21:45). They seek to apprehend him but are too intimidated by the crowds to take any immediate action, for, as the evangelist noted in 16:14 and 21:11, they considered Jesus to be a prophet.

The third story which Jesus tells the religious leaders is

an allegorized version of the parable of the great banquet.
Drawn from Q (Lk. 14:16-24) it reflects accommodation to the
context into which it has been placed. Another analogy, the
parable of the guest without a wedding garment, has been
joined to it and consequently also allegorized. Fused together
by the evangelist, they form a single narrative unit which
climaxes this series of stories spoken to the chief priests, elders
and Pharisees. The introductory formula, "The kingdom of
God is like . . .," which is peculiar to Matthew, begins to unveil
the crux of the matter: Israel's present situation is eschatologically critical. It is analogous to being invited to the
marriage festival of a king's son.[26] The invitations have already
been sent out, and on the day of the great festivities the servants are dispatched "to call those invited to the wedding
celebration" (22:3). When they refuse to come, the king repeats
the invitation; but there is no response. The evangelist has dis-
pensed with the individual excuses cited in Lk. 14:18ff. and
emphasized instead the sumptuous character of the meal: ". . .
my oxen and fatted cattle have been prepared." "Paying no
attention they went away, one to his own field, another to his
business; the rest seizing his servants insulted and killed them"
(22:5-6). This mistreatment and murder, which is missing in
the Lucan version, echoes the persecution of the wicked tenant
farmers in the previous story.

   In contrast to the preceding analogies, there is no
climactic question addressed to the hearers. Jesus himself
describes the severe reaction of the king: "And the king was
angry and sending his soldiers destroyed those murderers and
burned their city." Matthew is undoubtedly the author of this
allegorized reference to the destruction of Jerusalem in A.D.
70 and presents it as the grim consequence of the religious
leaders' rejection of God's messengers and their invitation to
the messianic banquet. They have not believed John the
Baptizer or responded to his call for genuine repentance; they
have refused to acknowledge the words and deeds of Jesus as
the eschatological work of God. Their own lives and the

institutions which they represent have been exposed to be as unfruitful and barren as the fig tree which Jesus cursed. On that account they will lose their heritage: "The kingdom of God will be given to a people who will produce its fruits."[27] According to the new invitation that is sent out by the king in 22:9-10, no distinctions will be made: both "bad and good" will be included, any and everyone living at the end of the streets or beyond the crossroads and junctions of the city. The banquet hall will be filled with guests.

At this point the second parable continues the story. The king enters to view his reclining guests and spies "a human being not wearing his wedding garment." Questioned and found unable to explain how he gained entrance, he is "bound hands and feet and cast into outer darkness" (22:13). This and not the destruction of the city is the climax and therefore also the point of the story. In view of the sinful past and the threatening future, what will be the decision of these religious leaders in the present?

For Matthew's contemporaries the first of the two analogies has already happened. Jerusalem has been destroyed, and the invitation to the great banquet is being issued by God's servants to all whom they find, both "the wicked and the good." The parable of the wedding guest without a garment is a warning to all who come to the dinner. Caught in the same tension between the sinful past and the threatening future, the church of Matthew, like the religious leaders of Judaism, must decide how they will respond to God's eschatological work in the present in order to be appropriately dressed for the great celebration when it finally takes place. "For," as Jesus concludes, "many are called but few chosen."

Four confrontations follow: the question concerning tribute to Caesar (22:15-22), the question concerning the resurrection (22:23-33), the question of the great commandment (22:34-40) and the question about David's son (22:41-6). These are incidents of controversy which manifest the hostility of the

religious leaders, especially the Pharisees. They have already
sought an opportunity to seize Jesus but have been prevented
by their fear of the masses. By means of the story of the
marriage feast he has attempted to show them the critical
nature of their position; but instead of a change of heart they
demonstrate increased determination "to ensnare Jesus by a
word" (22:15). Verse 16 contains the only reference to the
"Herodians" in the entire gospel. By including those aligned
with Herod and therefore sympathetic to Rome in the context
of a political question, the evangelist exposes the desperate and
bitter character of the growing conspiracy against Jesus. Their
duplicity is evident in the flattering preface: "Teacher, we
know that you are true and teach the way of God in truth and
you care for no one for you do not regard the appearance of
human beings; tell us therefore what does it seem to you? Is it
right to give tax to Caesar?" Aware of their maliciousness
Jesus does not hesitate to call them "hypocrites." The coin that
he asks for is specifically designated "the tax coin;" it bore the
offensive image of the emperor and was used for the payment
of taxes.[28] Since it is a coin with the figure and superscription
of Caesar, Jesus says, "Therefore, return to Caesar the things
of Caesar and to God the things of God." Evidently it is not too
difficult a matter to decide what belongs to Caesar and what
belongs to God. Their only response is to marvel and leave him
alone.

　　　　The next encounter involves the Sadducees who by
posing a concrete example of the practice of levirate marriage
attempt to demonstrate the absurdity of the idea of resurrection. A man who married died without children and left his
wife to his brother. He too died and left her to a third brother,
but he too died, and in succession four remaining brothers
married her and died. After them all the woman too finally
died: "In the resurrection therefore to which of the seven will
she be wife?" Jesus accuses them of a twofold error: they are ig-
norant of the Scriptures, and they do not know the power of
God. Their case in point is irrelevant because there is no such

supposed continuity between this mortal life and the ever-lasting life which God will share. There will be no marriage in the resurrection: "For in the state of the resurrection they neither marry nor are married but are like angels in heaven."[29]

Jesus then proceeds to contradict their denial of the resurrection by citing a text from the Torah, the only Scripture which the Sadducees appear to have acknowledged as canonical, which indicates that God and life are so intimately related that a denial of one necessarily involves the negation of the other: "Do you not know that which was spoken to you by God, "I am the God of Abraham, Isaac and Jacob? He is not the God of the dead but of the living." The evangelist's substitution of the participial clause, "that which was spoken to you by God," in place of Mark's ". . . in the book of Moses at the burning bush God said to him", stresses the existential rather than the historical character of the Old Testament.[30] In conclusion it is observed that the crowds heard and were astonished at his teaching.

Matthew's revision of Mk. 12:28-34 has changed the pericope of the question of the great commandment from a school debate to a polemical controversy, particularly through the omission of Mk. 12:32-4. The sympathetic inquirer, "one of the scribes," in the Marcan account has been replaced by "the Pharisees" who return after they have learned that Jesus silenced the Sadducees. One of them, a lawyer, puts Jesus to the test: "Teacher, what is the great command in the law?" In his answer the introductory words of the Shema, which is used in Mk. 12:29b, are missing. Omitting the fourth prepositional phrase of Deut. 6:5, "with your whole strength," Jesus simply replies, "you shall love the Lord your God in your whole heart and in your whole life and in your whole mind." The integrity of the human being's love is what is required. In the interpolation of verse 38, however, Jesus implies that the for-mulation of the lawyer's question is inadequate, "This is the great and *first* commandment. The other is like it." That is, there is not just one great commandment, namely Deut. 6:5.

There is another which stands alongside of it, Lev. 19:18, "You shall love your neighbor as yourself." In a fundamental contradiction of the lawyer's question Jesus concludes, according to the Matthean addition of verse 40, "On these *two commandments* the whole law and the prophets depend." Here is the very substance of the Old Testament. Indeed, they are the criteria by which the law and the prophets themselves are to be interpreted and evaluated.

The fourth and final confrontation with the religious leaders of Jerusalem, which is only a mild school debate in Mk. 12:35-37, has been sharpened into a polemical dialogue with the Pharisees. This time, however, Jesus himself formulates the question, "What do you think about the Messiah? Whose son is he?" Their brief reply, "Of David," is traditionally correct and can be supported by many Old Testament prophecies, some of which Matthew has quoted or alluded to in the course of his gospel.[31] It is challenged by Jesus' citation of Ps. 110:1 and his formulation of the ambiguity which it raises, "If David calls him Lord, how is he his son?" There is no response. No effort at resolution is made; the ambiguity remains. In this way before the culminating events of the gospel Matthew accentuates the discontinuity between the Son of David and Lord christologies. It was dramatized by Jesus' entry into Jerusalem riding on two donkeys; and the primacy of the one over against the other was affirmed by his healing the lame and the blind in the Temple "who are hated by David's soul." Now in 22:41-6, as the concluding episode of Jesus' Judaean ministry, its distinct subordination to the Lord christology is articulated by the quoted acknowledgment of David himself. In his forthcoming crucifixion as "the king of the Jews" it will be cancelled and with it his nationalistically oriented mission to the Jews.[32] Thus, this final confrontation with the Pharisees regarding the ambiguity of the Messiah's relationship to David is a fitting climax of the narrative of Book Five which recounts the events of Jesus' messianic career in his own country, "the land of Israel." In his editorial addition of verse 46 Matthew stresses the lordly superiority of Jesus over his enemies: "No one was able to answer him a word, neither did anyone from that day dare to question him any longer." It is an appropriate transition to the discourses of Book Five and especially the immediately following attack on "the scribes and the Pharisees."

FOOTNOTES

1 As he has previously done in 5:31f. Mt. 19:9 is a supplementation of 5:32 which completes the circle and makes the male as guilty of adultery as the female in the process of divorce. The variety of textual readings may result from the later scribal efforts at harmonization between 5:32 and 19:9.

2 See H. Braun, *Spätjüdisch-häretischer und frühchristlicher Radikalismus,* (Tübingen: J.C.B. Mohr (Paul Siebeck, 1957), II, pp. 108ff. and especially pp. 113f. Compare 1 Cor. 7:25ff.

3 See 11:25ff. and 18:3-4.

4 Compare Barth, *Matthew's Understanding of the Law,* pp. 96ff. Also Bornkamm, "End-Expectation," p. 29f.

5 For more details, see Jeremias, *The Parables of Jesus,* pp. 136ff.

6 E. Linnemann, *Jesus of the Parables,* p. 88.

7 For some enlightening remarks, see R.H. Lightfoot, *The Gospel Message of St. Mark,* (Oxford: At the University Press, 1950), pp. 45f.

8 It already bears such a character in the post-exilic period of Israel's history, as Zech. 14:4 attests.

9 See 27:51 for a parallel. Also 28:2 and 8:24 for other apocalyptic events marked by earthquakes.

10 See 1 Kings 1:38, Gen. 49:10f.

11 It is noteworthy that this chant of the masses is taken from Ps. 117 (118):25-6 which celebrates victory and which contains the verses (22-3) that Jesus will quote in 21:42.

12 See also 16:14.

13 Jeremiah's prophetic words and deeds will play a greater role in 27:3-10. See also 16:14.

14 See Mic. 4:6-7. Compare Lohmeyer, *Matthäus,* pp. 300f. and Hummel, *Auseinandersetzung,* pp. 96f. That the Son of David identity is finally inadequate is demonstrated by Jesus himself in 22:41ff. See also Bornkamm, *op. cit.,* p. 33.

15 R.H. Lightfoot, *op. cit.,* p. 45.

FOOTNOTES

16 The clause may be a later gloss, as some commentators think. For recent attempts to establish it as Marcan see: C.W.F. Smith, "No Time for Figs," *JBL* LXXIX, 1960, pp. 324f. and G. Münderlein, "Die Verfluchung des Feigenbaumes, " *NTS* (10), 1963, pp. 89ff.

17 Compare 3:10 and 7:19.

18 See Eliade, *Cosmos and History,* pp. 12ff., 141ff.

19 Matthew deletes the reference to the scribes in Mk. 11:27.

20 Hummel, *op. cit.,* p. 33, states that the parable is Matthew's device for linking the pericope of the question of authority (21:23-7) with the allegory of the wicked tenants (21:33-46). Hummel also considers the adverb "later" in verse 32 to project the accusation into Matthew's time and place against his Jewish contemporaries.

21 "When the season of fruits has arrived..." is Matthew's interpolation. It is strongly eschatological and echoes Mk. 11:13, which was omitted in the cursing of the fig tree.

22 Jeremias, *op. cit.,* p. 72. So also Jülicher, Klostermann and Lohmeyer.

23 Verse 41b is an editorial expansion of Mk. 12:9.

24 Trilling, *op. cit.,* p. 47. This is the most bitter expression Jesus has voiced against the leaders of Judaism. It foresees Israel superseded by a new people of God. See also Strecker's discussion, *op. cit.,* pp. 111, 169f. and Hummel, *op. cit.,* pp. 148f., 154.

25 The verse is omitted by the Bezae, Old Latin and Sinaitic Syriac manuscripts.

26 Since Luke's version refers only to "a great dinner," Matthew's allegorical features make the eschatological character of what is involved more pronounced. See also Lohmeyer, *op. cit.,* pp. 321f.

27 At the same time this judgment which Jesus pronounces is also intended by Matthew for the church to which he is addressing his gospel.

28 See McNeile, *Matthew,* p. 319. Lohmeyer, *op. cit.,* pp. 323ff. Stendahl, *Matthew,* p. 791, para. h.

29 Matthew has preferred to interpret the reality of the resurrection as a state of being rather than an event; the Marcan temporal particle "when" and its accompanying verbal clause, "they will arise from the dead," have been replaced by the noun "resurrection" introduced by the preposition "in" which denotes place or location. See Stendahl, *op. cit.,* p. 792, para. o.

30 Both of the O.T. quotations in Matthew's version are closer to the LXX text than Mark. See Stendahl, *School,* pp. 69ff. Matthew's peculiar use of the *hapax legomenon* "to marry as next of kin" is not found in the LXX reading. Stendahl thinks that it might have been used by Greek-speaking Judaism in Palestine or Syria.

31 2 Sam. 7:11ff.; Jer. 23:5ff., et al.

32 S. Johnson, "The David Royal-Motif in the Gospels," *JBL* LXXXVII, 1968, pp. 140ff. for a brief survey of the Davidic motif in Matthew and a different conclusion.

Chapter XIII

THE DISCOURSE OF BOOK FIVE

PART ONE: "A POLEMIC AGAINST THE SCRIBES AND PHARISEES"

Matthew 23:1 - 39

The discourse of Book Five, the last in the gospel, is unique in its bipartition of Jesus' teaching. The first part, chapter 23, is a vitriolic denunciation of the scribes and Pharisees spoken to "the crowds and his disciples." The second and longer part, chapters 24-5, consists of instruction on eschatology and is conveyed to the disciples privately (24:3).

All of the religious groups which have become conspicuous in the course of the gospel reflect the diverse and fragmented character of Judaism during the first century prior to the destruction of Jerusalem. Of all of them Jesus designates the scribes and the Pharisees to be the true leaders of Israel. According to 23:2, "they became seated on Moses' cathedra."[1] They are the true representatives of the Mosaic tradition. He openly acknowledges their authority and charges the Jewish masses as well as his disciples to submit to it: ". . . all things which they say to you, do and observe."[2]

In view of Jesus' attitude towards Moses and his encounters with those who represent Moses' authority, particularly the Pharisees, such a pronouncement is startling to say the least. Is Moses' chair to be so highly regarded when Jesus has overthrown four of six Mosaic injunctions, or their contemporary interpretations among the scribes and Pharisees, because they do not express the will of God for human health and freedom? What kind of authority does

Moses have when Jesus contradicts an ordinance that does not correspond to God's will for union and communion because he accommodated the law of God to the weaknesses of human beings? When Jesus concedes that the scribes and the Pharisees sit on Moses' seat, it can only mean that he considers them to be representatives of a very ambiguous authority, an authority that must be evaluated critically in terms of God's original intention for human beings.

Furthermore, such a concession must be viewed in the light of Jesus' condemnation of the Pharisees and scribes in 15:3ff. for nullifying God's commandment through "the tradition of the elders" by which they interpret Moses (15:6). His consequent warning to his disciples to beware of the leaven of the Pharisees and Sadducees is eventually grasped by the disciples to mean: "to guard against the *teaching* of the Pharisees and Sadducees" (16:12).

Finally it is to Peter and the community of disciples that Jesus presented the keys of the kingdom of God and its authority to bind and to loose. They have the freedom to conduct their life and to make their decisions according to the hermeneutical criteria he has taught them for the interpretation of the Old Testament law.

Why then should his disciples and the Jewish masses observe all that the scribes and Pharisees teach? This is in flat contradiction to all that has happened up to this point. Either Matthew is not in full control of his redactional work and has therefore produced a gospel shot through with inconsistencies and contradictions, or there is a purposeful motive behind the pronouncement of 23:2 which can only be grasped in the light of his composition as a whole and the distinctive viewpoint from which Jesus' life is being interpreted to his readers.

From the standpoint of Jesus' messianic career this concession of Moses' cathedra to the scribes and Pharisees is anachronistic. It is only after the destruction of the Temple that this group assumed the religious leadership of Judaism and established a way of life that became normative for all

Jews. The evangelist, therefore, is projecting the history of a post-70 development back into the life of Jesus. Jesus is made to acknowledge that the predecessors of Matthew's rabbinic contemporaries, the scribes and the Pharisees, were already during his lifetime the sole occupants of Moses' chair. Moreover, the masses and even his own disciples were charged by him to submit to their authority. Why? In view of all that has taken place in the course of the gospel, what is the purpose of this sudden change? Since it is intended for Matthew's readers, the only valid conclusion, it would appear, is that it attempts to demonstrate that the distinction which the scribes and Pharisees enjoyed during Jesus' ministry, which Jesus himself recognized, is no longer legitimate. Their privileged position as representatives of Moses has been forfeited by their rejection of Jesus and their subsequent participation in his crucifixion. Their lost estate and their bankruptcy are manifest after Jesus' death when they, along with the chief priests, appear before Pontius Pilate, the Roman governor, and address him as *kyrie* ("Lord"). Therefore, they no longer have the right to exercise any jurisdiction over the Jewish masses. The religious leadership of Israel which they once held has now passed to the community of Jesus' disciples.

This differentiation of position between the time of Jesus and the time of the evangelist is inherently supported by the gospel's eschatology, especially as it is conveyed by the introductory genealogy. Israel's history which begins with Abraham is culminated and concluded in its third epoch by the death of Jesus the Messiah. This end also marks the termination of the authority of the scribes and Pharisees. The new Israel which Jesus establishes with his disciples after his resurrection from the dead (28:16-20) is discontinuous with the old and therefore is no longer subordinate to the former occupants of Moses' cathedra.[3]

However, even when they were the official bearers of Mosaic authority, they did not employ the right hermeneutical criteria to interpret the law. Instead of leading the Jewish

masses to wholeness, union and freedom they only enslaved
them more. Thus although Jesus acknowledges their
authoritative position, his purpose is to pronounce judgment
on them and simultaneously their successors, the rabbis.[4] The
entire discourse is a masterful rhetorical construction of the
evangelist consisting of Q traditions and especially material
distinctively Matthean.

Jesus begins his speech by adopting an objective viewpoint: "The scribes and Pharisees have entered upon sitting on
Moses' chair. All things which they say to you, do and
observe." Such an initial point of departure will make his
judicial pronouncements which are to follow all the more
effective: "But do not do according to their works, for they say
but they do not." With this critical judgment half of their
authority is immediately shattered. These men who sit on
Moses' seat have no integrity! What makes it even worse is that
while they themselves do not practice what they teach "They
bind heavy burdens and place them on the shoulders of human
beings and will not lift a finger to move them." They are
heartless legalists. The works which they do perform only
confirm their lack of integrity for, "All their works they do in
order to be seen by human beings. For they broaden their
phylacterics and lengthen the fringes of their garments. They
love places of honor at dinner and the best seats in the
synagogues and greetings in the marketplace and to be called
'rabbi' by men."

All of this is opposed to the style of life which Jesus has
exemplified and taught, and Matthew utilizes this context in
order to have Jesus pause to present corresponding contrasts
for the community life of his followers. Three exhortations are
made in the second person plural: "Do not be called 'rabbi'
because you are all brothers. And 'father' you shall not call
(anyone) on earth for you have one heavenly Father. Neither
shall you call (anyone) 'leader' for you have one leader, the
Messiah." Such titles promote elitism, and Jesus has already
emphasized that there are no heirarchical structures in the

kingdom of God. Verse 11 is a doublet of 20:26, "The greater one among you will be your servant;" verse 12 is a wisdom saying, "But whoever exalts himself will be humbled and whoever humbles himself will be exalted."

After this momentary diversion he returns to his condemnation of the scribes and the Pharisees and with even more enmity pronounces a seven-fold series of woes upon them. If their authority has already been shattered by his accusation that there is no correspondence between their words and deeds, it will be demolished by these prophetic-like indictments. The first six appear to be divided into three pairs of judgments; each pair treats related aspects of their activity. The first two judge their ministry and mission. They are not fulfilling the fundamental purpose of their leadership and the authority that accompanies it. Their teaching produces greater bondage, and they as well as those over whom they exercise jurisdiction are its victims. Their missionary zeal has disastrous consequences for those who are converted by them to Judaism.

> Woe to you, scribes and Pharisees, hypocrites, for you lock the kingdom of God before human beings; for you do not enter neither do you permit those wanting to go in to enter.
> Woe to you, scribes and Pharisees, hypocrites, for you cross the sea and the dry land to make a single proselyte, a son of hell as yourselves.

The next two scrutinize the character and effects of their teaching. Their casuistry is distorted and absurd and succeeds only in diverting them from the original intention of the law.

> Woe to you, blind leaders of the blind, who say: "Whoever swears by the Temple, it is nothing; but whoever swears by the gold of the Temple, he is guilty." Blind fools, for which is greater, the gold or the Temple which sanctifies the gold? "And whoever swears by the altar, it is nothing; but whoever swears by the gift on it, he is guilty." Fools, for what is greater,

the gift or the altar which sanctifies the gift?

He who swears by the altar takes an oath on
it and everything on it.

He who swears by the Temple takes an oath
on it and the one who resides in it.

He who swears by heaven takes an oath on
the throne of God and the one seated on it.

Woe to you, scribes and Pharisees, hypocrites, for you tithe mint and dill and cummin and
you neglect the weightier matters of the law: justice,
mercy and faith. These things you should have done
without neglecting the others.

Blind leaders, you strain out the gnats and
drink down the camels.

The last pair expose the results of their pursuit of holiness.
Their religious quest produces a schizophrenic condition in
which they become more concerned about outward appearance than inner reality and truth.

Woe to you, scribes and Pharisees, hypocrites, for you clean the outside of the cup and the
plate, but the inside is full of robbery and self-
indulgence.

Blind Pharisee, first cleanse the inside of the
cup in order that the outside might become clean.

Woe to you, scribes and Pharisees, hypocrites, for you are like whitewashed tombs which
outwardly appear beautiful but inwardly are full of
dead men's bones and all uncleanness.

So also outwardly you appear righteous
before human beings but inwardly you are full of
hypocrisy and lawlessness.

The seventh and last woe stands by itself and serves as a point
of departure for the conclusion of the speech. As those who
disassociate themselves from the violent acts of their
forefathers, they only prove by their self-righteousness, self-
appraisal and lack of self-understanding that they are the true

children of those who killed the prophets.

> Woe to you, scribes and Pharisees, hypo-
> crites, for you build the graves of the prophets and
> you adorn the tombs of the righteous. And you say,
> "If we had been (alive) in the days of our fathers, we
> would not have been partners in the (spilling of the)
> blood of the prophets. So you testify against your-
> selves that you are the sons of those who murdered
> the prophets.

Acrimoniously Jesus urges them on: "Fill up the
measure of your fathers," and with bitter invective poses the
rhetorical question, "Snakes, offspring of vipers! How will you
flee from the judgment of hell?" "For that very purpose," — to
prevent any possible escape! — he adds, "I am sending you
prophets, wise men and scribes: some of them you will kill and
crucify; some of them you will scourge in your synagogues and
persecute from city to city." By looking ahead to the impending future the evangelist has Jesus anticipate the manner in
which his messengers and servants will be treated by these
leaders of Judaism. The experience of Matthew's contemporaneous Jewish Christian church may be echoed in these words.
All of this persecution belongs to the filling up of "the measure
of your fathers." All of it will be avenged, "from the blood of
Abel the righteous to the blood of Zechariah the son of
Barachiah whom you killed between the Temple and the
altar;" for Jesus affirms in 23:36, "Amen I say to you, all these
things will come upon this generation."

This long history of persecution and martyrdom which
begins with the murder of Abel has its *terminus ad quem* in the
killing of Zechariah "whom you killed between the Temple and
the altar." The phrase, "son of Barachiah," has been inserted
into this Q tradition for a more precise identification. Because
it creates more problems than it solves and because some
manuscript authorities, notably the Sinaiticus and Eusebius,
do not include it, it is tempting to dismiss it as a later scribal

interpolation.

"The son of Barachiah" could refer to the prophet Zechariah of Zech. 1:1, or one of the reliable witnesses Isaiah obtained in Is. 8:2. Due to error of one kind or another, it may also denote Zechariah, son of Jehoiada, of 2 Chron. 24:20ff. or the man of "pronounced hatred of wrong and love of liberty" described by Josephus in *The Jewish War* IV, 5, 4. Perhaps the prophet Zechariah of Zech. 1:1 should be eliminated first, for although he identifies himself as "the son of Barachiah," there is no record of his martyrdom which has survived in tradition. The Zechariah of Is. 8:2 is also an unlikely candidate for the same reason. The most logical prospect fitting the description of 23:35 is the Zechariah of 2 Chron. 24:20ff. who was in fact stoned "in the courtyard of the house of the Lord," and who as he was dying exclaimed, "May the Lord see and avenge!" In as far as his murder is cited in the last book of the Jewish canon, his martyrdom would be a most appropriate *terminus ad quem*. The difficulty is that the Septuagint, Matthew's Bible, refers to this man as Azariah, the son of Jodae the priest. If the evangelist in his use of this Q tradition knew that this Zechariah who was killed between the Temple and the altar was identifiable with the Zechariah of 2 Chron. 24:20ff., who in turn would be especially useful as the conclusion of the history of martyrdom in the Old Testament, why did he not insert "the son of Jodae" instead?[5] "Barachiah" may, of course, be an error resulting from a momentary lapse of memory; but the precision and care exhibited throughout the gospel make such an explanation doubtful.

The last identification possibility is almost equally attractive and has had many advocates.[6] According to Josephus, a Zechariah, the son of Baris, was unjustly tried and executed "in the middle of the Temple" prior to the destruction of Jerusalem. If this Zechariah is the person whom the evangelist has in mind, he would be equally suitable as a *terminus ad quem* of the history of martyrdom. All the blood unjustly shed from the beginning of the Old Testament to the time of the destruction of Jerusalem will be requited. Such an anachronism, however, is less justifiable than the seating of the scribes and Pharisees on Moses' chair during Jesus' lifetime. Moreover, there is no way of reconciling Matthew's "son of Barachiah" with Josephus' "son of Baris" and therefore also no explanation of why he wrote the one when he may have meant the other.[7]

The most likely alternatives seem to be a choice between regarding the phrase "son of Barachiah" as a later scribal addition and attributing a lapse of memory to the evangelist. In either case the phraseology and intent of 23:35 point to the Zechariah of 2 Chron. 24:20ff., the last of the martyrs of the Jewish Old Testament canon.

Having indicted those "who became seated on Moses' cathedra," the scribes and the Pharisees, Jesus culminates this first part of his final discourse with a condemnation of their citadel, Jerusalem, the city of David, the symbol of God's favor and the bearer of all the past glories and future hopes of Israel.

> Jerusalem, Jerusalem, killing the prophets and stoning those sent to you, how often I wanted to gather together your children as a hen gathers together her young under her wings and you would not. Behold your house is abandoned to you. For I say to you, you will by no means see me until you say, "Blessed is the one who comes in the name of the Lord.

Throughout his ministry Jesus the Messiah has labored to "gather together"[8] the lost sheep of Israel. The oppressed Jewish masses have followed him, and he has ministered to them; but their oppressors, the leaders of Judaism, have pursued and persecuted him. His career from the very beginning has been a life of rejection, above all in Judaea, "the land of Israel." At the eschatological moment he entered Jerusalem for messianic acclamation and divine judgment. The one he received from the masses, the other he pronounced on the Temple, the occupants of Moses' chair and now

Jerusalem. The city of David, which has been the city of God, is abandoned to its own fate, a fate that will be shared by the Temple and determined by the religious leaders. This is not a reaction in kind, "an eye for an eye." Jesus is not surrendering his messiahship, nor is he rejecting the Jews.[9] They will see him again, but only when their eyes are opened and they acknowledge him as, ". . . the one who comes in the name of the Lord."[10] In the meantime Jerusalem is left to suffer the dire consequences of desolation, willed not by God or his Messiah, but by the leaders of Judaism themselves.

PART TWO: "ON ESCHATOLOGY"

Matthew 24:1 - 25:46

The second part of Jesus' final discourse arises out of this indictment of Jerusalem. As Jesus withdraws from the Temple, the desolation of the holy city begins. When the disciples point to the buildings of the Temple, Jesus pauses to prophecy their ruination. The tragic consequences of his withdrawal will eventually become visible in their destruction: ". . . not one stone shall be left upon another which will not be torn down."

This announcement becomes the basis of the following speech on eschatology. Mk. 13 provides the framework, into which other materials of tradition are skillfully woven, as well as the setting. Jesus is seated or enthroned on the Mount of Olives. He addresses himself to all the disciples, not merely the four named in Mk. 13:3. The crowds are excluded. The mountain, the only one named in the gospel and located in Jerusalem has an eschatological character. From it the apocalyptic event of Jesus' entry into the holy city took place; on it he will now instruct his followers in the last things; and eventually, immediately prior to his arrest he will announce the beginning of the end.[11]

The disciple's question, "When will these things be *and*

what is the sign of your Parousia and the consummation of the age?" serves as the point of departure for Jesus' teaching. This is a reformulation of Mk. 13:4 which expresses more clearly the purpose and scope of Jesus' discourse. How closely are the two parts of the question related to each other? The first, "When will these things be?" seems to be intended to pursue Jesus' prediction of the devastation of the Temple, while the second half, "What is the sign of your Parousia and the consummation of the age?" appears to seek clarification on the nature of the end.

What is striking is that Jesus' reply does not take up these two questions individually. There is no return to the subject of the Temple destruction predicted in 24:2. It is as though the inquiry, "When will these things be?" has nothing to do with 24:2 and the judgment pronounced on the Temple; yet there is no other antecedent for "these things" except Jesus' prophecy concerning the Temple. It must therefore be assumed that both questions will be answered in relation to each other.

Jesus' immediate response is a warning: "Look out that no one deceives you!" Evidently "these things" which the disciples have inquired about refer to a pattern of apocalyptic events that is being used to forecast an imminent consummation. The razing of the Temple, which for Matthew's readers lies in the past, is included among them and may in fact be the fundamental sign. Concomitant occurrences and circumstances which belong to this apocalyptic scheme are enumerated by Jesus: the arising of false messiahs, wars and rumors of wars, famines, and earthquakes, *but* with the qualification that "all these things are the beginning of the birth pangs."[12] This produces a basic shift in the traditional pattern of apocalyptic eschatology in as far as these signs, including the devastation of the Temple, are no longer considered to be indications of the imminent end but only the commencement of the birth pangs of the new age.[13] In terms of the fourfold division of Israel's history conveyed by the gospel's opening genealogy this must refer to that time in the fourth and final epoch when the first faint signs of the new age that will emerge manifest themselves. These events of history and nature: false messiahs deceiving many, wars, famines, earthquakes, are the contractions of a new creation that is being born. "It is necessary that they happen, but the end is not yet" (24:6b).

According to 24:8, these birth pains will include the suffering of Jesus' disciples: "They will deliver you up to oppression and kill you and you will be hated by all nations on account of my name." Offense, betrayal and hatred — which Jesus experienced during his ministry — will run rampant. Many will be deceived by false prophets. Lawlessness and love-lessness will increase. The only hope of salvation, according to the evangelist's interpolation of Mk. 13:13b, is perserverance. At the same time "the good news of the kingdom must be proclaimed in the whole world for a witness to all nations." Only then will the goal be reached and only then will the present age — the fourth and last of Matthew's eschatology — be terminated (24:14). All of this, 23:4-14, belongs to Jesus' summary warning not to be led astray. It is the general framework of what is yet to be said. The end is not yet in sight, but the birth pains of the new creation have begun.

It is in 24:15 that Jesus returns to the matter of the Temple which evoked the disciples' substantive question and the discourse as a whole: "When, *therefore,* you see the abomination of desolation, which was spoken of through Daniel the prophet, standing in the holy place — let the reader understand[14] — then let those in Judaea flee into the mountains. Let the one on the roof not come down to take his things from the house and let the one in the field not turn back to fetch his cloak." The event of the Temple's destruction is not explicitly referred to again; it appears to be assumed. The prophecy drawn from Dan. 9:27 and 12:11, through the use of a part of Matthew's typical fulfillment formula, is implied to have been realized.[15] The abomination of desolation is standing in the holy place. The standards of the Roman legions and perhaps the images of Vespasian and Titus have been erected in the Temple site.[16] The readers of the gospel are reminded of the holocaust which Jesus predicted and the terrible events which accompanied it. They are paradigmatic of the consummation of history. Decisive action which involves abandonment of homes, fields and even clothing for the sake of speedy flight is the only effective response. The disciples must be free and unencumbered (24:16-9); and they should pray that seasonal conditions, such as winter, and religious observances, such as the sabbath, do not put additional restrictions on their freedom of movement.[17] Pregnant women and mothers nursing children will be at a great disadvantage. The horror of those days will intensify and will exceed that of any previous period in history: "For then there will be great affliction such as has not happened since the beginning of the world until now neither will ever be" (24:21). No one would survive at all if divine intervention did not shorten that time for the sake of the elect.

Under these frightful circumstances the disciples are to be especially wary of false messiahs and prophets. Even the elect will be in danger of being deceived (24:23-5). There will be seductive rumors of the Messiah's rendezvous, "Look, he is in the wilderness!" And in view of the traditional prophetic exhortation this will be extremely enticing.[18] Or "Look, he is in the secret place!" and the thought of joining him there will be very enticing. But, "Do not believe it!" Jesus warns. The Parousia — here he begins to answer the second part of the disciples' question — will be as swift and unexpected as the lightning which flashes across the sky (24:27). And the assembly of the elect will be as spontaneous as vultures gathering over a corpse.

The climax of Jesus' eschatological teaching and the explicit answer to the second half of the disciples' question: "What is the sign of your Parousia and the consummation of the age?" comes in 24:29-31 where the evangelist resumes his use of the Marcan outline. "Immediately after the affliction of

those days," when the birth pains have become almost un-
bearable, is the time when the new age will be born. There
will be a dazzling display of apocalyptic phenomena which
plunge the world into a primeval condition of chaos: ". . . the
sun will be darkened, and the moon will not give its light, and
the stars will fall from the sky." Last of all, ". . . the powers of
the heavens will be shaken!" These are the elemental forces
which have interfered with the freedom and apotheosis of
human beings.[19]

      This collapse of the heavenly luminaries corresponds to
the quake that reduced the earth to its original state of chaos at
the time of Jesus' death (27:51b) and which was followed by the
constitution of a new creation. Now at long last, after this
cosmic prelude, after "the powers of the heavens have been
shaken," the new age will come into being. The community of
authentic humanity will be born! Its birth, Jesus declares, will
be marked by "the sign of the Son of the Human Being in the
sky" (24:30). Since all of the luminaries have been extinguished
and the cosmos has been reduced to primordial darkness, "the
sign of the Human Being" must be a great light signalling the
dawn of a new day.[20] The sign of the birth of the Messiah was a
star which, when it reached its zenith point in the sky and stood
directly over where the child was, announced the beginning of
the messianic age. For the appearance of the Human Being to
inaugurate a completely new age the same identification
between sign and reality seems logical and appropriate.

      But in contrast to the Magi's rejoicing "with exceeding
great joy," "all the tribes of the earth will beat their breasts."
This fragmentary quotation derived from Zech. 12:12-4 is a
Matthean addition to the borrowed Marcan tradition and, like
its use in Rev. 1:7, depicts a world-wide reaction of remorse
and dread to this apocalyptic revelation. In their lamentation
"they will see the Son of the Human Being coming on the
clouds of heaven with power and great glory" (24:30b). Upon
his manifestation the community of the Human Being will be
consolidated by the angelic activity of gathering the elect from

the four corners of the earth (24:31).[21]

In 24:32-6 Jesus returns to the first part of the disciples' original inquiry and the question of "when." The analogy of the fig tree sprouting leaves and bearing fruit hints at a means of ascertaining the nearness of the end: "When you see *all* these things, you know it (the consummation) is at the gates." That "all these things" will take place is certain; the goal will be achieved. Heaven and earth will be dissolved, but the words of the Human Being, because they already are the reality they project, will never pass away. But no one knows the precise time of the dawning of this new day, "neither the angels, nor the son, *only* the Father."

The rest of the discourse consists of six analogies, drawn from different sources and contexts of tradition, which elucidate the style of life that this eschatological reality demands. First of all, the characterization of the time preceding the Parousia is derived from the Old Testament story of the Flood. In that time of crisis those who were completely absorbed in selfish and self-indulging pursuits, "eating and drinking, marrying and giving in marriage, "were swept away by the great cataclysm. "So will the Parousia of the Son of the Human Being be;" that is, according to 24:40f., a similar separation will occur: "Then two men will be in the field, one is taken and one is left. Two women will be grinding at the mill, one is taken and one is left." Vigilance, therefore, is necessary because no one knows the time of the Parousia: "If the housemaster knew at what hour the burglar comes, he would watch and not permit (him) to break into his house. On account of this be ready, for the Human Being is coming at an hour you do not expect." Like the faithful and wise servant of 24:45-51, the disciples have been entrusted with supervision. Responsibility is to be discharged with zealousness. Prudent conduct will be rewarded: "Blessed is that servant whom his master finds so doing when he comes" (24:46). But oppression and self-indulgence perpetrated by a reckless attitude arising out of the master's delay in returning will be prosecuted with severity:

"There will be weeping and gnashing of teeth."

The fourth and the fifth analogies elucidate two adjectives which have been used to characterize the responsible servant entrusted with supervision: "faithful and wise" (24:45). The distinctively Matthean parable of the Ten Virgins illustrates the meaning of being wise. "The kingdom of God will be analogous to . . ." the situation of ten virgins waiting for the bridegroom to come and inaugurate the wedding celebration. The wise five, because they were prepared, entered with him; the foolish five, who were not were excluded. The bridegroom's delay in the story echoes the church's consciousness of the tardiness of the Parousia. Such a circumstance, as the analogy shows, required prudent preparation and scrupulous watchfulness. Matthew's revision of the Q parable of the Talents concentrates on the necessity of exercising faithfulness or responsibility over all the gifts that have been received. In the light of the final reckoning this means investing in life and in living to the limits of capability, in spite of the contingencies involved. The reward is, "Enter into the joy of your Lord!" The timid soul, however, who fears to take any risks, loses the very future he is living and preserving himself for.

The analogy which terminates the discourse is actually a culminating "apocalyptic revelation." It provides a dramatic continuity for the mythological description of the Parousia of the Human Being in 24:29-31. The Human Being, who has come in his glory with all his angels, will sit on his throne and dispense justice.[22] His criteria for judgment, as 25:35f. shows, will be concrete deeds of love and mercy, the works which Jesus established throughout his teaching as the requirements of the law and God's will for all human beings.[23] All peoples will be gathered before him, and on the basis of his divine standard he will — at long last[24] — execute the great separation. Rejection and ostracism will be the fate of all those whose life and work did not contribute healing, freedom and reunion to their fellow human beings. For the righteous, that is, those who have followed the Human Being in performing deeds of justice, love and faith, the goal which Jesus foreshadowed at his transfiguration will have been realized: their participation in the apotheosis of the Human Being (13:43).

The end of Book Five is marked by the fifth and final use of the transition formula; the addition of the adjective "all" in 26:1 indicates that this is the conclusion of Jesus' teaching. As in previous instances the transition formula leads into a resumption of the narrative. What is continued in 26:2ff., however, stands outside of the Pentateuchal scheme of the literary framework. The fifth book has been concluded, but the gospel is not yet ended. To designate the remaining three chapters as "Epilogue," as is sometimes done, is to minimize their content. The death and resurrection of Jesus are not an afterthought but the consummation of the gospel. These eschatological events which shatter the continuity of history and with it Judaism's representation of Old Testament Israel also smash the Torah-like design of the book. Matthew's theology and literary construction are inextricably intertwined.

FOOTNOTES

1 The aorist verb "they sat" is probably intended to be ingressive, and from Matthew's vantage point looks back to the time after the destruction of the Temple when they assumed the leadership of Judaism. See Blass, Debrunner, Funk, *Greek Grammar,* p. 176, on "an extensive aorist meaning."

2 Verse 2 is often attributed to a strict circle of Jewish Christianity which continued to acknowledge the authority of the scribes and Pharisees. E. Haenchen, "Matthäus 23," *ZTK* 48 (1951), p. 40, and Hummel, *Auseinandersetzung,* p. 31. Perhaps it may be more correct to consider the evangelist to be its author for rhetorical reasons. See Barth's discussion, *Matthew's Understanding of the Law,* pp. 71f.

3 Compare Hummel, *op. cit.,* p. 32, and Bornkamm, "End Expectation," p. 21.

FOOTNOTES

4 Also Haenchen, *op. cit.,* pp. 47ff.

5 An old scholium on Matthew reads, "Zechariah, the son of Jodae." McNeile, *Matthew,* p. 340.

6 J. Wellhausen, *Einleitung in die ersten drei Evangelien,* Berlin, 2nd ed., 1911, pp. 118-23. Leo Baeck, "Secharja ben Berechja," *Monatschrift für Geschichte und Wissenschaft des Judentums,* p. 76 (1932), pp. 313ff. Strack-Billerbeck, *op. cit.,* I, 940f. Eb. Nestle, "Über Zacharias in Matt. 23," *ZNW* 6 (1905), pp. 198ff.

7 As Wellhausen himself admitted, *op. cit.,* p. 122, n. 1.

8 The verb, *episynagein,* echoes the word "synagogue" and is used again in 24:31 where the community of the Human Being will be gathered together by the angels of the Human Being.

9 Compare Trilling, *Das Wahre Israel,* pp. 67f.; Strecker, *Der Weg,* p. 113, and Hummel, *op. cit.,* p. 85.

10 This does not appear to be a reference to the Parousia, but to any indefinite time in the future.

11 Among the evangelists only Matthew employs the term "Parousia" (24:27, 37, 39) as well as the phrase "the consummation of the age" (13:39, 40, 49 and 28:20). The conjunction "and" which separates them in 24:3b implies a direct relationship between them. The Parousia is the sign of the end of the age.

12 Compare 4 Ezra 9:1ff. and 2 Bar. 27:1-15.

13 Compare Strecker, *op. cit.,* p. 239. Manfred Runge in his unpublished dissertation, *Endgeschehen und Heilsgeschichte im Matthäusevangelium,* at Greifswald, East Germany, 1962, investigates the eschatology of Mt. 24:5 and shows that the evangelist has detached the destruction of Jerusalem from the context of the final events of the age. See J. Rohde, *Rediscovering the Teaching of the Evangelists,* p. 107.

14 This clause may be intended to stress the veiled language that refers to the Roman standards and images which have been erected on the Temple site.

15 Compare 24:15 with 21:5, 13:35, 12:17, 8:17, et al.

16 See Josephus, *op. cit.,* VI, 6, 1 and Mishnah, Taanith 4, 6. For a critical discussion and other ancient references, G.R. Beasley-Murray, *A Commentary on Mark Thirteen,* (London: S.P.C.K., 1957), pp. 62-3.

17 Verse 20, as many commentators remark, may be an indication of the Jewishness of Matthew's church. See 1 Macc. 2:31-8. Compare Strack-Billerbeck, *Matthäus,* I, 952.

18 See Hos. 2:14; Is. 40:3, 41:19, 48:20f. and 51:3. Also Ezek. 20:34ff. "A return to the wilderness is a return to the grace of God." U. Mauser, *Christ in the Wilderness, Studies in Biblical Theology* No. 39, (Naperville: Allenson, 1963), p. 46.

19 See 1 Enoch. 18:13-6, 21:6, 72:1-37, 73:1-8, 75:1-3, 78:1-17, 79:1-6 and especially 80:1-8. Also 86:1, 88:1, 90:21-4 and The Secrets of Enoch 19:3-6.

FOOTNOTES

20 Compare Rev. 21:23-5. See McNeile, *op. cit.,* p. 352. Filson, *Matthew,* p. 256, seems to sense this when he asks, "Is the sign this brilliant light of his coming?"

21 See 13:39-41 for corresponding future eschatology.

22 Compare 1 Enoch 45:3, 51:2-3, 55:4, 61:8 and especially 62:5 and 69:27ff.

23 See also Stendahl, *Matthew* in Peake, p. 794, para. 692n. Jeremias *The Parables of Jesus,* pp. 206ff. estimates that the tradition is focused on the judgment of the heathen. But his is the supreme judgment for all human beings. Compare Test. Jos. 1:5-6, Test. Zeb. 7:1-8:3; 2 Enoch 9:1.

24 See 3:12 and 13:41ff.

Chapter XIV

THE CONSUMMATION
Matthew 26:2-28:20

The final narrative begins with Jesus' announcement of the coming Passover and his coincidental death: ". . . after two days the Passover happens and the Human Being is delivered up to be crucified." It is noteworthy that Matthew has recast into direct discourse what in Mark is a report and has added the clause, "and the Human Being is delivered up to be crucified." Evidently there is a meaningful association between the two events: the Passover and Jesus' death. The next reference, "after two days," may add eschatological significance. A parallel is found in the Jubilees midrash of Gen. 22:1ff., "after two days" the Passover and a sacrificial death. What makes its application to Matthew convincing is the subsequent development of this conjunction: the Passover and Jesus' sacrifice of himself constitute a new Exodus. Such a theme was already adumbrated in Jesus' hasty flight by night into Egypt at the time of Herod's slaughter of all the boys of Bethlehem and all the surrounding regions. The land of enslavement is Judaea! Jesus the Human Being will be delivered up on the night of Passover, and when he dies a new Exodus will occur. The first to be delivered will be the Old Testament saints who have been asleep in death, as well as Jesus himself. The disciples who follow the risen Jesus to Galilee and into the world beyond will also be redeemed from the bondage of Jerusalem as the Center of the world and from the religion of the scribes and Pharisees who sit on Moses' chair.

Four brief episodes follow each other quickly and set in motion the forces that will bring about a fulfillment of Jesus' opening announcement. The first is a scene of an assembly of the chief priests and elders plotting — under the leadership of the high priest himself — the death of Jesus (26:3ff.). The evangelist has altered Mark's cast of characters: the scribes, to whom the gospel is sympathetic, have been replaced by "the elders of the people" who will play a leading role in Jesus' execution.[1]

Jesus in the meantime is dining at the home of Simon the Leper in Bethany. An unidentified woman approaches and anoints him with an expensive perfume (26:12). To the disciples' reaction of indignation over this extravagant act Jesus replies, "The poor you always have with you, but me you do not." It must not be supposed that he is asserting the hopeless ineradicability of poverty in the world. What he is observing is that this is a very unusual circumstance. There is time enough to do something for the poor; but this woman has rightly discerned this moment — when his death is being planned by the leaders of the people — as the time for anointing his body for burial. It is an affirmation of his messiahship even in death, and therefore an act of faith. That is why, as Jesus acknowledges, ". . . that which she did will be spoken in her memory wherever the gospel is preached in the whole world."

The account of Judas' offer of betrayal follows. No motives are given; it is the meaning of his act that is important.[2] Matthew intimates it by replacing Mk. 14:11 with a fragmentary quotation drawn from Zech. 11:12, ". . . and they set out for him 30 pieces of silver" (26:15b). There is tragic irony here as there is also in the startling climax of his betrayal in 27:3-10. Unlike the context from which the Old Testament text has been derived, it is not the one who has, ". . . pitied the flock doomed for slaughter by those who traffic in sheep," who receives the 30 pieces of silver for services rendered. That would of course be Jesus, God's representative, who according to 9:36, "Seeing the crowds was moved to compassion for them because they were harrassed and oppressed like sheep without a shepherd." The money is given to Judas, a disciple who represents Jesus, but for the purpose of betraying his teacher and thereby terminating his office of shepherd and Messiah which he has been exercising with fierce loyalty.

Judas, in as far as he volunteers to betray Jesus, that is "to deliver him up," also represents "the land of Judah" which has repeatedly rejected him and will eliminate him by handing him over to the Romans for execution on a cross.[3] The use of the verb *paradidomi* is significant in this respect: it not only denotes Judas' act of betraying Jesus to the Jewish authorities but also their transfer of him to the judgment and sentencing of the Roman governor.[4]

One more brief episode follows. In an abbreviated Marcan tradition the evangelist presents Jesus sending his disciples "on the first day of Unleavened Bread" to prepare the Passover meal in Jerusalem. There are two noteworthy editorial additions. The pronoun *soi* ("for me") has been inserted at the end of 26:17. This is Jesus' Passover! The disciples make the preparations and even participate. But it is Jesus' Exodus meal because, according to the interpolation in 26:18, "my fulness of time is near."[5]

During the celebration that evening Jesus goes beyond his previous announcement in 26:2 that "the Human Being is delivered up to be crucified" and informs his disciples that it will be one of them who will hand him over. All of them, except one, use the epithet "Lord" in asking him, "Is it I?" Judas, according to Matthew's redaction, prefers the title "Rabbi" which he employs again at the moment of betrayal in the Garden of Gethsemane (26:49).[6] This refusal to acknowledge Jesus' Son of the Human Being-Son of God sovereignty corresponds to his intention to terminate Jesus' distinctive messiahship. (26:15).

Although this is a Passover meal there is no reference to a lamb being eaten; only bread and a cup are specified. The bread which the disciples are commanded to "eat" — the verb has been added to the Marcan tradition — is designated by Jesus to be his body. Their eating it gives them a share in his forthcoming sacrificial death and the Exodus it will inaugurate. By implication Jesus is the Passover victim, the lamb, that redeems them from their present bondage. The cup is of course closely related to its content, "the fruit of the vine," — as it is named in 26:29. It is a cup of blessing for it denotes the shedding of blood, the pouring out of a life, by which the past is cancelled and a new future with a new covenant is constituted (26:28). The disciples' drinking of the cup signifies their involvement in a destiny that Jesus is determining for them, as has already been expressed in 20:23, "You will indeed drink my cup." This incorporation into his life and destiny by their eating and drinking makes them true participants in a life-style that is now being culminated by a sacrificial death. More than ever being his disciples means taking up their cross and following him. At the same time, however, their eating and drinking together is a foretaste of that great feast which Jesus will celebrate with them when the community of the Human Being will have realized its apotheosis in the kingdom of the Father (26:29).[7]

Concluding the meal with a hymn, they leave Jerusalem and for the last time climb "into the Mount of Olives." On the mountain Jesus forewarns his disciples, "You will all be scandalized by me this night." The reason which he gives them is an Old Testament quotation, "For it is written, I will strike down the shepherd and the sheep will be scattered."[8] In the forthcoming historical event of Jesus' crucifixion God also will be a participant. This must be the scandal which Jesus is referring to in 26:31. Judas and the Jews will deliver him up to the Romans who in turn will nail him to the cross. But it is God who will slay him.

Earlier in the gospel (10:28) Jesus exhorted his disciples, "Do not fear those who kill the body but are unable to kill the soul. Rather fear the one who is able to destroy both

soul and body in hell." God, the one who is able to destroy both
soul and body in hell, will strike down the righteous shepherd.
He will not let the cup of divine wrath pass from the Son of the
Human Being-Son of God (26:39). He who would send more
than twelve legions of angels in rescue will destroy Jesus. In
view of his prayers in Gethsemane that is the death which he
dreads. It must be the desolation he expresses in his cry from
the cross, "My God, my God, why did you abandon me?"

In spite of this fearful death the Exodus which Jesus has
celebrated in the Passover meal with his disciples will take
place. He himself, by being raised from the dead, will conduct
it: "After I have been raised from the dead, I will precede you
into Galilee." There the dispersed disciples will be reconstituted by him to form the community of the Human Being,
the new people of God.

Peter, who seems to think that he has grasped all of this,
boasts that he above all will not be scandalized, even though he
has already taken offense previously at Jesus' substitution of a
suffering Messiah for one of power and glory. Jesus insists that
Peter will be so outraged that he will deny him three times. But
Peter persists in his bravado; even if it is necessary that he
should die with him, he will not deny him (26:35).

Jesus then leads his disciples into a field called Gethsemane. It is evidently the place of rendezvous with Judas and
the mob who will hand him over to the Jewish authorities
(26:45f.). Here he wishes to pray while he waits for the be-
trayer to arrive. Taking along Peter and the two sons of
Zebedee, the three who witnessed his transfiguration, he withdraws a short distance and begs them to watch with him. But
while he is praying they proceed to fall asleep. He turns to them
three times only to find them slumbering. He chides them, but
there is no indication they hear; he seems to be quite alone.
After praying that this cup might pass from him, he returns to
acknowledge, "My Father, if this (cup) is not able to pass away
except I drink it, let your will be done" (26:42). Jesus is putting
into practice the third petition of the prayer which he taught

his disciples in 6:9-13. There is a third prayer, but it is not quoted; it is only noted that it was the same as the second.

Reassured and resolute he turns to his disciples with the caustic rebuke, "Sleep and refresh yourselves in the future! See, the hour has arrived and the Human Being is delivered into the hands of sinners. Get up, let us be going. Look, the one who is betraying me has come." What he had been predicting to them since Peter's confession (16:21) will now begin to happen.

Judas arrives leading "a large crowd" sent by the priests and the elders of the people. He gives them the promised sign of identification by greeting Jesus with a kiss. The latter's response, which is peculiar to Matthew, expresses both intimate recognition and an acknowledgement of the purpose for which Judas came, "Friend, for that which you are here you are here!"[9] "Then," as if only by his consent, "approaching they laid hands on Jesus and apprehended him" (26:50).

One of the Twelve — he is not named! — rises to Jesus' defense by smiting the servant of the high priest with his sword and cutting off his ear. Jesus rejects this intervention and once again puts into practice what he has taught his disciples in 5:39ff. Retaliation in kind only perpetuates the cause and effect nexus; it is also not a response made in freedom. Moreover, according to the unique tradition of 26:53, it interferes with the will of the Father who could intervene with more than twelve legions of angels, which, according to 13:41 and 24:31, are at the disposal of the Human Being. The will of God must be carried out, and the Scriptures must be fulfilled. This is the last word which Jesus speaks to his disciples before his crucifixion.

He also reproaches the crowds who have accompanied Judas. Armed with swords and clubs at the instigation of the high priest and elders they are the very ones whom he taught in the Temple: "Daily I was seated in the Temple teaching and you did not arrest me."[10] He has served them with compassion because they are harrassed and oppressed as sheep without a shepherd, and now they have taken him prisoner. "All of this happened," the evangelist notes in an adaptation of Mk. 14:49b, "so that the writings of the prophets might be fulfilled" (26:56). This declaration corresponds to the fulfillment quotations scattered throughout the gospel: it interrupts the narrative and employs a similar introductory formula. But in contrast to the others it emphasizes what has been written and does not refer to any specific Old Testament text. What is beginning to happen at this point, according to Matthew, is a fulfillment of "the writings of the prophets." The Passion that will now take place will fulfill all of the divine promises made in these Scriptures. Perhaps it is this realization that induces the disciples to flight. They have been scandalized as Jesus predicted.

He is taken captive to the residence of the high priest where the Sanhedrin has already convened (26:57). Peter, who evidently has changed his mind about running away, enters the courtyard and seats himself among the servants in order "to see the end." He is determined, it seems, to remain true to the promise he made on the Mount of Olives.

Many false witnesses come forward in order to bear testimony against Jesus, but there is no agreement among them. Jesus cannot be convicted on the basis of false evidence. Finally, two are found who maintain that Jesus claimed to be able to destroy the Temple and to rebuild it in three days. No refutation is offered, neither is there any indication that these are false witnesses. Matthew, it seems, would prefer to have him indicted by testimony that is true but without a legal basis for conviction. Jesus remains silent, and the charge stands unchallenged. To elicit a response the high priest resorts to placing Jesus under oath, but for the purpose of answering another, more pointed question which he may have inferred from the testimony of the two witnesses: "Are you the Messiah, the Son of God?" Jesus' answer is not as straightforward as that of Mark's "I am," but neither is it evasive. His terse, "You said (it)," returns the question to the high priest unanswered.

He will reply but on his own terms and in his own way without being intimadated by the latter's adjurement. In this respect Jesus is once again acting according to his teaching of 5:33-7, ". . . do not swear at all . . ." His words, "Nevertheless I say to you. . ." introduce the response he concedes to make to the question which the high priest would force on him.[11] The Messiah title is set aside; he will only answer to it, as he stated earlier in 23:39, when he is greeted with the exclamation of faith: "Blessed is he who comes in the name of the Lord." Instead he replies, *"From now on* you will see the Son of the Human Being seated on the right hand of power and coming on the clouds of heaven" (26:64).[12] Jesus' enthronement as the authentic Human Being that God intended at creation will be especially manifest during his passion. It will not be a hidden reality visible to the eyes of faith. The high priest and the Sanhedrin seated with him will see it as his passion moves towards its climax in death on the cross. They, his enemies, are to know that genuine creaturehood is transfigured by suffering and death on behalf of others. At the same time Jesus also intimates that his enthronement lies in the future; it will not be realized until the time of the Parousia (24:29-31) when the Human Being community is constituted and he enters into an egalitarian lordship with all those who have followed him in the lifestyle that he has taught and lived.[13]

Upon hearing this affirmation the high priest evokes from the Sanhedrin the sentence of death. Open hostility supervenes as personal abuse and maltreatment are inflicted on him (26:67f.).

Peter in the meantime has been seated in the outer courtyard awaiting the outcome. The scene now shifts back to him. A maid approaches and identifies him as a companion of Jesus, but he thrusts it aside with a vigorous denial "before all" (26:69f.). Retreating to the "entrance" apparently in order to leave he is pointed out a second time by another servant girl. He resorts to an oath in order to escape involvement, but his Galilean dialect betrays his identity to the bystanders, and he feels compelled to disassociate himself by cursing and swearing. When the cock suddenly crows he remembers Jesus' prediction and goes out to weep bitterly.

After the priests and the elders have held counsel in order to determine how he is to be put to death, Jesus is delivered up to Pilate "the governor." This is evidently a crucial point in the narrative for the evangelist interrupts the Marcan sequence of events in order to insert a tradition that is his own and produces a certain climax in the gospel.

Judas returns to the priests and elders and in remorse attempts to repay the 30 pieces of silver with the admission that he has betrayed innocent blood (27:3f.). When the money is refused: "What is that to us? You see to it!" he throws it into the Temple, withdraws and hangs himself. The priests hesitate to deposit the amount in the treasury, "since it is the price of blood," and after some deliberation utilize it to purchase a potter's field, a place where potters dump their broken clay pots and vessels, which is to be used as a burial place for foreigners.[14]

For Matthew these actions, which fulfill certain Old Testament prophecies, express the cessation of the privileged position which the Jewish nation has enjoyed as the elect people of God. That is to say, Judas' act of throwing the 30 pieces of silver into the Temple is Judah's monetary settlement with Yahweh for services rendered and at the same time, as a result, the immediately effective cancellation of the contract binding both parties.[15] The money, however, does not remain in the Temple because of the priests' consciousness of guilt. Its employment in the purchase of a field duplicates the prophetic action of Jeremiah before the destruction of the first Temple in 586 B.C.[16] But because of the annulment of the covenant, there is no promise for the future, as there was formerly. The second Temple will also be destroyed, as Jesus predicted in 24:2. But the land will not be resettled; cities will not be rebuilt; crops will not be replanted. This potter's field, covered with the shards of the broken vessel of Israel,[17] will become a cemetery for the burial of — foreigners! Thus, tragically and ironically Israel has been dispossessed, and the promises of the Old Testament have been fulfilled and cancelled at the same time.

Pilate's interrogation produces nothing. In the face of the accusation of the priests and the elders Jesus remains silent. As no legal basis emerges for the execution of Jesus, Pilate, instead of releasing him, decides to let the Jews choose between "Jesus who is called Messiah" and "a notorious prisoner called Barabbas." The evangelist has formulated Pilate's question in such a way that the answer will necessarily bear a confessional character.

The scene is interrrupted by a note of warning sent to the Roman governor by his wife, "(Let there be) nothing between you and that righteous one, for I have suffered many things in a dream today on account of him." This brief tradition of 27:19, which has been interpolated into the narrative adopted from Mark, is peculiar to Matthew and uses a motif found at the beginning of the gospel. When Jesus' life was threatened by Herod the Great, the Magi were warned by a dream not to return to the king in Jerusalem.[18]

But Pilate is committed to the choice he has offered the Jews: "Which of the two do you wish I should release to you?" The crowds who are now also present have been swayed by the priests and the elders, and they choose Barabbas. Pilate's responsive question is once again phrased in such a way that the answer will be confessional in one way or another: "What then shall I do with Jesus who is called Messiah?" The reply in unison is, "Let him be crucified." No reason is given to his final question: "What wrong did he do?" Instead they cry out more vigorously, "Let him be crucified."

Matthew's propensity for the exoneration of the Roman governor is apparent in the insertion of the special tradition of 27:24f. Pilate uses the Jewish ritual of purging oneself of innocent blood to affirm his own guiltlessness.[19] Yet the point is not his innocence but the guilt which the Jews willingly assume and with it the divine curse pronounced on the shedding of innocent blood.[20] The substitution of *pas ho laos* ("all the people") in 27:25 in place of "the crowds" who appear in 27:20 suggests that the evangelist is implicating the whole nation of God's elect people.[21] All Israel is involved in this tragic moment: ". . . all the people (of God) said, 'His blood be on us and on our children' ".[22] Implicitly acknowledging Jesus' innocence in their cry, "all the people," in tragic contrast to Jeremiah's trial where they interceded on behalf of the prophet's life, demand that the death sentence be carried out.[23]

Only after the Jews have assumed the guilt of Jesus' death is Barabbas released to them. Jesus, after being scourged — a Roman practice administered before the execution took place — is handed over to the soldiers to be crucified. Before leading him away for execution they make sport of him and so add to his misery and suffering. According to the evangelist's interpolation, they dressed him in a crimson cloak, set a woven crown of thorns on his head, put a reed in his right hand and fell on their knees before him in mock worship (27:28f.). Matthew poses the bitter irony of the derisive adoration which Jesus receives from his executioners as the "King of the Jews."

A man by the name of Simon of Cyrene is pressed into service to bear the cross to a place outside the city called Golgotha. The customary anesthetizing drink is offered to Jesus, but after tasting it he refuses to drink it. This is "wine mixed with wormwood."[24] Jesus chooses to retain full control of himself and his senses. Even though he is being nailed to a cross he remains free to the end.

After he has been raised up on the cross, he is stripped of his last possession. The soldiers divide his garments by the casting of lots, "and seating themselves they were observing him there."[25] They are the ones who place the charge for which he is being executed above his head: "This is Jesus the King of the Jews" (27:37). At the beginning of the gospel the Magi came from the East to worship Jesus "the King of the Jews": and they presented him with their gifts: gold, frankincense and myrrh. Now at the end of his life his Roman crucifiers, who have deprived him of his clothes and sit under the cross staring at his naked and lonely condition, raise the title by which he was first called for the last time.

The evangelist notes briefly that two thieves were crucified with him and then turns to describe the mood of derision and ridicule that prevails. Those walking by blaspheme him, and in the words of Ps. 22(21:8)7 adopted from Mark, ". . . are shaking their heads" and taunting him with their mockery. In 27:40b the conditional clause, "If you are God's son," has been inserted before the imperative, "Come down from the cross." The word echoes the second temptation of the devil spoken on the pinnacle of the Temple in Jerusalem (4:6).

Three individual expressions of contempt are attributed to "the priests with the scribes and elders."[26] Their words, in contrast to the mockery of "those passing by," are not addressed to Jesus but are spoken in the third person singular as though these Jewish leaders were carrying on a conversation among themselves which they nevertheless want Jesus to overhear (27:42f.). Their condescending admissions are sadistic in the very truth which they convey: "He saved others; he is unable to save himself." "He is the king of Israel; let him come down from the cross and we shall believe him."[27] "He has trusted in God; let him now save him, if he wants him, for he said, 'I am God's son.' " Jesus' freedom is severely restricted: he is not able to save himself; he cannot descend from the cross; God cannot and will not deliver him in this moment. Nevertheless to the very end he retains the final jurisdiction over his life and breath (27:50).

Jesus' desolation becomes more complete as the two thieves, who are crucified and dying with him, identify with the bystanders and religious leaders and add reproach of their own (27:44). Darkness falls upon "the whole earth". The creation itself is announcing the impending catastrophe.

The end comes quickly. After maintaining complete silence throughout his crucifixion, Jesus shouts a grief-stricken cry of absolute desolation: "My God, my God, why did you abandon me?"[28] He is beginning to taste of the bitter cup that he dreaded to drink (26:39, 42).

Some of the bystanders misinterpret Jesus' cry as an invocation of Elijah. How such confusion is possible is difficult to understand, at least in the Marcan version where the words of address, "Eloi, Eloi" have little resemblance to the Hebrew forms of Elijah: "Eliyahu" or "Eliya". It is Matthew who renders the misunderstanding more plausible by substituting "Eli, Eli." The possibility which suggests itself, therefore — in view of what appears to be so deliberate a misinterpretation — is that it is a literary device intended by Mark to serve as a foil in order to express the fulfillment of Ps. 69 (68:22)21. Matthew, who does not avoid the tradition yet attempts to ease its difficulty, seems to ignore the note of fulfillment — even though he borrows the words appropriated from Ps. 69 — and to retell the story for the sake of making another point. There is a more direct relationship between the misunderstanding of the cry and the singular action that follows: "And immediately one of them" rushes to offer Jesus a sponge soaked with cheap wine (27:48). It does not matter to the evangelist who this is; the intent appears to be charitable, perhaps to help Jesus to stay alive until Elijah intervenes. The rest of the bystanders reject this interference in favor of waiting for the miracle of divine intervention. Perhaps in the very last minute he will be saved by the coming of Elijah, the forerunner of God.

But there is no divine intervention, at least not in the form in which it is expected. Deserted by God as well as human beings and denied even a final act of charity, Jesus cries out with a great voice (27:50). In contrast to the shout of 27:46 this is an inarticulate scream, not of fear and despair but of lord-ship.[29] In one final earth-rending shriek Jesus consumes all the vitality that is still within him and in a great last exhalation sends forth *to pneuma* ("his spirit"). In freedom the Son of the Human Being-Son of God terminates his life, discharging the divine breath that has been residing in him.

At his expiration the veil of the Temple is torn in two from top to bottom.[30] God exits from his/her dwelling place, the Temple on Mount Zion, and thus consummates the withdrawal Jesus began in 23:38, "Behold, your house is abandoned to you!"[31] With this departure divine judgment falls upon Israel, for this is the moment in which the history of God's people is culminated. The death of Jesus is also the death of Israel.

Concomitantly the earth also collapses: "and the earth was shaken and the rocks were split." The world is plunged into the night of its original primeval silence.[32] The judgment that falls on Israel overwhelms all "the inhabitants of the earth for iniquity."[33] In view of the solidarity of humanity all are involved in the guilt of killing the new man, the bearer of the divine humanity that the Creator destined for all human beings. The death of Jesus, according to Matthew's apocalyptic mythology, constitutes the ontological end of the creation and its history.

A new creation follows this cataclysmic event: "The tombs were opened and many bodies of the holy ones being asleep were raised." With the resurrection of the Old Testament saints there is a reconstitution of all things.[34] The new age which they anticipated in their prophecies has dawned, and they are its first participants.

Matt. 27:53 continues this apocalyptic sequence of events with the stipulation, "and coming out of the tombs *after his resurrection* they came into the holy city and were made visible to many." According to tradition, Jesus is the first to have been raised from the dead, so it is natural for the evangelist to specify the priority of his resurrection. Yet in one respect the saints precede him, although they do not emerge from their tombs until after his resurrection. Causally linked to Jesus' death, their awakening is the result of his final exhalation. His is the breath that "breathes into these dead ones" and makes them live again. It is an echo of Ezek. 37:9-12 in 27:52f. that supports the probability of such a connection. For after being awakened from the sleep of death by his divine breath, they must await his own exit from the grave so that he can lead them, in accordance with Ezek. 37:12, "I am opening your tombs, and I will lead you up from your tombs and I will lead you into the land of Israel."[35] In this way the messiahship of Jesus is sustained, and the history of the Old Testament Israel is continued.

The connection between Jesus' death and these attendant apocalyptic phenomena is perceived by "the centurion and those with him observing Jesus." The former may be the same centurion who approached Jesus earlier in the gospel and who in interceding on behalf of his servant boy acknowledged the authority of Jesus' word.[36] The latter are the soldiers who crucified him, cast lots for his garments and who, according to the redaction of 27:36, "seating themselves were observing him there (on the cross)." On the basis of what they observe they are overwhelmed with respect and spontaneously confess, "Truly this was God's Son!" Once again the evangelist's irony is apparent. At the beginning of Jesus' life the Magi from the East were the first to interpret the significance of the rising star and to follow it until "it stood above where the child was. And seeing the star they rejoiced with a great joy . . . and falling they worshipped . . ." the King of the Jews. At the end of his life the very Roman soldiers who crucified him "seeing the earthquake and the things happening were greatly reverent" and acknowledged him as God's Son. In this way the gospel's tendency toward universalism has made full circle. As Jesus had said in response to the centurion's faith in 8:11f., "Many will come from the east and west and dine with Abraham, Isaac and Jacob in the kingdom of God, but the sons of the kingdom will be cast into outer darkness . . ."

There were also "many women" who, having followed Jesus from Galilee in order to minister to him, watched from a distance (27:55). Three of them are named: Mary Magdalene, Mary the mother of James and Joseph and the mother of the sons of Zebedee.[37] Two of them, Mary Magdalene and "the

other Mary" are mentioned again in 27:61 and 28:1. The designation of the latter as "the other Mary" can only refer to "Mary
the mother of James and Joseph" in 27:56 and may be a literary
abbreviation. As the mother of James and Joseph she must be
the Mary who is mentioned in 13:55 as Jesus' mother; and
James and John, her sons, must be two of the four brothers of
Jesus who are named in the same text.[38] Why Matthew does
not identify her more directly as Jesus' mother is not clear.
Since she and Mary Magdalene appear at the consummation
of the gospel witnessing Jesus' death, burial and resurrection,
they may serve to establish the historical integrity of these
climactic events in the creedal tradition that Matthew's church
has received.[39] At the beginning of the gospel Mary became
"the virgin", the embodiment of Mother Israel who gave birth
to the Messiah. Perhaps she continues this representation and
along with Mary Magdalene symbolizes the mother church of
Jerusalem and its witness.

      The burial of Jesus is undertaken by Joseph of
Arimathea who emerges here for the first time and is described
by Matthew as "a rich man" who "had become a disciple of
Jesus" (27:57). Receiving the body from Pilate he proceeds to
bury it in a new tomb which he had hewn out of the rock for
himself. This act discloses the nature of his faith, for it was
contrary to Jewish law to bury anyone judged and executed as
a criminal — especially one cursed because he was hanged on a
tree (Deut. 21:22f.) — in a tomb that represents the continuity
of the fathers of Israel.[40] After rolling a great stone before the
entrance, he departs leaving behind the two Marys who,
according to the evangelist's insert, "seated themselves over
against the tomb."

      "On the following day which is after the preparation"
the chief priests and the Pharisees approach Pilate in order to
request that the tomb in which Jesus has been buried be sealed
and guarded. The time reference with which Matthew begins
this episode is an indirect designation of the sabbath. The
Pharisees, by conducting this business with Gentiles, are

transgressing the same commandment they accused Jesus of breaking when he restored a withered arm on the sabbath and they in reaction began to plot his destruction (12:14). Furthermore, in addressing Pilate, the representative of Rome and Roman oppression, as "Lord," the title which the Jews reserved for God alone, they reveal their alienation. God has vacated the Temple, and they have no other Lord except Caesar. The third day is drawing near; and since Jesus had predicted his resurrection "after three days," as they say — perhaps their peculiar timetable reflects the sign of Jonah which Jesus gave them in 12:40, for Jesus nowhere predicted that he would rise "after three days" — their aim, as they explain, is to prevent the disciples from stealing the corpse and subsequently deceiving the people with the announcement of his resurrection. Such an occurrence, they claim, would make "the final deception (of the disciples) worse than the first." What the first one was is not stated, but it clearly implies the delusion of Jesus' messiahship.

This uniquely Matthean tradition (27:62-6), which reintroduces the Pharisees for the first time since chapter 23, reflects Jewish slander which is more appropriately located in the evangelist's context than in the historical circumstances surrounding Jesus' burial. Its inclusion in the gospel, along with its sequel in 28:11-5, is Matthew's attempt to refute the charge, perhaps rabbinic in origin, that Jesus' resurrection is the deliberate ruse of his disciples who, having disposed of his body, proclaimed the miracle of his resurrection.[41] Pilate gives his approval to their request: the tomb is sealed and a guard is posted.

The gospel culminates in Jesus' resurrection from the dead. The narrative of this event, however, is terse and restrained. In this respect the end is like the beginning. Jesus' origin was explicated with utmost brevity: he was created by the holy Spirit, and he was adopted by Joseph. Nothing of the circumstances of his birth beyond time and place were reported. The conclusion of the gospel is similarly brief. The circumstances of Jesus' resurrection remain shrouded in mystery. Unlike the account of the transfiguration there is no description of his exalted being or his resurrected body. There is no indication of a discontinuity that would separate him from his disciples or prevent their recognizing him. Nothing is said that might possibly reduce or detract from the wonder of the event. Apocalyptic mythology and the report of the empirical experiences of seeing, touching and hearing are combined to affirm its reality and meaning.

The time is dawn on the first day of the week, the day after the sabbath, by inference the eighth day. Two women — the evangelist's preference for two is once again apparent! — come to view the tomb. Mary Magdalene and "the other Mary," the mother of Jesus, are the witnesses to the crucial events of Jesus' death, burial and resurrection. Upon their arrival at the sepulcher another apocalyptic event takes place: "And look, a great earthquake happened." This is the culminating seismic occurrence in the gospel, and it stands back to back with the earthquake of Jesus' death. While the earlier one manifested judgment effecting the collapse of the creation, this subsequent quake denotes Jesus' resurrection from the dead, his leading the awakened saints out of their graves and the beginning of a new creation. None of these events is described or explicated. The apocalyptic mythology simply and with great restraint conveys the reality of this divine reconstitution.

Accompanying the earthquake is the descent of the angel of the Lord who seats himself on the great stone that he has rolled away from the entrance of the tomb. The language which Matthew utilizes to describe him: "His appearance was like lightning and his garment white as snow!" enhances the apocalyptic character of this consummation. His purpose is to serve as the agent of revelation. At the beginning of the gospel he appeared in dreams as the bearer of divine communication. Now at this reconstitution he becomes an apocalyptic manifestation visible to those guarding the tomb as well as the women who have come to view it. Evidently what he represents and what he discloses are to be understood as empirical realities. As the agent of revelation he unveils the empty tomb and announces the event of Jesus' resurrection from the dead.

For those guarding the tomb who represent Jesus' enemies this apocalyptic event is simultaneously their judgment: "From fear of him the guards *eseisthesan* ("were shaken") and became as dead men."[42] Nothing is said to them, but they see the revelation of the empty tomb and concomitantly experience the shattering collapse of their lives.

The two women, on the other hand, who have also witnessed this apocalyptic manifestation, are exhorted and re-assured, "Stop being afraid! For I know you are seeking the crucified Jesus." Without pause the angel discloses the meaning of what has happened: "He is not here for he was resurrected, as he said. Come look at the place where he was laid." Beckoned to enter the empty tomb for their own empirical confirmation, they are commissioned to serve as bearers of this revelation to the disciples: "Go quickly and say to his disciples, 'He was raised from the dead and see he is pre-ceding you into Galilee; there you will see him.' " What Jesus predicted to his disciples has been fulfilled.[43] The Exodus has begun. Jesus has been delivered from the ultimate bondage of death. Jerusalem, which has been abandoned by God and is therefore as devoid of the divine presence as the empty tomb is to be left behind. Jesus, the conqueror of death and the embodiment of life, is returning to Galilee. It is only by par-ticipating in this Exodus, by following Jesus to Galilee, that the disciples will see him.

Overwhelmed with fear and joy the women begin to run from the tomb in order to obey the angel's command. Unexpectedly, the risen Jesus manifests himself to them and thereby upholds the testimony of the angel. No description of his resurrected appearance is given. The women respond to his greeting by drawing nearer, and as if to certify the reality of their experience, they grasp his feet. Only then do they worship him. Hearing is added to the sense experiences of sight and touch. Jesus repeats and upholds the charge of the angel: "Stop being afraid! Go report to my brothers that I am departing into Galilee. There they will see me." What is new in his self-disclosure is his designation of his disciples as siblings; it is the first time in the gospel that he refers to them in this way. They are to be informed that he has been raised from the dead and that as a result he has received his kingdom. But more than ever they are to know that he places himself in a horizontal relationship to them. They are his brothers and sisters, his equals; and by their joining him in his Exodus to Galilee they are to become his comrades.

In the meantime some of the guards return to Jerusalem in order to report their experience of this apocalyptic revelation (28:11). A meeting of the Sanhedrin is convened, and in mutual counsel the chief priests and the elders agree to bribe the soldiers to conceal the truth of Jesus' resurrection by spreading the lie that the disciples stole his body during the night while they were asleep. By promising to deal with any difficulties that might be raised by Pilate who had agreed to seal the tomb and post the guard they reveal themselves to be suppressors of the truth as well as collaborators with Rome. "Taking the money they did as they were taught;" and that, according to the evangelist, is how the slanderous rumor that Jesus' resurrection is to be explained by the disciples' theft of his corpse got started. "This very word began to spread among the Jews to this day." The designation "Jews" reflects contemporaneous usage. Yet because of its employment after the resurrection it may be intended to emphasize the lost estate of "the sons of the kingdom." The continuity of Old Testament Israel now belongs to Jesus and his followers.

This is the point of the final episode in the gospel. The eleven remaining disciples follow Jesus into Galilee and ascend *eis to oros* ("into the mountain") which had been predesignated by him. It is the mountain of his sovereignty, the *axis mundi* on which the new creation of the Son of the Human Being-Son of God has already become visible. There they

encounter the risen Jesus. Like the two Marys they have no
difficulty in recognizing him, and they respond in worship. But
in contrast to them, some have doubts. What kind of doubts is
not made explicit; most likely, however, they are doubts about
the reality of his resurrection from the dead. Jesus does not
attempt to resolve their uncertainties and perplexities. It is as
though he is not even aware of them, for he proceeds to
announce to them the event of his enthronement: "There was
given to me all authority in heaven and on earth." By means of
this paraphrase of Dan. 7:14 he identifies himself with the Son
of the Human Being who comes on the clouds of heaven to
receive his divinely-appointed rule.[44] The vision of the
prophet, he intimates, has been fulfilled. The Human Being
has been enthroned on God's right hand. The age of the rule of
authentic humanness has commenced.

At the same time, however, as he also exclaimed before
the high priest in 26:64, the Human Being is only approaching
his rule for it is not an elitist reality which he exercises alone.
His disciples who have joined him in his Exodus share it. But
all peoples and nations are to participate in it. Therefore, it is
necessary that the eleven descend from the mountain and go
out into the world in order to make disciples of all nations, so
that finally and irrevocably they may all be enthroned
together.

The original wording of the Great Commission, as
some have advocated, may have been a poetically structured
quatrain with its own peculiar rhythm.[45]

There was given to me all authority in heaven and on earth.
Going therefore make disciples of all nations in my name.
Teaching them to observe all things I commanded you.
And look, I am with you all the days to the consummation of the age.

There is a certain correspondence between the first and the
fourth lines which enclose the actual mission charge. The one

who is seated on the right hand of power and therefore has all authority in heaven and on earth is also the "*I am* with you" or Emmanuel until the age consummates in the Parousia of the Human Being.[46] The second and third lines, which convey the mission charge, have a parallelism of their own. Both begin with participles: "Going," "teaching," which express sequential activities. "Going" implies a mission which fulfills itself in calling men, women and children to "hope in his name" (12:21) as well as to participate in the life, freedom and love of the Human Being-Servant of the Lord. Making disciples of all nations also means handing down Jesus' teaching which effects health and wholeness by integrating confessing his name and doing deeds of righteousness.[47] That necessarily includes baptism! Making disciples of all nations in his name means teaching them to follow Jesus who submitted to John's baptism in order to fulfill all righteousness. Thus originally the command to baptize may have been implicitly understood rather than explicitly expressed.[48] If this is so, the trinitarian formula: "in the name of the Father and of the Son and of the Holy Spirit," which belongs to the rite of baptism, may also not have been included. As has often been pointed out, it is not transmitted by Eusebius in his quotation of the Great Commission.

The Great Commission is also Jesus' response to his disciples' doubts. For it is in obedience to this charge, in their leaving behind even this mountain and going out into the world, that their doubts will be resolved. When they venture "into the country beyond" — as in the episode of 14:22-33 — they will experience the reality of the one who is "I AM" coming to them and demonstrating sovereignty over chaos. And when, like Peter, they join him in exercising that sovereignty they will know that he is indeed the Human Being who has been enthroned on the right hand of God, the one who has cast out judgment by triumphing over death and the power of evil.

Eleven ascended into the mountain; twelve descend.

Jesus does not remain behind on the mount; nor does he ascend into heaven: "Look, I am with you all the days to the consummation of the age." He joins himself to the company of the eleven, and as the twelfth reconstitutes Israel. At the same time he imparts his Son of the Human Being-Son of God identity to them, for they are all his comrades in carrying out the Great Commission which he has just issued. Now the Human Being is no longer an individual; he has become a community or a communion in which all its participants have an equal share in his lordship. They are what he is, and what he has done they will do because he will be with them. Their mission, therefore, cannot fail even as his did not fail; but in order for it to reach its culmination they, like him, must take up their cross and pass through suffering and death. Only through defeat can victory be gained. The goal that God has ordained will be realized. When the fourth and final age is terminated, the community of authentic humanity will emerge from the womb of Mother History and will enjoy the life of God forever. For the destiny of the community of the Human Being is the same as that of the individual Human Being. As he was metamorphosed into God on the high mountain in Galilee, they too will be apotheosized and shine as the sun in the kingdom of God.

FOOTNOTES

1 See 26:47, 57; 27:1, 3, 12, 41.

2 See E. Auerbach, *Mimesis. The Representation of Reality in Western Literature,* (Garden City, New York: Doubleday Anchor Books, 1957), pp. 8ff., where a significant characteristic of Bible stories is delineated: motives as well as purpose so often remain unexpressed.

3 It is possible that Matthew, like Paul in Gal. 3:13, is conscious of the curse of Deut. 21:22f. and implies it as a major factor in handing Jesus over to the Romans for crucifixion in order to eliminate any future possibility of a Jewish following.

FOOTNOTES

4 See 26:15, 21, 46, 48; 27:2, 3, 4, 26.

5 This is also Israel's fullness of time, for Jesus also represents the people of God. Compare Strecker, *Der Weg,* p. 88.

6 Matthew eliminated Peter's use of this title as it appears in Mk. 9:5; in his gospel it is a title used by Jesus' enemies.

7 See also 13:43. Perhaps it is also significant that Matthew has added the prepositional phrase, "with you," in 26:29 echoing the words of 1:23 and 28:20. Jesus is Emmanuel, "God with us."

8 Lohmeyer, *op. cit.,* p. 364, best explains the unusual construction: *eph ho parei* as an ellipsis which can best be rendered as "So you have come for that which you have come." Also Blass, Debrunner, Funk, *Greek Grammar,* p. 158.

10 For the possibility that 26:52 is a quotation taken from the Targum of Is. 50:11, see H. Kosmala, "Matthew xxvi 52 - A Quotation from the Targum," *N.T.* 4 (1960), pp. 3-5.

11 See 11:24 for the use of the same clause introduced by the same adversative conjunction.

12 Matthew has added the initial prepositional phrase, "From now on . . ."

13 Compare H.E. Tödt, *The Son of Man,* pp. 80ff. The prior or primary reality is the present enthronement, but alongside of that stands the future enthronement. Ps. 110:1 is placed before Dan. 7:13-4 and results in a dialectical eschatology that also involves the reality of the one and the many, Jesus and the community of his followers.

14 Matthew knows of a current tradition associated with "a field of blood" and may have identified this as the field purchased by the priests. See Acts 1:18f.

15 See J.W. Doeve, *Jewish Hermeneutics,* pp. 185ff. Stendahl, *School,* pp. 121ff. Gundry, *The Use of the Old Testament in St. Matthew's Gospel,* pp. 122ff.

16 See Jer. 32:9-15.

17 See Jer. 18:1ff.

18 Stendahl, *Matthew* in Peake, p. 796, para. 694e. Also Trilling's discussion of 27:19, *Das Wahre Israel,* pp. 48ff.

19 See Deut. 21:6-8 and Ps. 26(25)6. Also Lohmeyer, *op. cit.,* p. 385 and n. 3 on the Greek and Latin witnesses to this practice.

20 See 2 Sam. 1:16, Jer. 51(28):35 and especially 26(33):15.

21 For the same phrase, see Josephus, *Ant.* XI, 133. Also Jer. 26(33):7-16 where it is used three times. Matthew's expansion of the Marcan text appears to have been influenced by the parallel event of Jeremiah's trial.

22 Hummel, *Auseinandersetzung,* claims this is a formula out of the legal language of the O.T.

23 Again see Jer. 26(33):7-16 and Matt. 16:14.

FOOTNOTES

24 The participial clause "mixed with wormwood" is an editorial addition which echoes Ps. 69(68:22)21 and gives further evidence of reflection on the O.T. contributing to the expansion of the passion narrative. So also 27:35.

25 See Ps. 22(21:19)18. The substitution of the aorist for the present tense in Mk. 15:24 is a closer approximation of the LXX text. See Gundry, *op. cit.*, p. 62.

26 The last of these is a Matthean interpolation taken from Ps. 22(21:9)8. See Strecker, *op. cit.*, pp. 28f.

27 It is noteworthy that the conditional particle, "if," is missing here, while it is used in 27:40. Some manuscripts also include it in 27:42 but it appears to be a scribal insertion intended to ease the difficulty of the text.

28 The text of 27:46 is extremely problematic with the manuscripts offering many variants. For different explanations of the difficulties involved, McNeile, *Matthew*, p. 421; Lohmeyer, *op. cit.*, p. 394. Since it is my opinion that Matthew did not know Hebrew, I do not consider the change here to have been made on the basis of the Hebrew text of Ps. 22(21):1 but on the basis of the subsequent confusion of the "Eloi, Eloi" with Elijah. To make this more understandable Matthew substitutes "Eli, Eli" but goes on to return the rest of the quotation as cited by Mark. "Lema," I think, is the original reading of the Marcan text and has been adopted by Matthew along with the verb. Also Strecker, *op. cit.*, p. 27.

29 Compare Joel 3:16.

30 Hummel, *op. cit.*, p. 84, also finds a connection between Jesus' death and the rending of the veil.

31 Thus, with God's withdrawal Mount Zion and the Temple lose their status as the absolute Center of the earth.

32 For O.T. and intertestamental examples of this apocalyptic motif see: Mic. 1:3f., Is. 24:1-20, 1 Enoch 1:4-9, Test. Lev. 4:1ff., Assump. Mos. 10:3 and 4 Ez. 7:30.

33 See Is. 26:21.

34 The identity of "the holy ones" is problematic, but see Zech. 14:5 and Dan. 7:22, 27.

35 See the LXX text of Ezek. 37:12. This connection between Ezek. 37:9-12 and Matt. 27:52f. is also supported by J. Grassi, "Ezek. 37:1-14 and the N.T.," *NTS*(11) Jan. 1965, pp. 162ff. See especially p. 163 where Grassi notes the correspondence between the Ezekiel panel of the resurrection at the saints.

36 The fact that Matthew changes the word "centurion" in Mk. 15:39 to "leader of a hundred" which is the same term appearing in the Q tradition of 8:5 suggests a possible identification of the two.

37 The last of the three has been substituted for Salome in Mk. 15:40.

38 Compare with Mk. 6:3 and 15:40.

39 Compare 1 Cor. 15:3-8.

FOOTNOTES

40 Strack-Billerbeck, *Matthäus* I, 1049, and Stendahl, *Matthew* in Peake, p. 797, para. 695a. Perhaps Is. 53:9 as well as the typology of the rich Joseph burying his father Israel are implicitly intended here.

41 See J. Klausner, *Jesus of Nazareth,* (London: Allen, Unwin & Co., 1925), pp. 18-54. Also R. Travers Herford, *Christianity in the Talmud and Midrash,* (Clifton, New Jersey: Reference Book Publishers, 1966), pp. 35-96, 344-69, 401-36.

42 Compare Dan. 10:7ff., Rev. 1:17 and 4 Ez. 10:29ff.

43 See 16:21, 17:22f., 20:18f. and especially 26:32.

44 See Lohmeyer, "Mir ist gegeben alle Gewalt," *In Memoriam Ernst Lohmeyer,* ed. by W. Schmauch, (Stuttgart: Evangelisches Verlagswerk, 1951), pp. 34f., 47, on the use of Dan. 7:13f. in 28:18. Also Trilling, *op. cit.,* pp. 6ff. and 34ff.

45 H. Kosmala, "The Conclusion of Matthew," *Annual of Swedish Theological Institute* (1965), pp. 140-5.

46 See Trilling, *op. cit.,* and G. Barth, *Matthew's Understanding of the Law,* p. 135, on "I am with you . . ."

47 O. Michel, "Abschluss des Matthäusevangeliums," *Evangelische Theologie* 1 (1950-51), p. 24. Also Barth, *op. cit.,* p. 133.

48 See Lohmeyer, *op. cit.,* p. 39.

INDEX OF BIBLICAL REFERENCES

OLD TESTAMENT

23:5ff. - 215
26(33):7-16 - 258
26(33):15 - 258
31:1-4 - 82
31:15 - 68
32:9-15 - 258
51(28):35 - 258

Ezekiel
12:2 - 171
20:34ff. - 233
26:1-3 - 149
37:1-4 - 259
37:9-12 - 248, 259
37:12 - 249, 259

Daniel
2 - 45, 52
2:35 - 45

5:6 - 184
5:9 - 66
7 - 45, 52
7:13f. - 260
7:13-4 - 258
7:13-8 - 129
7:14 - 255
9:27 - 227
10:7ff. - 260
12:11 - 227

Hosea
2:14 - 233
6:6 - 41, 143
11:1 - 68
14:1 - 63

Joel
3:16 - 259

Amos
1:9-12 - 149
1:13 - 63

Micah
1:3f. - 259
4:6-7 - 214
5:1 - 67

Zechariah
1:1 - 223
9:9 - 61
11:12 - 236
12:12-4 - 229
14:4 - 31, 214
14:5 - 259

Malachi
3:1 - 71, 140
4:5-6 - 71

INTERTESTAMENTAL LITERATURE

2 Esdras (4 Ezra)
7:30 - 259
9:1ff. - 233
10:29ff. - 260

1 Enoch
1:4-9 - 259
18:13-6 - 233
21:6 - 233
24:1-6 - 45
45:3 - 234
51:2-3 - 234
52:1-6 - 45
55:4 - 234
61:8 - 234
62:5 - 234
69:27ff. - 234
72:1-37 - 233
73:1-8 - 233
75:1-3 - 233
77:4 - 45
78:1-17 - 233
79:1-6 - 233
80:1-8 - 233
86:1 - 233
88:1 - 233
90:21-4 - 233
93:3-91:17 - 45, 126, 129
93:3b - 183
93:5 - 183

93:7 - 183
93:8 - 183

2 Enoch
9:1 - 234
19:3-6 - 233
24:1-33:1 - 126
33:1 - 130

2 Baruch
27:1-15 - 233
53-74-45,49,52,129
53:1 - 49
53:6 - 49
56:1-16 - 50
57:1 - 50
58:1 - 50
59:1-12 - 50
60:1 - 50
61:1-8 - 50
62:1-8 - 50
63:1-11 - 50
64:1-10 - 50
66:1-8 - 50
67:1-6 - 50
68:4-8 - 50
69:1 - 50
72:2 - 50
73:2 - 51
74:2 - 51

The Testaments of
the XII Patriarchs

T. Reuben
4:6-9 - 64
4:11 - 64
6:1-4 - 64

T. Simeon
4:1 - 58
5:1-3 - 64

T. Levi
4:1ff. - 259
18:3-4 - 184

T. Judah
14:2-15:6 - 64
18:2 - 64

T. Zebulon
7:1-8:3 - 234

T. Dan
5:1 - 58

T. Naphtali
6:1-6 - 129,182

NEW TESTAMENT

An index of chapter and verse references to Matthew is hardly necessary since the chapter by chapter interpretation in this book proceeds according to the structure of the gospel and every left page cites the major section that is being treated.

NON-CANONICAL WRITINGS

INDEX OF AUTHORS

Iber, G., 24

Jeremias, Joachim, 43, 44, 63, 113, 129, 158, 190, 191,
     214, 215, 234
Johnson, Marshall D., 62, 63
Johnson, Sherman E., 215
Josephus, Flavius, 44, 223, 233, 258

Kee, Howard Clark, 38
Kilpatrick, G.D., 82
Kingsbury, Jack D., 24, 63, 83, 158
Klausner, Joseph, 260
Klostermann, E., 130
Knox, John, 113
Koester, Helmut, 25
Kosmala, Hans, 64, 114, 258, 260
Kraeling, Carl H., 44
Krentz, Edgar, 83
Kuhn, Karl G., 63
Kümmel, W.G., 44

Lenski, Gerhard, 43
Lightfoot, R.H., 214
Linnemann, Eta, 44, 129, 158, 214
Ljungmann, H., 112, 113
Lohmeyer, Ernst, 63, 81, 82, 113, 114, 129, 183, 214,
     215, 258, 259, 260
Lowe, John, 184

Manson, T.W., 112, 114
Marxsen, Willi, 24, 25
Mauser, Ulrich, 233
McNeile, A.H., 82, 215, 233, 234, 259
Metzger, Bruce M., 81
Michel, Otto, 24, 190, 260
Moore, George Foote, 63
Moule, C.F.D., 82, 158
Münderlein, G., 215

Nestle, Eberhard, 233
Neusner, Jacob, 150

Perrin, Norman, 25, 113
Philostratus, 35

Robinson, Theodore H., 63
Rohde, Joachim, 24, 233
Runge, Manfred, 233
Russell, D.H., 45, 184

Schlatter, Adolf, 183, 184
Schniewind, Julius, 113, 138

Schweizer, Eduard, 82, 113, 184
Sjoberg, Gideon, 43
Smith, C.W.F., 215
Stendahl, Krister, 63, 81, 82, 113, 114, 129, 150,
    183, 190, 215, 234, 258, 260
Strack-Billerbeck, 82, 114, 150, 233, 260
Strecker, Georg, 24, 25, 63, 64, 81, 82, 112, 114, 129, 130
    149, 150, 158, 183, 184, 190, 215, 233, 258, 259
Streeter, B.H., 25, 128, 184
Suetonius, 81
Suggs, M. Jack, 24, 112, 150, 184

Tödt, Heinz Eduard, 138, 150, 258
Trilling, Wolfgang, 24, 82, 83, 112, 138, 183, 184, 190
    215, 233, 258, 260

von Dobschütz, Ernst, 45
von Hofman, J.C.K., 63

Waetjen, Herman C., 62, 63
Walker, N., 82
Wellhausen, Julius, 233
Wimsatt, Jr., W.K., 25
Windisch, Hans, 112

Zahn, Theodor, 63, 82, 129